TOP
STOCKS

THIRTY-FIRST EDITION

2025

MARTIN ROTH'S

BEST-SELLING ANNUAL

TOP STOCKS

THIRTY-FIRST EDITION

2025

A SHAREBUYER'S GUIDE TO
LEADING AUSTRALIAN COMPANIES

WILEY

This thirty-first edition first published in 2025 by John Wiley & Sons Australia, Ltd
First edition published as *Top Stocks* by Wrightbooks in 1995
New edition published annually

ISBN: 978-1-394-24883-4

A catalogue record for this book is available from the National Library of Australia

Registered Office
John Wiley & Sons Australia, Ltd. Level 4, 600 Bourke Street, Melbourne, VIC 3000, Australia

For details of our global editorial offices, customer services, and more information about Wiley products visit us at www.wiley.com.

Wiley also publishes its books in a variety of electronic formats and by print-on-demand. Some content that appears in standard print versions of this book may not be available in other formats.

Cover image: © vadymstock/Adobe Stock

Cover design by Wiley

Charts created using MetaStock

The author and publisher would like to thank Alan Hull (author of *Active Investing*, Revised Edition, *Trade My Way* and *Invest My Way*; www.alanhull.com) for generating the five-year share-price charts.

Set in Adobe Garamond Pro 10/12pt by Straive, Chennai, India

Printed in Singapore
M128628-1_011024

Contents

Preface   *vii*

Introduction   *xv*

PART I: the companies

Accent Group Limited	2	CSL Limited	48
Acrow Limited	4	Data#3 Limited	50
Adairs Limited	6	Elders Limited	52
AGL Energy Limited	8	Evolution Mining Limited	54
Amotiv Limited	10	Fiducian Group Limited	56
ANZ Group Holdings Limited	12	Fortescue Limited	58
ARB Corporation Limited	14	Gold Road Resources Limited	60
Aristocrat Leisure Limited	16	Grange Resources Limited	62
ASX Limited	18	GWA Group Limited	64
Australian Ethical Investment		IDP Education Limited	66
Limited	20	Iluka Resources Limited	68
Beacon Lighting Group Limited	22	Insurance Australia Group Limited	70
BHP Group Limited	24	IPH Limited	72
Brambles Limited	26	JB Hi-Fi Limited	74
Breville Group Limited	28	Johns Lyng Group Limited	76
CAR Group Limited	30	Jumbo Interactive Limited	78
Clinuvel Pharmaceuticals Limited	32	Lindsay Australia Limited	80
Cochlear Limited	34	Lovisa Holdings Limited	82
Codan Limited	36	Lycopodium Limited	84
Coles Group Limited	38	Macmahon Holdings Limited	86
Collins Foods Limited	40	Macquarie Group Limited	88
Commonwealth Bank of Australia	42	Mader Group Limited	90
Computershare Limited	44	Magellan Financial Group Limited	92
Credit Corp Group Limited	46	Medibank Private Limited	94

Metcash Limited	96
Monadelphous Group Limited	98
Monash IVF Group Limited	100
National Australia Bank Limited	102
Netwealth Group Limited	104
NIB Holdings Limited	106
Nick Scali Limited	108
Nine Entertainment Company Holdings Limited	110
NRW Holdings Limited	112
Objective Corporation Limited	114
Origin Energy Limited	116
Perpetual Limited	118
Pinnacle Investment Management Group Limited	120
Platinum Asset Management Limited	122
Premier Investments Limited	124
Pro Medicus Limited	126
PWR Holdings Limited	128
Ramelius Resources Limited	130
REA Group Limited	132
Reece Limited	134
Reliance Worldwide Corporation Limited	136
Ricegrowers Limited	138
Ridley Corporation Limited	140
Rio Tinto Limited	142
Santos Limited	144
Schaffer Corporation Limited	146
Servcorp Limited	148
Smartgroup Corporation Limited	150
Southern Cross Electrical Engineering Limited	152
Steadfast Group Limited	154
Super Retail Group Limited	156
Supply Network Limited	158
Technology One Limited	160
Wesfarmers Limited	162
Westpac Banking Corporation	164
WiseTech Global Limited	166
Woolworths Group Limited	168

PART II: the tables

A	Market capitalisation	173	I	Year-on-year return on equity growth	181
B	Revenues	174	J	Debt-to-equity ratio	182
C	Year-on-year revenues growth	175	K	Current ratio	183
D	EBIT margin	176	L	Price/earnings ratio	184
E	Year-on-year EBIT margin growth	177	M	Price-to-NTA-per-share ratio	185
F	After-tax profit	178	N	Dividend yield	186
G	Year-on-year earnings per share growth	179	O	Year-on-year dividend growth	187
H	Return on equity	180	P	Five-year share price return	188

Preface

This latest edition of *Top Stocks* arrives at a time when many investors are concerned about the direction of the stock market. Reasons for continuing volatility seem to abound.

Interest rates and inflation remain at persistently elevated levels. Consumer confidence is ebbing. The wars in Ukraine and the Middle East bring fears of widening conflicts. Many are talking of a housing crisis. Could a recession be on the way?

As I have noted in earlier editions, *Top Stocks* is written for times such as these, when the future is cloudy. Because, no matter the direction of the stock market, numerous fine companies continue to emerge in Australia, offering investors great prospects. *Top Stocks 2025* showcases many such companies.

They are often smaller to medium-sized corporations. Some will be unfamiliar to investors. But all meet the stringent *Top Stocks* criteria, including solid profits and moderate debt levels.

Of course, such stocks could not withstand the tidal wave of a substantial market sell-off. They too would be affected. But they should be affected less. And if they are good companies they will continue to thrive and to pay dividends. And they will bounce back faster than many others.

This is the 31st annual edition of *Top Stocks*, and guiding investors towards value stocks has been one of the paramount aims of the book from the very first edition. Indeed, one of the rationales for the book has always been to highlight the truth that Australia boasts many excellent companies that enjoy high profits — and growing profits — regardless of the direction of the markets.

Despite the title, *Top Stocks* is actually a book about companies. Right from the start it has been an attempt to help investors find the best public companies in Australia, using strict criteria. These criteria are explained fully later. But, in essence, all companies in the book must have been publicly listed for at least five years and must have been making a profit and paying a dividend for each of those five years.

They must also meet tough benchmarks of profitability and debt levels. It is completely objective. The author's own personal views count for nothing. In addition, share prices have never been relevant.

Of the 84 companies in *Top Stocks 2025* — four fewer than in last year's edition — fully 61 reported a higher after-tax profit in the latest financial year (June 2024 for most of them), including three that achieved triple-digit profit growth and a further 39 with double-digit growth. In addition, 58 achieved higher earnings per share and 57 paid a higher dividend.

And though share prices are not relevant for selection to *Top Stocks*, 46 of the companies in the book have provided investor returns — share price appreciation plus dividends — of an average of at least 10 per cent per year over a five-year period.

Energy transition

Each year I try to identify trends among the companies of *Top Stocks*. Certainly one of the biggest recently has been the rush towards decarbonisation and renewable energy. A growing number of companies are trying to align themselves with this movement.

Here are some examples from *Top Stocks*:

- AGL Energy is investing heavily in renewable energy assets.
- Australian Ethical Investment invests in companies involved in green energy. Its new Infrastructure Debt Fund provides capital for key renewable energy developments.
- BHP Group is restructuring its operations in order to gain greater exposure to what it believes are mega-trends of decarbonisation and electrification.
- Fortescue Metals is involved in green energy projects in many countries through its Energy division.
- Iluka Resources is a global leader in the mining and processing of a range of rare earth minerals that are key components for a growing number of high-tech industries.
- Lycopodium is involved in two battery recycling schemes and is also working with government and academic bodies on the development of new energy storage technologies. It has developed new methods of reducing the carbon footprint of gold mining operations.
- Monadelphous Group is involved in large-scale renewable energy projects through its Zenviron joint venture.
- Origin Energy manages a series of wind and solar energy developments and is also involved in battery projects for energy storage.
- PWR Holdings is working with electric car manufacturers for the supply of sophisticated cooling technology. It is also involved in developments in storage batteries for alternative energy systems.
- Rio Tinto is involved in the massive Oyu Tolgoi copper-gold mine development in Mongolia. In Argentina it has acquired the Rincon lithium project and it has expressed its interest in acquiring further copper and lithium assets.

- Southern Cross Electrical Engineering expects a growing amount of work from renewable energy projects. In May 2024 it received the largest initial contract in its history, the $160 million Collie battery project in Western Australia.
- Wesfarmers holds half the equity in Covalent Lithium, which is constructing a $1.9 billion mine and refinery in Western Australia with the goal of producing 50 000 tonnes of lithium hydroxide annually for use in lithium batteries.

Cars and trucks

A surprising number of companies in *Top Stocks* have some kind of involvement with cars and trucks. The shares of some of these companies have been excellent long-term performers:

- Amotiv, the new name for GUD Holdings, is an important manufacturer of products for the automotive aftermarket and accessories sector.
- ARB is a prominent manufacturer of specialty automotive accessories and an international leader in specialised equipment for four-wheel-drive vehicles.
- CAR Group is the market leader in online automotive advertising.
- Insurance Australia Group is one of Australia's leading vehicle insurers, with brands that include NRMA Insurance and RACV Home and Motor Insurance.
- Lindsay Australia is a prominent trucking company.
- PWR Holdings has a particular specialty in the manufacture of cooling systems for racing car teams and high-performance automobile companies.
- Schaffer manufactures leather goods for the automobile industry through its 83 per cent–owned subsidiary Automotive Leather.
- Smartgroup has important businesses providing vehicle novated leasing and fleet management services.
- Super Retail Group manages the Supercheap Auto chain, the largest and most profitable of its four businesses.
- Supply Network is a leading supplier of truck and bus parts.

Car and truck companies

	5-year share price return (% p.a.)
Amotiv	6.2
ARB	18.1
CAR Group	21.0
Insurance Australia Group	1.0
Lindsay Australia	24.2
PWR Holdings	16.8
Schaffer	12.1
Smartgroup	0.2
Super Retail Group	17.3
Supply Network	49.8

High-tech companies

For some years in *Top Stocks* I have been talking about the rise and rise of high-tech companies in Australia. They are generally small companies — though large enough to be in the All Ordinaries Index of Australia's 500 largest stocks — and it can sometimes be difficult for outsiders to understand just how they make their money. Thus, many investors avoid them.

But technology has infiltrated just about every facet of our lives, and the best of these companies are set to continue growing. It is worth taking the time to learn more about them.

Profit growth (and share price acceleration) for many of these companies has been outstanding. They are often on high price-earnings ratios, but that reflects the market's belief that high levels of growth will continue. Dividend yields can be low. Nevertheless, they should be on the radar of all serious investors.

High-tech companies

	5-year share price return (% p.a.)
Codan	27.5
Computershare	14.8
Data#3	25.2
Objective	27.8
Technology One	24.8
WiseTech Global	26.5

Small stocks

A particular attraction of *Top Stocks* is the manner in which the book places the spotlight on smaller, emerging companies, many of which have just ascended into the rankings of the top 500 stocks. Some of these companies continue to rise, offering solid gains to astute investors.

A special example is the medical imaging software company Pro Medicus. It entered *Top Stocks 2006* at a share price of $1.15 and a market capitalisation of $108.5 million. It appears in this latest edition of the book at a price of $155.16 and a market capitalisation of $16.2 billion.

Another example is Codan, a technology company with a specialty in several niche products. It entered *Top Stocks 2016* at a price of $0.89. In this latest edition it is priced at $15.08.

Supply Network is a provider of truck and bus parts for transport companies, with operations throughout Australia and New Zealand. It entered the book only in *Top Stocks 2020* at a price of $3.99. It appears in *Top Stocks 2025* at a price of $28.80. In fact, over a period of five years it is the top-performing stock in the book. (See Table P.)

Pinnacle Investment Management first appeared in *Top Stocks 2021* at $5.25. It is in this latest edition at $16.42.

A final example: WiseTech Global appeared for the first time only in *Top Stocks 2023*, priced at $59. Two years later, in *Top Stocks 2025*, it is $122.94.

Here are several smaller companies that are appearing in *Top Stocks* for the first time:

- Acrow is a prominent supplier of support services for the construction sector.
- Mader Group is a specialist in mobile and fixed plant equipment maintenance and support. Its key business is the supply of tradespeople for the maintenance of heavy mobile equipment in the resources and energy sectors.
- Southern Cross Electrical Engineering is a leading national provider of specialised electrical, instrumentation, maintenance and communication services.

Who is *Top Stocks* written for?

Top Stocks is written for all those investors wishing to exercise a degree of control over their portfolios. It is for those just starting out, as well as for those with plenty of experience but who still feel the need for some guidance through the thickets of more than 2000 listed stocks.

It is not a how-to book. It does not give step-by-step instructions to 'winning' in the stock market. Rather, it is an independent and objective evaluation of leading companies, based on rigid criteria, with the intention of yielding a large selection of stocks that can become the starting point for investors wishing to do their own research.

A large amount of information is presented on each company, and another key feature of the book is that the data is presented in a common format, to allow readers to make easy comparisons between companies.

It is necessarily a conservative book. All stocks must have been listed for five years even to be considered for inclusion. It is especially suited for those seeking out value stocks for longer-term investment.

Yet, perhaps ironically, the book is also being used by short-term traders seeking a goodly selection of financially sound and reliable companies whose shares they can trade.

In addition, there are many regular readers, who buy the book each year, and to them in particular I express my thanks.

What are the entry criteria?

The criteria for inclusion in *Top Stocks* are strict:

- All companies must be included in the All Ordinaries Index, which comprises Australia's 500 largest stocks (out of more than 2000). The reason for excluding smaller companies is that there is often little investor information available on them and some are so thinly traded as to be almost illiquid. In fact, the 500 All Ordinaries companies comprise, by market capitalisation, more than 95 per cent of the entire market.

- It is necessary that all companies be publicly listed since at least the end of 2019 and have a five-year record of profits and dividend payments each year.
- All companies are required to post a return-on-equity ratio of at least 10 per cent in their latest financial year.
- No company should have a debt-to-equity ratio of more than 70 per cent.
- It must be stressed that share price performance is NOT one of the criteria for inclusion in this book. The purpose is to select companies with good profits and a strong balance sheet. These may not offer the spectacular share-price returns of a high-tech start-up or a promising rare earths miner, but they should also present less risk.
- There are several notable exclusions. Listed managed investments are out, as these mainly buy other shares or investments. Examples are Australian Foundation Investment Company and all the real estate investment trusts.
- A further exclusion are the foreign-registered stocks listed on the ASX. There is sometimes a lack of information available about such companies. In addition, their stock prices tend to move on events and trends in their home countries, making it difficult at times for local investors to follow them.

It is surely a tribute to the strength and resilience of Australian corporations that, once again, despite the volatility of recent years, so many companies have qualified for the book.

Changes to this edition

A total of 19 companies from *Top Stocks 2024* have been omitted from this new edition.

Two, Altium and CSR, were taken over. One, Brickworks, reported a big interim loss and another, Telstra Group, saw its debt-to-equity ratio rise above the 70 per cent limit for this book.

The remaining 15 excluded companies had return-on-equity ratios that fell below the required 10 per cent:

Baby Bunting Group
Bapcor
Beach Energy
BlueScope Steel
Clover Corporation
Enero Group
Hansen Technologies
Harvey Norman Holdings
IGO
Lifestyle Communities
Michael Hill International

Mineral Resources
PeopleIn
Seek
Woodside Energy Group

There are 15 new companies in this book (although eight of them have appeared in earlier editions of the book, but were not in *Top Stocks 2024*).

The new companies in this book are:

Acrow*
AGL Energy
Brambles
Evolution Mining
Gold Road Resources*
Macmahon Holdings
Mader Group*
Monash IVF Group*
Origin Energy
Perpetual
Ramelius Resources*
Ricegrowers*
Schaffer Corporation
Southern Cross Electrical Engineering*
Westpac Banking Corporation

* Companies that have not appeared in any previous edition of *Top Stocks*.

Appearing in every edition of *Top Stocks*

Just one company has appeared in all 31 editions of *Top Stocks*: Commonwealth Bank of Australia.

Commonwealth Bank entered the original edition of the book in 1995 at a share price of $9.17 and a market capitalisation of around $11 billion. It is in the latest edition at a share price of $143.47 and a market capitalisation of nearly $240 billion.

In fact, such has been its growth that it has now become the largest company in the book (and also on the ASX) by market capitalisation, overtaking BHP, which held that title in virtually every previous edition of the book.

Once again it is my hope that *Top Stocks* will serve you well.

Martin Roth
Melbourne
September 2024

Introduction

The 84 companies in this book have been placed as much as possible into a common format, for ease of comparison. Please study the following explanations in order to get as much as possible from the large amount of data.

The tables have been made as concise as possible, though they repay careful study, as they contain large amounts of information.

Note that the tables for the banks have been arranged a little differently from the others. Details of these are given later in this Introduction.

Head

At the head of each entry is the company name, with its three-letter ASX code and the website address.

Share-price chart

Under the company name is a long-term share-price chart, to September 2024, provided by Alan Hull (www.alanhull.com), author of *Invest My Way*, *Trade My Way* and *Active Investing*.

Small table

Under the share-price chart is a small table with the following data.

Sector

This is the company's sector as designated by the ASX. These sectors are based on the Global Industry Classification Standard — developed by S&P Dow Jones Indices and Morgan Stanley Capital International — which aims to standardise global industry sectors. You can learn more about these at the ASX website.

Share price

This is the closing price on 6 September 2024. Also included are the 12-month high and low prices, as of the same date.

Market capitalisation

This is the size of the company, as determined by the stock market. It is the share price multiplied by the number of shares in issue. All companies in this book must be in the All Ordinaries Index, which comprises Australia's 500 largest stocks, as measured by market capitalisation.

Price/earnings ratio

The price/earnings ratio (PER) is one of the most popular measures of whether a share is cheap or expensive. It is calculated by dividing the share price — in this case the closing price for 6 September 2024 — by the earnings-per-share figure. Obviously the share price is continually changing, so the PER figures in this book are for guidance only.

Dividend yield

This is the latest full-year dividend expressed as a percentage of the share price. Like the price/earnings ratio, it changes as the share price moves. It is a useful figure, especially for investors who are buying shares for income, as it allows you to compare this income with alternative investments, such as a bank term deposit or a rental property.

Price-to-NTA-per-share ratio

The NTA-per-share figure expresses the worth of a company's net tangible assets — that is, its assets minus its liabilities and intangible assets — for each share of the company. The price-to-NTA-per-share ratio relates this figure to the share price.

A ratio of one means that the company is valued exactly according to the value of its assets. A ratio below one suggests that the shares are a bargain, though usually there is a good reason for this. Profits are more important than assets.

Some companies in this book have a negative NTA-per-share figure — as a result of having intangible assets valued at more than their net assets — and a price-to-NTA-per-share ratio cannot be calculated.

See Table M, in the second part of this book, for a little more detail on this ratio.

Five-year share price return

This is the approximate total return you could have received from the stock in the five years to September 2024. It is based on the share price appreciation or depreciation plus dividends, and is expressed as a compounded annual rate of return.

Dividend reinvestment plan

A dividend reinvestment plan (DRP) allows shareholders to receive additional shares in their company in place of the dividend. Usually — though not always — these shares are provided at a small discount to the prevailing price, which can make them quite attractive. And of course no broking fees apply.

Many large companies offer such plans. However, they come and go. When a company needs finance it may introduce a DRP. When its financing requirements become less pressing it may withdraw it. Some companies that have a DRP in place may decide to deactivate it for a time.

The information in this book is based on up-to-date information from the companies. But if you are investing in a particular company in expectations of a DRP be sure to check that it is still on offer. The company's own website will often provide this information.

Company commentary

Each commentary begins with a brief introduction to the company and its activities. Then follow the highlights of its latest business results. For the majority of the companies these are their June 2024 results, which were issued during July and August 2024. Finally, there is a section on the outlook for the company.

Main table

Here is what you can find in the main table.

Revenues

These are the company's revenues from its business activities, generally the sale of products or services. However, it does not usually include additional income from such sources as investments, bank interest or the sale of assets. If the information is available, the revenues figure has been broken down into the major product areas.

As much as possible, the figures are for continuing businesses. When a company sells a part of its operations the financial results for the sold activities are separated from the core results and reported as a separate item. This can mean that the previous year's results are restated — also excluding the sold business — to make year-on-year comparisons more valid.

Earnings before interest and taxation

Earnings before interest and taxation (EBIT) is the firm's profit from its operations before the payment of interest and tax. This figure is often used by analysts examining a company. The reason is that some companies have borrowed extensively to finance their activities, while others have opted for alternative means. By expressing profits before interest payments it is possible to compare more precisely the performance of these companies.

Note that the EBIT figures in this book are calculated by adding together the company's pre-tax profit and its interest payments — both figures that are given in company financial reporting. Some analysts prefer a net interest payments amount — that is, interest payments minus interest receipts. This is not done for this book.

You will also find many companies using a measure called EBITDA, which is earnings before interest, taxation, depreciation and amortisation.

EBIT margin

This is the company's EBIT expressed as a percentage of its revenues. It is a gauge of a company's efficiency. A high EBIT margin suggests that a company is achieving success in keeping its costs low.

Gross margin

The gross margin is the company's gross profit as a percentage of its sales. The gross profit is the amount left over after deducting from a company's sales figure its cost of sales: that is, its manufacturing costs or, for a retailer, the cost of purchasing the goods it sells. The cost of goods sold figure does not usually include marketing or administration costs.

As there are different ways of calculating the cost of goods sold figure, this ratio is better used for year-to-year comparisons of a single company's efficiency, rather than in comparing one company with another.

Many companies do not present a cost of goods sold figure, so a gross margin ratio is not given for every stock in this book.

The revenues for some companies include a mix of sales and services. Where a breakdown is possible, the gross profit figure will relate to sales only.

Profit before tax/profit after tax

The profit before tax figure is simply the EBIT figure minus interest payments. The profit after tax figure is, of course, the company's profit after the payment of tax, and also after the deduction of minority interests. Minority interests are that part of a company's profit that is claimed by outside interests, usually the other shareholders in a subsidiary that is not fully owned by the company. Many companies do not have any minority interests, and for those that do it is generally a tiny figure.

As much as possible, I have adjusted the profit figures to exclude non-recurring profits and losses, which are often referred to as significant items. It is for this reason that the profit figures in *Top Stocks* sometimes differ from those in the financial media, where profit figures often include significant items.

Significant items are those that have an abnormal impact on profits, even though they happen in the normal course of the company's operations. Examples are the profit from the sale of a business, the expenses of a business restructuring, the write-down of an asset, an inventory write-down or a bad-debt loss. These are all generally one-off expenses.

Significant items are controversial. It is often a matter of subjective judgement as to what is included and what excluded. After analysing the accounts of hundreds of companies while writing the various editions of this book, it is clear that different companies use varying interpretations of what is significant.

Further, when they do report a significant item there is no consistency as to whether they use pre-tax figures or after-tax figures. Some report both, making it easy to adjust the profit figures in the tables in this book. But difficulties arise when only one figure is given for significant items.

In normal circumstances most companies do not report significant items. But investors should be aware of this issue. It sometimes causes consternation for readers of *Top Stocks* to find that a particular profit figure in this book is substantially different from that given in a media report or by some other source.

It is also worth noting my observation that a growing number of companies present what they call an underlying profit (called a cash profit for the banks), or even a so-called normalised profit, in addition to their reported (statutory) profit. This underlying profit will exclude not only significant items but also discontinued businesses and sometimes other related items. Where all the relevant figures are available, I have generally used these underlying figures for the tables in this book.

As already noted, when a company sells or terminates one of its businesses it will now usually report the profit or loss of that business as a separate item. It will also usually back-date its previous year's accounts, to exclude that business, so worthwhile comparisons can be made of continuing businesses.

The tables in this book usually refer to continuing businesses only.

Earnings per share
Earnings per share is the after-tax profit divided by the number of shares. Because the profit figure is for a 12-month period the number of shares used is a weighted average of those on issue during the year. This number is provided by the company in its annual report and its results announcements.

Cashflow per share
The cashflow per share ratio tells — in theory — how much actual cash the company has generated from its operations.

In fact, the ratio in this book is not exactly a true measure of cashflow. It is simply the company's depreciation and amortisation figures for the year added to the after-tax profit, then divided by a weighted average of the number of shares. Depreciation and amortisation are expenses that do not actually utilise cash, so can be added back to after-tax profit to give a kind of indication of the company's cashflow.

By contrast, a true cashflow — including such items as newly raised capital and money received from the sale of assets — would require quite complex calculations based on the company's statement of cashflows.

However, many investors use the ratio as this book presents it, because it is easy to calculate, and it is certainly a useful guide to approximately how much funding the company has available from its operations.

Dividend

The dividend figure is the total for the year, interim and final. It does not include special dividends. The level of franking is also provided.

Net tangible assets per share

The NTA per share figure tells the theoretical value of the company — per share — if all assets were sold and all liabilities paid. It is very much a theoretical figure, as there is no guarantee that corporate assets are really worth the price put on them in the balance sheet. Intangible assets such as goodwill and patent rights are excluded because of the difficulty in putting a sales price on them, and also because they may in fact not have much value if separated from the company.

Note that this book includes right of use assets as intangible assets. Not all analysts do. (A right of use asset is, essentially, a company's contractual right to use a particular asset, such as a lease for a property.)

As already noted, some companies in this book have a negative NTA, due to the fact that their intangible assets are so great, and no figure can be listed for them.

Where a company's most recent financial results are the half-year figures, these are used to calculate this ratio.

Interest cover

The interest cover ratio indicates how many times a company could make its interest payments from its pre-tax profit. A rough rule of thumb says a ratio of at least three times is desirable. Below that and fast-rising interest rates could imperil profits. The ratio is derived by dividing the EBIT figure by net interest payments. Some companies have interest receipts that are higher than their interest payments, which turns the interest cover into a negative figure, so it is not listed.

Return on equity

Return on equity is the after-tax profit expressed as a percentage of the shareholders' equity. In theory, it is the amount that the company's managers have made for you — the shareholder — on your money. The shareholders' equity figure used is an average for the year.

Debt-to-equity ratio

This ratio is one of the best-known measures of a company's debt levels. It is total borrowings minus the company's cash holdings, expressed as a percentage of the shareholders' equity. Some companies have no debt at all, or their cash position is greater than their level of debt, which results in a negative ratio, so no figure is listed for them.

Where a company's most recent financial results are the half-year figures, these are used to calculate this ratio.

Current ratio

The current ratio is simply the company's current assets divided by its current liabilities. Current assets are cash or assets that can, in theory, be converted quickly into cash. Current liabilities are normally those payable within a year. Thus, the current ratio measures the ability of a company to repay in a hurry its short-term debt, should the need arise. The surplus of current assets over current liabilities is referred to as the company's working capital.

Where a company's most recent financial results are the half-year figures, these are used to calculate this ratio.

Banks

The tables for the banks are somewhat different from those for most other companies. EBIT and debt-to-equity ratios have little relevance for them, as they have such high interest payments (to their customers). Other differences are examined below.

Operating income

Operating income is used instead of sales revenues. Operating income is the bank's net interest income — that is, its total interest income minus its interest expense — plus other income, such as bank fees, fund management fees and income from activities such as corporate finance and insurance.

Net interest income

Banks borrow money — that is, they accept deposits from savers — and they lend it to businesses, homebuyers and other borrowers. They charge the borrowers more than they pay those who deposit money with them, and the difference is known as net interest income.

Operating expenses

These are all the costs of running the bank. Banks have high operating expenses, and one of the keys to profit growth is cutting these expenses.

Non-interest income to total income

Banks have traditionally made most of their income from savers and from lending out money. But they are also working to diversify into new fields, and this ratio is an indication of their success.

Cost-to-income ratio

As noted, the banks have high costs — numerous branches, expensive computer systems, many staff, and so on — and they are all striving to reduce these. The cost-to-income ratio expresses their expenses as a percentage of their operating income, and is one of the ratios most often used as a gauge of efficiency. The lower the ratio drops the better.

Return on assets

Banks have enormous assets, in sharp contrast to, say, a high-tech start-up whose main physical assets may be little more than a set of computers and other technological equipment. So the return on assets — the after-tax profit expressed as a percentage of the year's average total assets — is another measure of efficiency.

PART I
THE COMPANIES

Accent Group Limited

ASX code: AX1   www.accentgr.com.au

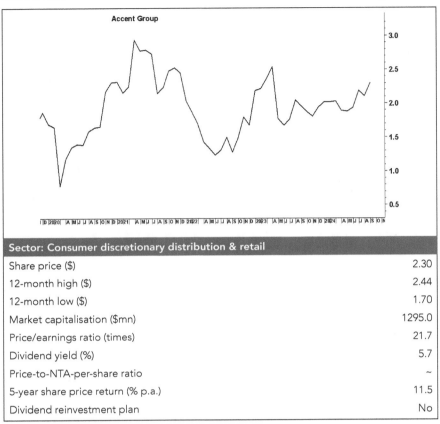

Accent Group

Sector: Consumer discretionary distribution & retail	
Share price ($)	2.30
12-month high ($)	2.44
12-month low ($)	1.70
Market capitalisation ($mn)	1295.0
Price/earnings ratio (times)	21.7
Dividend yield (%)	5.7
Price-to-NTA-per-share ratio	~
5-year share price return (% p.a.)	11.5
Dividend reinvestment plan	No

Sydney company Accent Group, which started in 1988 as a small wholesale distributor based in New Zealand, is today a prominent footwear, apparel and accessories wholesaler and retailer. It has grown rapidly through a series of mergers and acquisitions and operates across 20 different retail banners, with exclusive distribution rights in Australia and New Zealand for 14 international brands. Its brands include The Athlete's Foot, Platypus Shoes, Hype DC, Skechers, Merrell, CAT, Vans, Dr. Martens, Saucony, Timberland, HOKA, Superga, Subtype, Stylerunner, Nude Lucy, Glue Store and UGG.

Latest business results (June 2024, full year)

Sales edged up but the company experienced a double-digit decline in profits as it was hit by inflationary pressures and weakening consumer discretionary spending. Retail sales rose 6.3 per cent, or 1.7 per cent on a like-for-like basis, with wholesale revenues down 17 per cent. The company reported pleasing strength in newer brands that included Nude Lucy, Stylerunner, HOKA and UGG, together with a continuing strong performance from Skechers, The Athlete's Foot and Hype DC. New Zealand sales, representing 11 per cent of the total, grew by 5 per cent. During the year the company opened 93 new stores and closed 19, and at June 2024 it operated 863 stores and 32 websites. Note that the June 2024 year comprised 52 weeks, compared to 53 weeks for the July 2023 year.

Outlook

Accent maintains its ambitious long-term growth strategy and expects profits to continue rising, although it is cautious about the near-term outlook as discretionary consumer spending continues to be hurt by cost of living pressures. In response, it has initiated a program aimed at delivering operational and cost efficiencies over the three years to June 2027. It plans to open at least 50 new stores during the June 2025 year. It sees great potential in apparel sales, and has been achieving significant growth with its Nude Lucy women's lifestyle apparel brand, with 36 stores and websites operating, and plans for more. It is now testing the American market for this brand with a US-focused website. Its Stylerunner apparel brand is also seeing solid growth, with 10 new stores soon to join the 28 existing outlets. Profits also continue to grow for its key The Athlete's Foot brand, with a network of 99 corporate stores and 60 franchise stores. Its contactable customer database grew by 400 000 customers in the June 2024 year to 10.2 million customers, and the company is expanding its series of loyalty programs for them.

Year to 30 June*	2023	2024
Revenues ($mn)	1409.0	1448.1
Retail (%)	86	89
Wholesale (%)	14	11
EBIT ($mn)	140.2	112.3
EBIT margin (%)	10.0	7.8
Gross margin (%)	55.2	55.8
Profit before tax ($mn)	119.6	84.4
Profit after tax ($mn)	88.7	59.5
Earnings per share (c)	16.16	10.61
Cash flow per share (c)	45.22	40.76
Dividend (c)	17.5	13
Percentage franked	100	100
Net tangible assets per share ($)	~	~
Interest cover (times)	7.3	4.3
Return on equity (%)	20.1	13.8
Debt-to-equity ratio (%)	27.1	29.2
Current ratio	1.1	1.0

*2 July 2023

Acrow Limited

ASX code: ACF

www.acrow.com.au

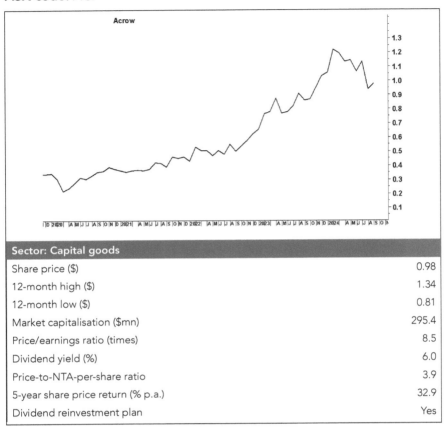

Sector: Capital goods	
Share price ($)	0.98
12-month high ($)	1.34
12-month low ($)	0.81
Market capitalisation ($mn)	295.4
Price/earnings ratio (times)	8.5
Dividend yield (%)	6.0
Price-to-NTA-per-share ratio	3.9
5-year share price return (% p.a.)	32.9
Dividend reinvestment plan	Yes

Sydney-based Acrow, formerly known as Acrow Formwork and Construction Services, was founded in the United Kingdom in 1936, with Australian activities starting in 1950. It is a prominent supplier of support services for the construction industry. Its core businesses are the provision of formwork — temporary or permanent casings where fresh concrete is poured — and of scaffolding supplies and services. In November 2023 it acquired MI Scaffold and in March 2024 it acquired Benchmark Scaffolding & Edge Protection.

Latest business results (June 2024, full year)

Underlying revenues and profits rose, in a good result for the company, with strength across most areas of operation. The high-margin Formwork division saw sales up 19 per cent, with all states delivering growth, apart from Queensland, and a milestone achievement in the award of a $5 million contract for the Melbourne North-East Link project, the largest equipment supply deal in the company's history. The Industrial Services division achieved 78 per cent growth in revenues, reflecting the two acquisitions during the year, along with a strong organic performance. By contrast, the small Commercial Scaffold division, which rents out scaffolding systems for large construction projects, suffered from a second-half decline in demand, with sales for the year down 15 per cent.

Outlook

Acrow has specialties in several key areas of the construction sector and benefits from the continuing strength of infrastructure developments in Australia. Around half of its revenues are generated in Queensland, and it is working to strengthen its position in other states, particularly New South Wales and Victoria. It has particular expertise in the industrial sector, supporting major oil, gas and mining companies with on-site labour and scaffolding supply. It is also strengthening and expanding its existing fields of operation. It is achieving success with Jumpform, its new jacking system business for the construction of lift shaft cores in multi-storey buildings. It is also boosting its exposure to heavy-duty screen systems for major construction activity, with 57 project wins and $15.9 million in revenues in the June 2024 year, and is realising a growing amount of cross-selling business across its formwork, scaffolding, jacking system and screen system activities. The two recent acquisitions are both based in Queensland and are highly complementary and bring new capabilities to Acrow, especially in complex scaffolding projects within the mining and marine sectors. The company is now seeking further acquisitions. Its early forecast is for revenue growth of around 20 per cent for June 2025, with double-digit profit growth.

Year to 30 June	2023	2024
Revenues ($mn)	168.5	215.3
Formwork (%)	61	56
Industrial services (%)	24	33
Commercial scaffold (%)	15	10
EBIT ($mn)	37.7	53.7
EBIT margin (%)	22.4	24.9
Profit before tax ($mn)	33.2	46.1
Profit after tax ($mn)	30.5	33.0
Earnings per share (c)	11.64	11.54
Cash flow per share (c)	17.46	18.80
Dividend (c)	4.4	5.85
Percentage franked	94	100
Net tangible assets per share ($)	0.28	0.25
Interest cover (times)	8.4	7.1
Return on equity (%)	32.7	27.1
Debt-to-equity ratio (%)	45.1	48.7
Current ratio	1.1	1.2

Adairs Limited

ASX code: ADH   investors.adairs.com.au

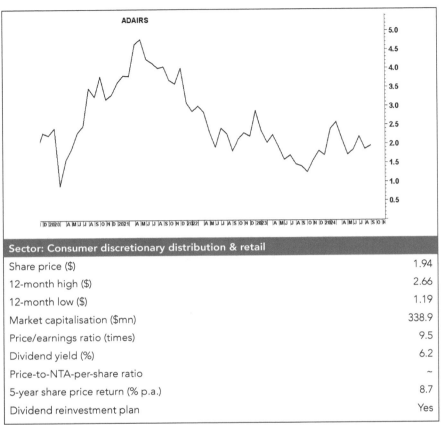

Sector: Consumer discretionary distribution & retail	
Share price ($)	1.94
12-month high ($)	2.66
12-month low ($)	1.19
Market capitalisation ($mn)	338.9
Price/earnings ratio (times)	9.5
Dividend yield (%)	6.2
Price-to-NTA-per-share ratio	~
5-year share price return (% p.a.)	8.7
Dividend reinvestment plan	Yes

Melbourne-based home furnishings specialist Adairs dates back to 1918 and the opening of a store in Prahran, Melbourne. It has since grown into a nationwide chain of stores specialising in bed linen, bedding, towels, homewares, soft furnishings, children's furnishings and some bedroom furniture. It has also expanded to New Zealand, and it manages a flourishing online business. It operates the Brisbane-based Mocka online furniture and homewares business and the Melbourne-based furniture and bedding retailer Focus on Furniture. At June 2024 it operated 171 Adairs stores and 25 Focus stores.

Latest business results (June 2024, full year)

Revenues fell and profits were down for the third straight year, as Adairs was hit by inflationary pressures and a slowdown in consumer spending. Adairs stores saw sales down 4.1 per cent and underlying EBIT falling 9.4 per cent, with reduced customer traffic and a disappointing performance for the company's range of fashion bed linen. Focus on Furniture reported an 8.7 per cent decline in sales, despite opening two new stores, and was also hurt by rising costs, with underlying EBIT falling 28.8 per cent. Nevertheless, though just 22 per cent of total turnover, the Focus business contributed a third of underlying EBIT. A recovery in the underperforming Mocka operation saw sales up 5.7 per cent as new products and enhanced promotions delivered increased average order values. Underlying EBIT for Mocka soared from $1.5 million in the June 2023 year to $6.5 million. Having spent $20 million to take operational control from DHL of its National Distribution Centre in September 2023, Adairs achieved cost savings of $4 million. Note that the June 2024 year comprised 53 weeks, compared to 52 weeks for June 2023.

Outlook

Adairs manages popular brands with high levels of customer recognition and loyalty. With an addressable Australian home furnishings market of some $12 billion it sees solid scope for growth. Nevertheless, it is cautious about the near-term outlook, with discretionary consumer spending weak and the economic outlook uncertain. It is working to reduce its cost base and expects further benefits as it transitions to a new warehouse management system at its National Distribution Centre. It benefits from the strength of its Linen Lover loyalty program, with one million members, who are responsible for 85 per cent of company sales. It has upgraded its Mocka online business and expects continuing growth from existing and new channels. It expects to open six new Adairs stores and three new Focus stores during the June 2025 year.

Year to 30 June*	2023	2024
Revenues ($mn)	621.3	594.4
Adairs (%)	69	70
Focus (%)	23	22
Mocka (%)	8	8
EBIT ($mn)	71.3	66.9
EBIT margin (%)	11.5	11.3
Gross margin (%)	45.9	47.5
Profit before tax ($mn)	57.6	50.7
Profit after tax ($mn)	40.2	35.5
Earnings per share (c)	23.35	20.47
Cash flow per share (c)	57.32	55.25
Dividend (c)	8	12
Percentage franked	100	100
Net tangible assets per share ($)	~	~
Interest cover (times)	5.4	4.2
Return on equity (%)	20.1	16.7
Debt-to-equity ratio (%)	36.4	28.7
Current ratio	1.0	0.8

*25 June 2023

AGL Energy Limited

ASX code: AGL

www.agl.com.au

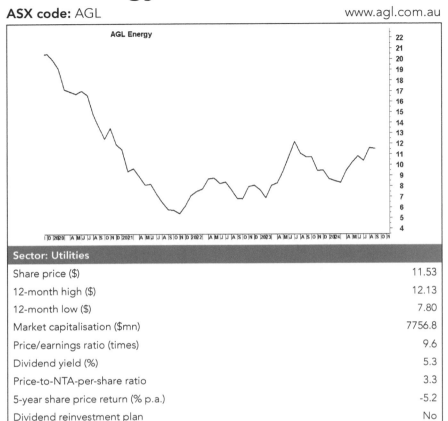

Sector: Utilities	
Share price ($)	11.53
12-month high ($)	12.13
12-month low ($)	7.80
Market capitalisation ($mn)	7756.8
Price/earnings ratio (times)	9.6
Dividend yield (%)	5.3
Price-to-NTA-per-share ratio	3.3
5-year share price return (% p.a.)	-5.2
Dividend reinvestment plan	No

Sydney-based power generator and supplier AGL Energy is one of Australia's oldest companies, founded in 1837 as Australian Gas Light. Having closed the Liddell black coal power plant in New South Wales in 2023, it now operates three major coal- and gas-fired power stations — the Bayswater black coal power plant in New South Wales, the Loy Yang brown coal mine and power plant in Victoria and the Torrens gas power plant in South Australia. Its growing portfolio of renewable assets includes wind power generation in South Australia, Queensland, New South Wales and Victoria, hydro-electric power generation in Victoria and New South Wales, and solar power in New South Wales. Through its wholesale and retail businesses AGL supplies electricity and gas to more than four million business and residential customers in most states of Australia. It also maintains pool generation sales — electricity sold into the National Electricity Market. In addition, it operates a small telecommunications business.

Latest business results (June 2024, full year)

Profits surged, thanks to rising electricity prices and a greatly improved performance at the company's power stations. Total electricity customer sales volumes actually fell by nearly 5 per cent from the previous year, with gas sales volumes down 22.5 per cent, due to milder weather and competitive market conditions. Electricity demand was also hurt by the increasing use of rooftop solar generation by residential customers. Electricity and gas customer numbers rose 3 per cent to 4.1 million, with 344 000 telecommunications customers, up 18 per cent.

Outlook

Having benefited from rising energy prices and some significant productivity gains, AGL believes that profits have likely peaked. A combination of inflationary pressures, funding for strategic growth initiatives, rising depreciation and amortisation charges, and strong competition mean that earnings might decline, and the company's early forecast is for an after-tax profit in the June 2025 year of $530 million to $730 million. AGL is investing heavily in renewable energy projects as it works towards the closure of the Bayswater power station by 2033 and the Loy Yang A power station by 2035. Its development pipeline of renewable assets has grown to 6.2 gigawatts, with a goal of 12 gigawatts of generating capacity by 2035. Its 250-megawatt Torrens Island Battery began operations in August. In August 2024 it announced the acquisition for a combined total of $250 million of Firm Power, which has 21 battery energy storage system projects in development, and Terrain Solar, which is developing six solar projects.

Year to 30 June	2023	2024
Revenues ($mn)	14 157.0	13 583.0
Electricity (%)	43	53
Generation sales to pool (%)	33	22
Gas (%)	18	17
EBIT ($mn)	643.0	1482.0
EBIT margin (%)	4.5	10.9
Gross margin (%)	20.4	29.4
Profit before tax ($mn)	375.0	1157.0
Profit after tax ($mn)	281.0	812.0
Earnings per share (c)	41.77	120.70
Cash flow per share (c)	149.98	231.74
Dividend (c)	31	61
Percentage franked	0	0
Net tangible assets per share ($)	2.88	3.46
Interest cover (times)	2.5	4.8
Return on equity (%)	4.8	15.4
Debt-to-equity ratio (%)	53.4	33.1
Current ratio	1.1	1.1

Amotiv Limited

ASX code: AOV

amotiv.com

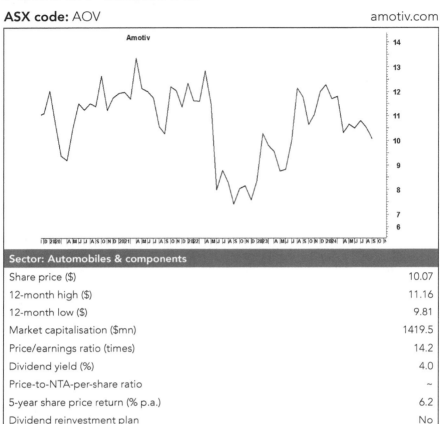

Sector: Automobiles & components	
Share price ($)	10.07
12-month high ($)	11.16
12-month low ($)	9.81
Market capitalisation ($mn)	1419.5
Price/earnings ratio (times)	14.2
Dividend yield (%)	4.0
Price-to-NTA-per-share ratio	~
5-year share price return (% p.a.)	6.2
Dividend reinvestment plan	No

Amotiv, the new name for GUD Holdings, is based in Melbourne and was founded in 1940. Following the sale of its Davey water pumps and water treatment products business, it now solely manufactures and distributes a wide range of specialist products for the automotive aftermarket and accessories sector, with a large portfolio of several dozen brands. It operates primarily in Australia and New Zealand, though with a small but rapidly growing exposure to other international markets.

Latest business results (June 2024, full year)

Revenues and profits rose in a solid result, with strength in all divisions. During the year the company restructured its operations and it now segments its many businesses into three divisions. The best result came from the Lighting, Power & Electrical division, with double-digit gains in sales and profits, although this partly reflected acquisitions during the year. The 4WD Accessories and Trailering division benefited from growing vehicle sales in Australia, partially offset by weakness in New Zealand. The Powertrain & Undercar division, which specialises in a variety of products that include heavy-duty filters, fuel pumps, clutches and brakes, was helped by some price increases and increased demand for most products, despite warehousing issues that hurt brake sales. Total international sales — excluding New Zealand — jumped 52 per cent to represent 9 per cent of total turnover. The Davey water products subsidiary was divested in September 2023, and the results in the table have been adjusted to exclude this business.

Outlook

Amotiv estimates that the total addressable market for its products in Australia and New Zealand is currently worth some $8.4 billion. With a market share of only around 9 per cent, it sees considerable scope for growth. It also benefits as the number of cars in Australia rises, from around 21 million at present to an estimated 23 million by 2030, and with the average car age also edging up, from 11.9 years to an estimated 12.5 years. It has a variety of strategies for growth. Its Infinitev subsidiary is a leader in the recycling and repurposing of electric vehicle batteries, and Amotiv is making a substantial investment to boost this business. One of the company's goals is to become a global leader in automotive lighting. In November 2023 it acquired Swedish lighting specialist Rindab, and it plans to use this new subsidiary as a base for expansion throughout Europe. It has also established manufacturing facilities in South Africa, which it views as a key automotive manufacturing hub for global markets.

Year to 30 June	2023	2024
Revenues ($mn)	916.5	987.2
4WD accessories & trailering (%)	36	35
Lighting, power & electrical (%)	31	33
Powertrain & undercar (%)	33	32
EBIT ($mn)	157.9	168.5
EBIT margin (%)	17.2	17.1
Gross margin (%)	43.2	44.1
Profit before tax ($mn)	126.9	141.0
Profit after tax ($mn)	93.7	99.8
Earnings per share (c)	66.49	70.84
Cash flow per share (c)	100.40	107.33
Dividend (c)	39	40.5
Percentage franked	100	100
Net tangible assets per share ($)	~	~
Interest cover (times)	5.3	6.4
Return on equity (%)	10.8	10.9
Debt-to-equity ratio (%)	45.2	35.2
Current ratio	2.3	2.0

ANZ Group Holdings Limited

ASX code: ANZ

www.anz.com.au

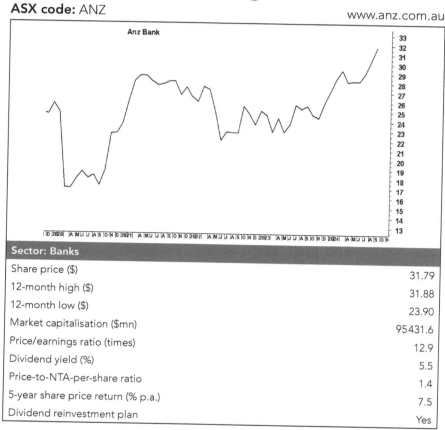

Sector: Banks	
Share price ($)	31.79
12-month high ($)	31.88
12-month low ($)	23.90
Market capitalisation ($mn)	95431.6
Price/earnings ratio (times)	12.9
Dividend yield (%)	5.5
Price-to-NTA-per-share ratio	1.4
5-year share price return (% p.a.)	7.5
Dividend reinvestment plan	Yes

Melbourne-based ANZ has its roots in the establishment of the Bank of Australasia in London in 1835. It is today one of the country's four banking giants and one of our largest companies. It is a market leader in New Zealand banking, and it is also active in the Pacific region. It is acquiring the banking business of Queensland-based Suncorp.

Latest business results (March 2024, half year)

A competitive home loans market and a decline in the bank's net interest margin drove profits down. The bank was also hurt by both rising operating expenses and the cost of strategic initiatives. The core Australia Retail division saw revenues and profits fall, despite an increase in lending volumes. The Institutional division achieved a small rise in income but with profits edging down as corporate finance and transaction banking lending volumes fell. The Australia Commercial division recorded declines in income and profits as an unfavourable deposit mix sent the net interest margin down, along with higher net funding costs and asset margin contraction. The fourth major division, representing New Zealand operations, actually achieved a modest increase in profits, with home loan growth more than offsetting a contraction in business lending, along with higher earnings on capital.

Outlook

ANZ has received federal government approval for its takeover of Suncorp's banking business — announced in July 2022 — and it is now working to complete the transaction. The acquisition will add an estimated $47 billion in home loans to ANZ's portfolio, along with some $45 billion in deposits and $11 billion in commercial loans. It could also provide annual cost synergies of around $260 million, along with 1.2 million new customers. ANZ continues to invest in digital technology to simplify its operations, and in particular to reduce the processing time for home loan applications. Technological advances include its flagship retail banking platform, ANZ Plus, which provides smoother customer transactions and boosts the personal banking business. This now has more than 690 000 customers and $14 billion in deposits. The Institutional division has achieved success with its payments platform operation, which is facilitating some $164 trillion in annual payments, and this business continues to grow. ANZ is also investing more in expanding and strengthening its Commercial division, which services some 650 000 small businesses. With the bank subject to inflationary pressures, it is investing in a range of productivity measures, and achieved around $200 million in cost savings in the March 2024 half.

Year to 30 September	2022	2023
Operating income ($mn)	18 547.0	20 893.0
Net interest income ($mn)	14 874.0	16 581.0
Operating expenses ($mn)	9579.0	10 139.0
Profit before tax ($mn)	9200.0	10 509.0
Profit after tax ($mn)	6515.0	7405.0
Earnings per share (c)	228.80	246.82
Dividend (c)	146	175
Percentage franked	100	76
Non-interest income to total income (%)	19.8	20.6
Cost-to-income ratio (%)	51.6	48.5
Return on equity (%)	10.1	10.9
Return on assets (%)	0.6	0.7
Half year to 31 March	2023	2024
Operating income ($mn)	10 528.0	10 347.0
Profit before tax ($mn)	5398.0	5062.0
Profit after tax ($mn)	3821.0	3552.0
Earnings per share (c)	127.60	118.30
Dividend (c)	81	83
Percentage franked	100	65
Net tangible assets per share ($)	21.69	22.09

ARB Corporation Limited

ASX code: ARB   www.arb.com.au

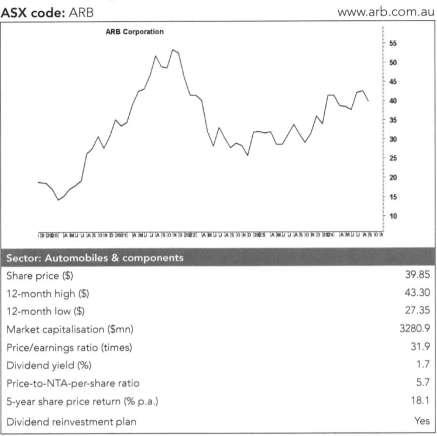

Sector: Automobiles & components	
Share price ($)	39.85
12-month high ($)	43.30
12-month low ($)	27.35
Market capitalisation ($mn)	3280.9
Price/earnings ratio (times)	31.9
Dividend yield (%)	1.7
Price-to-NTA-per-share ratio	5.7
5-year share price return (% p.a.)	18.1
Dividend reinvestment plan	Yes

Melbourne-based ARB, founded in 1975, is a prominent manufacturer of specialty automotive accessories, and an international leader in the design, production and distribution of specialised equipment for four-wheel-drive (4WD) vehicles. These include its Air Locker air-operated locking differential system, as well as a wide range of other products, including bull bars, roof racks, tow bars, canopies and the Old Man Emu range of suspension products. It operates a network of 74 ARB-brand stores throughout Australia. It has established manufacturing facilities in Thailand and it exports to more than 100 countries.

Latest business results (June 2024, full year)

Profits staged a solid recovery after the double-digit decline of the previous year. ARB's strongest business, representing 58 per cent of total company turnover, is Australian aftermarket sales to its own stores and to other ARB stockists, and these grew 5.4 per cent for the year. Price rises and operational efficiencies helped generate a boost to profit margins. Exports represent a further third of sales, and these fell 6.5 per cent, with weakness in the US auto sector compounded by reduced demand from ARB's major American wholesale customer. Original equipment manufacturer

(OEM) sales to local vehicle manufacturers showed exceptional strength, with revenues surging by more than 40 per cent.

Outlook

ARB believes it can achieve higher sales and profits in the June 2025 year, even in an environment of slowing consumer spending. Branded ARB stores play a significant role in the company's domestic aftermarket sales. It did not open any new Australian stores during the June 2024 year, but plans three by June 2025 and upgrades to others. It has also opened its first store in New Zealand. A strategic partnership with Ford Australia provides it with early access to Ford vehicle designs and the opportunity to market a complete range of accessories as new vehicles are released. With rising overseas demand, the company is seeing a recovery in export sales. It is implementing a series of growth initiatives in the key US market. It has acquired a 30 per cent interest in Off Road Warehouse (ORW), an American 4WD accessories retailer, enabling this business to expand its store network. It has also launched a new direct-to-consumer eCommerce website and has initiated a new partnership with Toyota USA. The company also expects further growth in OEM sales. At June 2024 ARB had no debt and more than $56 million in cash holdings. In September 2024 it announced that it would raise its stake in ORW from 30 per cent to 50 per cent and that ORW would acquire 42 retail stores under the 4 Wheel Parts banner.

Year to 30 June	2023	2024
Revenues ($mn)	671.2	693.2
EBIT ($mn)	123.8	143.1
EBIT margin (%)	18.4	20.6
Gross margin (%)	42.8	45.8
Profit before tax ($mn)	122.1	141.4
Profit after tax ($mn)	88.5	102.7
Earnings per share (c)	107.92	124.91
Cash flow per share (c)	139.50	159.50
Dividend (c)	62	69
Percentage franked	100	100
Net tangible assets per share ($)	6.40	6.98
Interest cover (times)	87.3	363.2
Return on equity (%)	15.2	16.2
Debt-to-equity ratio (%)	~	~
Current ratio	4.2	4.1

Aristocrat Leisure Limited

ASX code: ALL

ir.aristocrat.com

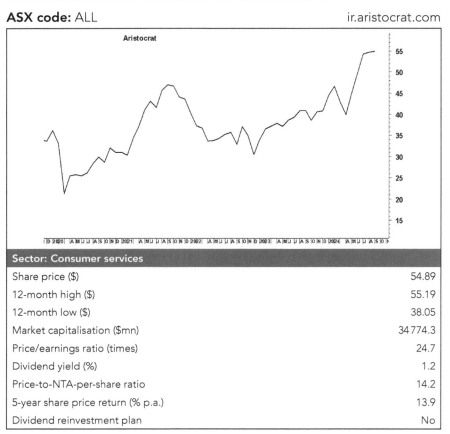

Sector: Consumer services	
Share price ($)	54.89
12-month high ($)	55.19
12-month low ($)	38.05
Market capitalisation ($mn)	34774.3
Price/earnings ratio (times)	24.7
Dividend yield (%)	1.2
Price-to-NTA-per-share ratio	14.2
5-year share price return (% p.a.)	13.9
Dividend reinvestment plan	No

Sydney-based Aristocrat, founded in 1953, is one of the world's leading developers of hardware and software for the gaming industry. It divides its activities into three operating units. Aristocrat Gaming provides casino games to customers in more than 300 gaming jurisdictions around the world. Pixel United is involved in the development of games for electronic mobile devices. The third unit, Aristocrat Interactive, provides customers with online gaming, known as real money gaming (RMG).

Latest business results (March 2024, half year)

Continuing strength in the key North American casino market generated another good result for Aristocrat. Gaming revenues comprise some 56 per cent of total company turnover, and sales and profits both rose. This business was also helped by some strong demand from Asian customers, boosting profit margins in the region. Pixel United represents about 41 per cent of turnover, with sales largely flat from the March 2023 period, although a strong focus on operational efficiencies generated a double-digit rise in profits. Nevertheless, Pixel United profitability remains substantially below that for the gaming business. The very small Aristocrat Interactive business unit reported fast-growing sales and profits.

Outlook

Aristocrat enjoys a strong position in the global gaming industry, with high market shares in many regions. With an estimated addressable market of more than US$400 billion, it sees substantial potential for growth. It has a particular goal of doubling the value of the company every five years. Nevertheless, this remains a competitive business, and the company is highly dependent on a continuing stream of attractive new and enhanced products. To develop these it must recruit and retain large numbers of highly skilled creative specialists and technology experts, and this has been one of its key challenges. Consequently, its design and development budget remains high at around 12 per cent to 13 per cent of annual revenues. It sees some of the best growth prospects from the RMG sector, and has announced a target of becoming one of the world's leading gaming platforms for global online RMG. In April 2024 it completed the US$1.2 billion acquisition of NeoGames, a leader in the RMG business, and it expects its Aristocrat Interactive division to make an increasingly important contribution, with particular potential for the iLottery product. Aristocrat is also working to rationalise its Pixel United business in order to boost its profit margins. With much of its income coming from outside Australia, Aristocrat's earnings are heavily influenced by currency rate trends.

Year to 30 September	2022	2023
Revenues ($mn)	5573.7	6295.7
EBIT ($mn)	1582.5	1824.1
EBIT margin (%)	28.4	29.0
Profit before tax ($mn)	1327.7	1670.4
Profit after tax ($mn)	1000.9	1454.1
Earnings per share (c)	150.77	222.49
Cash flow per share (c)	206.57	280.94
Dividend (c)	52	64
Percentage franked	100	100
Interest cover (times)	6.9	44.9
Return on equity (%)	20.2	22.8
Half year to 31 March	2023	2024
Revenues ($mn)	3080.4	3269.6
Profit before tax ($mn)	852.8	961.7
Profit after tax ($mn)	653.0	711.3
Earnings per share (c)	99.10	110.80
Dividend (c)	30	36
Percentage franked	100	100
Net tangible assets per share ($)	3.46	3.86
Debt-to-equity ratio (%)	~	~
Current ratio	3.3	3.1

ASX Limited

ASX code: ASX www.asx.com.au

Sector: Financial services	
Share price ($)	63.10
12-month high ($)	68.69
12-month low ($)	53.98
Market capitalisation ($mn)	12 234.3
Price/earnings ratio (times)	25.8
Dividend yield (%)	3.3
Price-to-NTA-per-share ratio	11.0
5-year share price return (% p.a.)	-2.8
Dividend reinvestment plan	No

Sydney-based ASX (Australian Securities Exchange) was formed in 1987 through the amalgamation of six independent stock exchanges that formerly operated in the state capital cities. Each of those exchanges had a history of share trading dating back to the 19th century. Though originally a mutual organisation of stockbrokers, in 1998 ASX became a listed company, with its shares traded on its own market. It expanded in 2006 when it merged with the Sydney Futures Exchange. Today it provides primary, secondary and derivative market services, along with clearing, settlement and compliance services. It is also a provider of a range of comprehensive market data and technical services.

Latest business results (June 2024, full year)

Revenues rose in a buoyant market environment but underlying earnings were down, as a 15 per cent jump in operating expenses — notably staffing costs — reduced profits. ASX categorises its operations into four broad divisions. The best result came from the Markets division, with revenues up 7.9 per cent as market volumes rose, and with notably strong performances from 90-day bank bill futures and three-year and 10-year treasury bond futures. The Technology and Data division was also firm, with revenues up 5.9 per cent, thanks especially to continuing growth in demand for equities and futures market data. By contrast, the Listings division suffered a 4.8 per cent decline in revenues, with 56 new listings, compared to 57 in the previous year and 217 in the June 2022 year. The Securities and Payments division recorded a 1.1 per cent fall in revenues, owing to reduced activity in cash equities clearing and settlement services.

Outlook

ASX's profits are highly geared to levels of market activity. The company also enjoys a degree of protection in its operations, with little effective competition for many of its businesses. Rising costs have resulted in part from ASX's aborted plans to replace its Clearing House Electronic Subregister System (CHESS), as well as from the necessity to boost staff numbers to meet increasingly stringent regulatory requirements. The company forecasts further increases in costs of 6 per cent to 9 per cent in the June 2025 year. It plans another replacement to CHESS, to be delivered from 2026 by global technology provider Tata Consultancy Service. It is working to develop new products, and in July 2024 introduced three environmental futures contracts that allow customers to price and hedge emissions reduction risk. It sees a solid pipeline of companies waiting to list as market conditions improve.

Year to 30 June	2023	2024
Revenues ($mn)	1010.2	1034.3
Markets (%)	29	30
Securities & payments (%)	26	25
Technology & data (%)	24	25
Listings (%)	21	20
EBIT ($mn)	1037.4	1144.5
EBIT margin (%)	102.7	110.7
Profit before tax ($mn)	706.4	681.5
Profit after tax ($mn)	491.1	474.2
Earnings per share (c)	253.69	244.85
Cash flow per share (c)	273.89	265.50
Dividend (c)	228.3	208
Percentage franked	100	100
Net tangible assets per share ($)	5.80	5.73
Interest cover (times)	~	~
Return on equity (%)	13.2	12.9
Debt-to-equity ratio (%)	~	~
Current ratio	1.1	1.1

Australian Ethical Investment Limited

ASX code: AEF   www.australianethical.com.au

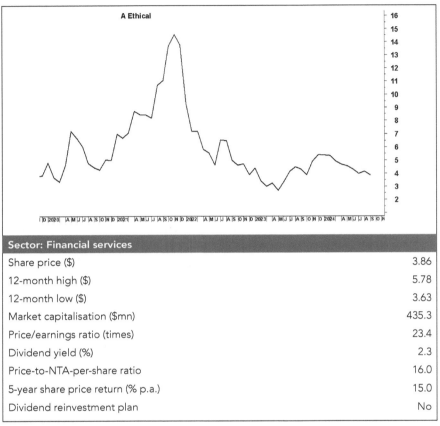

Sector: Financial services	
Share price ($)	3.86
12-month high ($)	5.78
12-month low ($)	3.63
Market capitalisation ($mn)	435.3
Price/earnings ratio (times)	23.4
Dividend yield (%)	2.3
Price-to-NTA-per-share ratio	16.0
5-year share price return (% p.a.)	15.0
Dividend reinvestment plan	No

Australian Ethical, based in Sydney, was founded in 1986. It is a wealth management company that specialises in investments in corporations that meet a set of ethical criteria. It operates a range of wholesale and retail funds — including superannuation — that incorporate Australian and international shares, emerging companies and fixed interest. In 2024 it acquired the fixed income business Altius Asset Management. The company donates up to 10 per cent of its profits to charities and activist groups through its Australian Ethical Foundation.

Latest business results (June 2024, full year)

Buoyant financial markets helped deliver a sparkling rise in revenues and profits, bolstered by a full-year contribution from Christian Super, acquired in 2023. Net inflows of $0.61 billion were up 30 per cent from the previous year, and a solid investment performance elevated funds by $0.63 billion. Consequently, funds under management at June 2024 of $10.4 billion were up from $9.2 billion a year earlier. The company received a small performance fee from the outperformance of its

Emerging Companies Fund. Careful cost management limited the growth in expenses and, with revenues rising at a faster pace, profit margins expanded.

Outlook

Australian Ethical is a small company but is a leader in the trend towards ethical investment. In a growing marketplace, with many major financial institutions launching their own ESG (environmental, social and governance) funds, Australian Ethical has attracted attention because of its perceived independence. The company's pledge is that it seeks out positive investments that support its three pillars of people, planet and animals. Its Ethical Charter gives details of the criteria it uses for its investments, and it provides a public list of the companies in which it is prepared to invest. It is working to achieve growth and is actively seeking diversification opportunities, including appropriate acquisitions. Its $5.5 million acquisition of Altius Asset Management from Australian Unity will strengthen its capabilities in fixed income investing and boost funds under management by around $2 billion. In February 2024 it launched its Infrastructure Debt Fund to provide capital for key renewable energy developments. Inhouse projects for the transition of its superannuation administration and its custody and investment administration are expected to deliver annual savings of around $4 million on operating expenses. Nevertheless, Australian Ethical remains heavily exposed to volatile financial markets, and its businesses could be hurt in any sustained downturn. At June 2024 the company had no debt and more than $26 million in cash holdings.

Year to 30 June	2023	2024
Revenues ($mn)	81.1	100.5
EBIT ($mn)	15.9	19.6
EBIT margin (%)	19.6	19.5
Profit before tax ($mn)	15.8	19.5
Profit after tax ($mn)	11.8	18.4
Earnings per share (c)	10.57	16.52
Cash flow per share (c)	11.70	17.52
Dividend (c)	7	9
Percentage franked	100	100
Net tangible assets per share ($)	0.22	0.24
Interest cover (times)	~	~
Return on equity (%)	45.9	64.8
Debt-to-equity ratio (%)	~	~
Current ratio	2.0	2.3

Beacon Lighting Group Limited
ASX code: BLX   www.beaconlighting.com.au

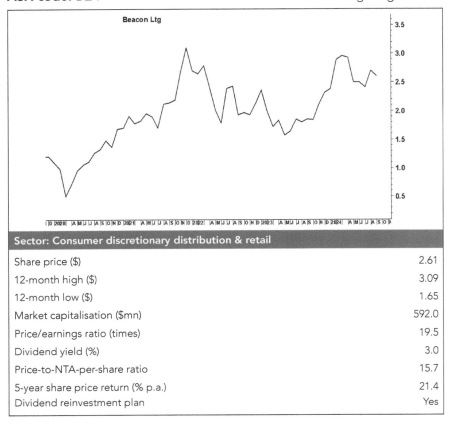

Sector: Consumer discretionary distribution & retail

Share price ($)	2.61
12-month high ($)	3.09
12-month low ($)	1.65
Market capitalisation ($mn)	592.0
Price/earnings ratio (times)	19.5
Dividend yield (%)	3.0
Price-to-NTA-per-share ratio	15.7
5-year share price return (% p.a.)	21.4
Dividend reinvestment plan	Yes

Melbourne-based lighting specialist Beacon dates back to the launch of the first Beacon Lighting store in 1967. It steadily expanded throughout Australia, and today has 126 stores — two of them franchised — supplying a wide range of lighting fixtures and light globes, as well as ceiling fans. Its Beacon Commercial division supplies many commercial projects, including volume residential developments, apartment complexes, aged care facilities, hotels and retail fit-outs, with five sales offices around Australia. The Beacon International business operates sales offices in Hong Kong, Germany and the US, with a support office in China.

Latest business results (June 2024, full year)

Sales rose but profits fell, as inflationary pressures and rising distribution and marketing expenses bit into margins. Seven new stores were opened during the year. In addition, the June 2024 year represented 53 weeks, compared to 52 weeks for the previous year, and on a like-for-like basis 2024 sales were in line with 2023. In an environment of weakened consumer confidence, the company's focus on trade sales proved rewarding, with trade sales in stores rising by 27 per cent and online trade sales up by 42 per cent. Beacon Commercial boosted sales by 14 per cent, with strong demand from volume residential builders. The small Beacon International division achieved single-digit sales growth.

Outlook

Beacon's business is closely linked to trends in the housing market. With renovation activity in decline the company could suffer, as households are hit by cost of living pressures and cut back on discretionary spending. Much of its product range is imported, so it is also vulnerable to currency fluctuations and supply chain disruptions. In response, Beacon has a variety of strategies for growth. It plans to open five new stores during the June 2025 year, in Victoria and New South Wales, with a long-term aspirational target of around 195 stores nationwide. It will continue its successful focus on boosting services to trade customers, estimating the trade market in Australia for its products as worth $2.1 billion annually. Initiatives include the roll-out of further trade-specific products, dedicated trade rooms at its stores, trade seminars, a trade training program and enhanced internet platforms to facilitate online business. Trade revenues have risen strongly to represent around a third of relevant sales, and the company hopes to raise this to 50 per cent by June 2028. The Beacon International division continues to expand its marketing efforts in North America, Europe and Asia for Beacon's fan and lighting products.

Year to 30 June*	2023	2024
Revenues ($mn)	312.0	323.1
EBIT ($mn)	54.8	51.8
EBIT margin (%)	17.6	16.0
Gross margin (%)	67.7	69.0
Profit before tax ($mn)	48.2	43.3
Profit after tax ($mn)	33.6	30.1
Earnings per share (c)	15.05	13.35
Cash flow per share (c)	28.82	28.75
Dividend (c)	8.3	7.9
Percentage franked	100	100
Net tangible assets per share ($)	0.12	0.17
Interest cover (times)	9.2	7.2
Return on equity (%)	23.8	19.1
Debt-to-equity ratio (%)	1.2	~
Current ratio	1.7	1.7

*25 June 2023

BHP Group Limited

ASX code: BHP   www.bhp.com

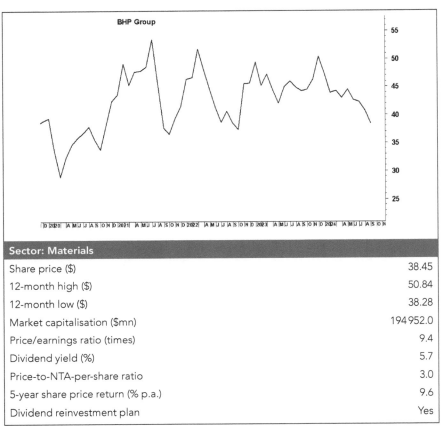

Sector: Materials	
Share price ($)	38.45
12-month high ($)	50.84
12-month low ($)	38.28
Market capitalisation ($mn)	194 952.0
Price/earnings ratio (times)	9.4
Dividend yield (%)	5.7
Price-to-NTA-per-share ratio	3.0
5-year share price return (% p.a.)	9.6
Dividend reinvestment plan	Yes

Melbourne-based resources giant BHP was founded as Broken Hill Proprietary in 1885. In 2001 it merged with another resources major, Billiton, which dated back to 1851. Today it segments its operations into five broad product areas — iron ore, copper, coal, nickel and potash —with activities in many countries.

Latest business results (June 2024, full year)

Rising levels of production for iron ore and copper, along with higher prices, generated an increase in revenues and profits for BHP, offsetting weakness in coal. The mainstay iron ore business saw revenues and profits up 13 per cent on just a small increase in production. Such is the company's strength in iron ore, including its low production costs, that it contributed around two-thirds of total EBIT. Copper revenues rose by 16 per cent, with profits jumping 29 per cent, thanks to higher prices as well as the addition of South Australian copper miner OZ Minerals, acquired in May 2023. Coal revenues fell 30 per cent and profits crashed by 54 per cent as production fell. The company's small nickel business was hit by lower prices and fell into the red, with a subsequent US$2.7 billion after-tax impairment charge. In July 2024 BHP announced the temporary suspension of its nickel operations. Note that BHP reports its results in US dollars. The Australian dollar figures in this book — converted at prevailing exchange rates — are for guidance only.

Outlook

BHP is restructuring its operations in order to gain greater exposure to what it believes are mega-trends of decarbonisation and electrification. It is placing a particular emphasis on copper developments, expecting demand to grow steadily over the longer term, and is already one of the world's leading producers. It plans to double copper production in South Australia and in July 2024 it announced a US$2.1 billion plan to work with Canada's Lundin Mining to develop copper mines in the Vicuña region of Chile and Argentina. With nickel prices falling, it is suspending operations at its Western Australia Nickel business operation, though it will invest up to US$300 million annually to support a potential restart. Its high-margin iron ore business remains very dependent on Chinese economic trends, with signs that steel production there may have peaked. BHP is investing heavily in its Jansen potash project in Canada, with initial production now expected by the end of 2026, in order to meet global fertiliser demand that the company believes could double from present levels by the 2040s.

Year to 30 June	2023	2024
Revenues ($mn)	80 323.9	84 330.3
Iron ore (%)	44	50
Copper (%)	30	33
Coal (%)	20	14
EBIT ($mn)	35 016.4	37 645.5
EBIT margin (%)	43.6	44.6
Profit before tax ($mn)	31 941.8	34 315.2
Profit after tax ($mn)	20 029.9	20 697.0
Earnings per share (c)	395.53	408.39
Cash flow per share (c)	544.70	566.69
Dividend (c)	261.43	219.61
Percentage franked	100	100
Net tangible assets per share ($)	12.83	12.88
Interest cover (times)	15.3	16.7
Return on equity (%)	30.2	30.6
Debt-to-equity ratio (%)	20.4	16.7
Current ratio	1.2	1.7

Brambles Limited

ASX code: BXB   www.brambles.com

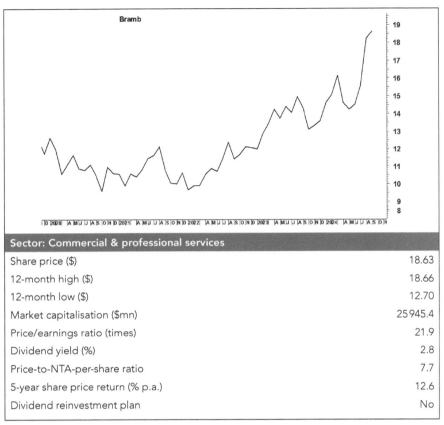

Sector: Commercial & professional services	
Share price ($)	18.63
12-month high ($)	18.66
12-month low ($)	12.70
Market capitalisation ($mn)	25 945.4
Price/earnings ratio (times)	21.9
Dividend yield (%)	2.8
Price-to-NTA-per-share ratio	7.7
5-year share price return (% p.a.)	12.6
Dividend reinvestment plan	No

Sydney-based Brambles has a history that dates back to 1875, when Walter Bramble opened a butcher's business, later expanding into transportation and logistics. Today, following a long series of acquisitions, it is the global leader in pallets, crates and container pooling services under the brand name CHEP (Commonwealth Handling Equipment Pool, a term used by the Australian government to designate pallets and other assets left in Australia by the United States Army after World War II). It owns approximately 347 million pallets, crates and containers and operates through a network of more than 750 service centres in 60 countries.

Latest business results (June 2024, full year)

In a volatile business environment Brambles enjoyed gains in revenues and profits, driven especially by price increases designed to mitigate the impact of inflation. Overall volumes were up 1 per cent. Profits rose at a faster pace than revenues, reflecting productivity benefits and gains from supply chain initiatives. The company saw growth in all regions, with CHEP Americas delivering a 24 per cent jump in profits on a 7 per cent sales increase, thanks especially to a sharp reduction in pallet losses as the company introduced enhanced asset control measures. CHEP EMEA (covering Europe, the Middle East and Africa) achieved a 17 per cent gain in profits, with revenues up 9 per cent, due to price increases and asset efficiency. CHEP Asia-Pacific reported a 2 per cent profit increase on sales growth of 6 per cent, with benefits from new customer contracts and volume growth. Brambles reports its results in US dollars. The Australian dollar figures in this book — converted at prevailing exchange rates — are for guidance only.

Outlook

Brambles is heavily influenced by trends in global trade and, more generally, by the global economy. More than half its revenues come from the Americas, and it is affected by the high expenses of these operations, with profit margins below those prevailing elsewhere, and it is working to drive down costs. It has initiated structural changes to incentivise the effectual use of its pallets, and this transformation program has generated significant improvements to asset efficiency, with consequent cost benefits. Further cost savings are being derived from a series of automation investments at the company's network of service centres. It is also working to expand its regions of operation. The company's early forecast is for sales growth of 4 per cent to 6 per cent in the June 2024 year, with profits rising by 8 per cent to 11 per cent.

Year to 30 June	2023	2024
Revenues ($mn)	9069.9	9917.3
CHEP Americas (%)	55	55
CHEP EMEA (%)	36	37
CHEP Asia-Pacific (%)	9	8
EBIT ($mn)	1603.3	1924.2
EBIT margin (%)	17.7	19.4
Profit before tax ($mn)	1409.1	1706.5
Profit after tax ($mn)	980.6	1181.7
Earnings per share (c)	70.65	84.93
Cash flow per share (c)	149.16	172.26
Dividend (c)	39.5	51.99
Percentage franked	35	35
Net tangible assets per share ($)	2.17	2.41
Interest cover (times)	9.4	10.0
Return on equity (%)	24.8	25.6
Debt-to-equity ratio (%)	69.5	51.4
Current ratio	0.5	0.6

Breville Group Limited

ASX code: BRG

www.brevillegroup.com

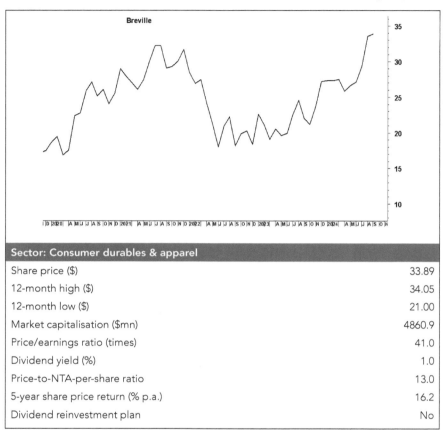

Sector: Consumer durables & apparel	
Share price ($)	33.89
12-month high ($)	34.05
12-month low ($)	21.00
Market capitalisation ($mn)	4860.9
Price/earnings ratio (times)	41.0
Dividend yield (%)	1.0
Price-to-NTA-per-share ratio	13.0
5-year share price return (% p.a.)	16.2
Dividend reinvestment plan	No

Sydney-based Breville Group traces its origins to the production of the first Breville radio in 1932. It later moved into the home appliance business and was subsequently acquired by Housewares International. In 2008 Housewares changed its name to Breville Group, and today the company is a leading designer and distributor of small electrical kitchen home appliances under various brands, including Breville, Sage, Lelit, Baratza and Kambrook. Breville sells its products in some 80 countries, and international business is responsible for around 80 per cent of company turnover. Premier Investments hold 28 per cent of Breville's equity.

Latest business results (June 2024, full year)

Despite a slowdown in consumer spending in its main markets, Breville was able to post further gains in sales and profits, and with a marked strengthening in the second half. With earnings growing at a faster pace than sales, profit margins were higher. New products played an important role in the good result, and there was particularly strong demand worldwide for coffee-making equipment. The best performance came from the Europe/Middle East/Africa region, where sales grew 8.5 per cent on a constant currency basis. The Americas sector saw sales up 2.9 per cent, and both regions achieved double-digit gains in the second half. Asia-Pacific sales fell 6.4 per cent, despite a second-half recovery that was led by coffee equipment, and despite a strong performance from South Korea. Breville's Distribution division sells products designed and developed by third parties, and represents about 13 per cent of total turnover. It recorded a 2.7 per cent decline in sales, though with a double-digit rise in profits.

Outlook

Breville has been achieving great success with its strategy of developing premium home appliances for the American, European and Asia-Pacific markets. North America alone now represents half of company revenues and Europe has passed the Asia-Pacific region as the second-largest market. The company regards coffee in particular as offering great potential. Its 2022 acquisition of premium Italian coffee equipment manufacturer Lelit and the 2020 purchase of coffee grinder manufacturer Baratza have made Breville a force in the international specialty coffee equipment sector. Its beanz.com coffee bean business, run in partnership with specialty coffee roasters, is active in Australia, the US and the UK, with further countries to follow. New products that are performing well include the Barista Impress range of espresso machines, the InFizz range of carbonated water and soda makers and the Paradice food processor. The company also continues steadily to enter new markets.

Year to 30 June	2023	2024
Revenues ($mn)	1478.6	1530.0
EBIT ($mn)	172.7	188.1
EBIT margin (%)	11.7	12.3
Gross margin (%)	35.0	36.4
Profit before tax ($mn)	151.0	165.7
Profit after tax ($mn)	110.2	118.5
Earnings per share (c)	77.23	82.69
Cash flow per share (c)	109.57	124.41
Dividend (c)	30.5	33
Percentage franked	100	100
Net tangible assets per share ($)	2.11	2.60
Interest cover (times)	8.2	9.4
Return on equity (%)	15.9	14.6
Debt-to-equity ratio (%)	15.8	~
Current ratio	2.6	2.3

CAR Group Limited

ASX code: CAR cargroup.com

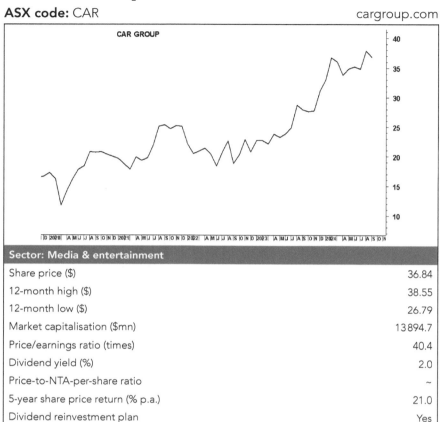

Sector: Media & entertainment	
Share price ($)	36.84
12-month high ($)	38.55
12-month low ($)	26.79
Market capitalisation ($mn)	13 894.7
Price/earnings ratio (times)	40.4
Dividend yield (%)	2.0
Price-to-NTA-per-share ratio	~
5-year share price return (% p.a.)	21.0
Dividend reinvestment plan	Yes

CAR Group, formerly known as Carsales.com, was founded in Melbourne in 1997 and has grown to become the market leader in online automotive advertising. It also operates specialist websites for the sale of other goods that include boats, motorcycles, trucks, construction equipment, farm machinery, caravans and tyres. It has expanded abroad, with interests in automotive businesses in the US, Asia and Latin America, and these operations now generate more than half of company turnover. The Investments division manages tyre marketing and vehicle inspection businesses. A smaller division provides a diverse range of data services for customers, including research and reporting, valuations, appraisals, website development and photography services.

Latest business results (June 2024, full year)

Strong growth across all key businesses helped deliver further solid gains in revenues and profits. Australian online advertising achieved a 13 per cent rise in sales, with strength in each key customer area. North American operations also reported a 13 per cent sales boost, overcoming challenging market conditions. Latin American businesses were particularly strong as CAR Group raised its ownership of Brazil's Webmotors from 30 per cent to 70 per cent. Asian revenues were up 15 per cent, with continuing strong progress in the South Korean Encar business.

Outlook

CAR Group primarily does business in four countries — Australia, the US, Brazil and South Korea — that it calculates offer a total addressable market of some $10.3 billion annually, and it sees significant scope for long-term growth. However, with Australia viewed as a largely mature market, the best future expansion could come from abroad. The company's early forecast is for continuing good growth for the June 2025 year in North America and Asia, with strong growth in Latin America. Trader Interactive — acquired for nearly $2 billion — is an American leader in the provision of digital markets for commercial and recreational vehicles and industrial equipment. CAR Group is already generating synergies from this business through introducing its own technology, developing new products and acquiring more customers. It is also introducing new systems and technology to Webmotors, which is the leading automotive digital marketplace in Brazil, and is realising significant expansion in dealer numbers. Together with banking giant Santander it manages a streamlined auto loan application business in Brazil that is achieving very fast growth. It also expects continuing strong progress in its Korean Encar operation — which is that country's leader in automotive classifieds — thanks especially to increased uptake of the company's Guarantee vehicle inspection service.

Year to 30 June	2023	2024
Revenues ($mn)	781.2	1098.7
Australia — online advertising (%)	45	36
North America (%)	23	25
Latin America (%)	4	17
Asia (%)	13	11
Investments (%)	8	6
EBIT ($mn)	416.0	524.0
EBIT margin (%)	53.3	47.7
Profit before tax ($mn)	360.1	438.0
Profit after tax ($mn)	278.2	344.0
Earnings per share (c)	78.11	91.25
Cash flow per share (c)	108.16	132.32
Dividend (c)	61	73
Percentage franked	73	50
Net tangible assets per share ($)	~	~
Interest cover (times)	8.7	7.3
Return on equity (%)	13.6	11.6
Debt-to-equity ratio (%)	31.2	33.7
Current ratio	1.8	2.0

Clinuvel Pharmaceuticals Limited

ASX code: CUV   www.clinuvel.com

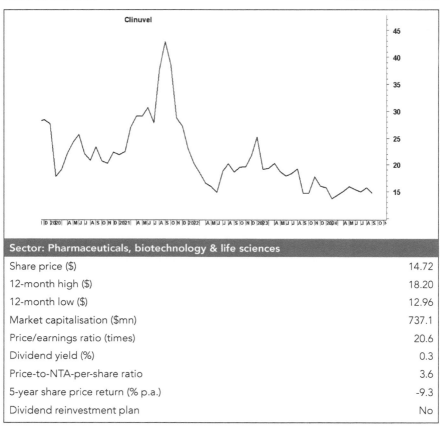

Sector: Pharmaceuticals, biotechnology & life sciences	
Share price ($)	14.72
12-month high ($)	18.20
12-month low ($)	12.96
Market capitalisation ($mn)	737.1
Price/earnings ratio (times)	20.6
Dividend yield (%)	0.3
Price-to-NTA-per-share ratio	3.6
5-year share price return (% p.a.)	-9.3
Dividend reinvestment plan	No

Melbourne-based biopharmaceutical company Clinuvel dates back to 1987, when scientists devised technologies for the protection of skin using human hormones. Today it is a global company with a focus on developing drugs for the treatment of various skin disorders. Its lead therapy afamelanotide — known as Scenesse — has been shown to be effective in treating severe phototoxicity — intolerance of light — in many badly affected patients. It has been approved by regulators for commercial distribution in many countries. The company is also developing other drugs.

Latest business results (June 2024, full year)

Clinuvel reported double-digit increases in sales and profits, in another good result, as Scenesse demand continued to rise, with a growing number of patients, prescribing doctors and centres administering treatment. The company reported a 90 per cent retention rate among patients. In the US the number of specialty treatment centres rose from 50 to 85. A 19 per cent increase in costs followed a sharp rise in personnel expenses as the company recruited new specialists, with an eye to future expansion.

Outlook

Scenesse reduces the severity of phototoxic skin reactions in patients with a rare light intolerance condition known as erythropoietic protoporphyria. Such patients can experience severe pain from sun exposure, as well as swelling and scarring of exposed areas of the body such as the face and hands, with hospitalisation and powerful pain killers sometimes necessary. Scenesse is the first drug developed for this condition. It was launched in Europe in 2016 and in the US in 2020 and the company is actively seeking to have it approved in other countries. During 2025 it expects to expand its American treatment centre numbers to 120. A new partnership with rare diseases specialist Valentech Pharma has enabled access to patients in Latin America. In addition, Clinuvel is involved in a series of drug trials. It has launched highly promising tests in the US to determine whether Scenesse can be used to treat vitiligo, a skin disorder where patches of skin become pale or white. It is also working on the development of a range of over-the-counter skin protection products, based on Scenesse. It has developed a new drug, Prénumbra, a liquid formulation of Scenesse, and has begun studies on using this drug in the treatment of arterial ischaemic stroke. It is developing a third drug, Neuracthel, which it believes could have applications in the treatment of neurological, endocrinological and degenerative diseases. At June 2024 Clinuvel had no debt and cash holdings of more than $183 million.

Year to 30 June	2023	2024
Revenues ($mn)	78.3	88.2
EBIT ($mn)	45.6	50.7
EBIT margin (%)	58.2	57.5
Profit before tax ($mn)	45.6	50.7
Profit after tax ($mn)	30.6	35.6
Earnings per share (c)	61.94	71.51
Cash flow per share (c)	63.54	73.80
Dividend (c)	5	5
Percentage franked	100	100
Net tangible assets per share ($)	3.31	4.04
Interest cover (times)	~	~
Return on equity (%)	21.1	19.4
Debt-to-equity ratio (%)	~	~
Current ratio	7.4	8.8

Cochlear Limited

ASX code: COH

www.cochlear.com

Sector: Health care equipment & services	
Share price ($)	288.75
12-month high ($)	350.32
12-month low ($)	237.69
Market capitalisation ($mn)	18 911.4
Price/earnings ratio (times)	53.0
Dividend yield (%)	1.4
Price-to-NTA-per-share ratio	16.1
5-year share price return (% p.a.)	6.9
Dividend reinvestment plan	No

Sydney-based Cochlear, founded in 1981, has around 60 per cent of the world market for cochlear bionic-ear implants, which assist the communication ability of people suffering from severe hearing impediments. It also sells the Baha bone-anchored hearing implant, as well as a range of acoustic products. With manufacturing facilities and technology centres in Australia, Europe and North America, it has sales in over 180 countries, and overseas business accounts for more than 90 per cent of revenues and profits.

Latest business results (June 2024, full year)

Sales and profits rose again in a good result, with growth across all business units. Cochlear implant sales rose 9 per cent to 48 040 units, with revenues up 14 per cent. The roll-out of the Nucleus 8 sound processor in the US and Western Europe continued to contribute to the good result, with particular strength among the seniors segment. Emerging market unit sales rose by 5 per cent, with strength in China, Brazil and Eastern Europe partially offset by declines in India and Argentina. Service revenues grew by 15 per cent, thanks especially to the continuing growth in Nucleus

8 processor sales. Acoustics sales rose by 7 per cent, with strong demand for the Osia implant, which was launched in the US in December 2023.

Outlook

Cochlear continues to launch new products at an impressive rate, with a high level of research and development spending, and this is helping it maintain its market leadership. It expects Nucleus 8 sound processor sales to remain firm, with strong demand also for the Osia implant. However, it sees a slowdown in Services division growth. A particular recent marketing focus has been adults and seniors in developed markets, which it regards as its biggest opportunity, given the large and growing market size and a current penetration rate of only about 3 per cent. The company points to research suggesting that good hearing is an important contributor to healthy ageing. In particular, it notes a 2023 report that found cognitive decline slowing by 48 per cent for a group of older adults with a degree of hearing loss and at risk of cognitive decline, after they had worn hearing aids for three years. At June 2024 Cochlear had no debt and cash holdings of more than $513 million. The company's early June 2025 forecast is for revenues growth of around 10 per cent, with an after-tax profit of $410 million to $430 million.

Year to 30 June	2023	2024
Revenues ($mn)	1936.1	2235.6
Cochlear implants (%)	58	59
Services (%)	30	30
Acoustics (%)	12	11
EBIT ($mn)	412.6	494.0
EBIT margin (%)	21.3	22.1
Gross margin (%)	74.3	74.5
Profit before tax ($mn)	403.2	484.8
Profit after tax ($mn)	305.2	356.8
Earnings per share (c)	464.09	544.43
Cash flow per share (c)	587.11	673.97
Dividend (c)	330	410
Percentage franked	54	75
Net tangible assets per share ($)	17.27	17.97
Interest cover (times)	~	~
Return on equity (%)	17.8	19.9
Debt-to-equity ratio (%)	~	~
Current ratio	2.4	2.3

Codan Limited

ASX code: CDA   www.codan.com.au

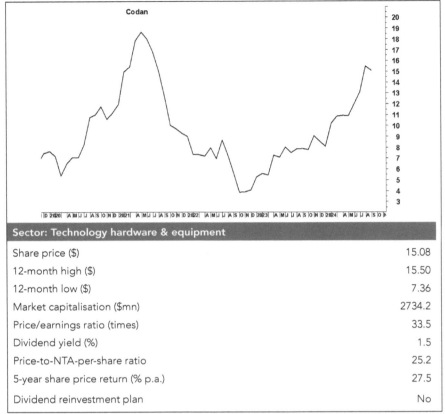

Sector: Technology hardware & equipment	
Share price ($)	15.08
12-month high ($)	15.50
12-month low ($)	7.36
Market capitalisation ($mn)	2734.2
Price/earnings ratio (times)	33.5
Dividend yield (%)	1.5
Price-to-NTA-per-share ratio	25.2
5-year share price return (% p.a.)	27.5
Dividend reinvestment plan	No

Adelaide electronics company Codan was founded in 1959. Its fast-growing Communications division produces high-frequency communication equipment for military and public safety use. The Metal Detection division is a leading world manufacturer of metal-detecting products, including Minelab detectors for hobbyists, gold detectors for small-scale miners and landmine detectors for humanitarian applications. Codan sells to more than 150 countries, and overseas sales represent around 90 per cent of company revenues. It has manufacturing sites and sales offices in Australia, Canada, Denmark, the UK and the US.

Latest business results (June 2024, full year)

Sales and profits rebounded from the previous year's decline, when a sharp decline in metal detector sales, due mainly to significant disruptions in African markets, hurt the result. This time metal detector revenues were up by 25 per cent, thanks especially to a series of new models and the company's success in expanding its sales channels throughout Europe and North America. African sales, representing nearly a third of the total, also recovered. Communications division sales rose 19 per cent, with a particularly strong contribution from the Zetron business, which supplies emergency and mission-critical communications equipment. The division also benefited from two acquisitions during the year.

Outlook

Codan is a significant force in two niche high-tech product areas. The Communications division held an order book of $197 million at June 2024, up 21 per cent from a year earlier, and the company's early forecast was for revenues growth for this division of 10 per cent to 15 per cent in the June 2025 year. The Zetron business is expected to continue growing strongly as Codan invests in a new generation of products. Following success in winning large military contracts in Europe and South Korea, Codan is working to have its tactical communications products accepted into defence-related communications programs in North America. The December 2023 acquisition of US wireless broadcast equipment specialist Wave Central is part of Codan's strategy for enhancing its tactical communications radio and wireless technology. Its metal detectors dominate the African artisanal gold mining sector, and it is also a significant force in recreational markets in Europe and North America. It is achieving success in boosting its presence with leading retailers and on digital platforms, helped by a range of new products that have been well received, and expects continuing growth in metal detector sales in the June 2025 year. It is also achieving continuing solid demand for landmine detecting equipment and is involved in humanitarian efforts in Ukraine.

Year to 30 June	2023	2024
Revenues ($mn)	456.5	550.5
Communications (%)	60	59
Metal detection (%)	39	40
EBIT ($mn)	88.0	114.0
EBIT margin (%)	19.3	20.7
Gross margin (%)	54.6	55.4
Profit before tax ($mn)	82.6	104.5
Profit after tax ($mn)	67.8	81.4
Earnings per share (c)	37.46	44.95
Cash flow per share (c)	53.42	63.23
Dividend (c)	18.5	22.5
Percentage franked	100	100
Net tangible assets per share ($)	0.52	0.60
Interest cover (times)	16.5	12.1
Return on equity (%)	17.5	19.1
Debt-to-equity ratio (%)	12.7	16.9
Current ratio	1.7	1.7

Coles Group Limited

ASX code: COL　　　　　　　　　www.colesgroup.com.au

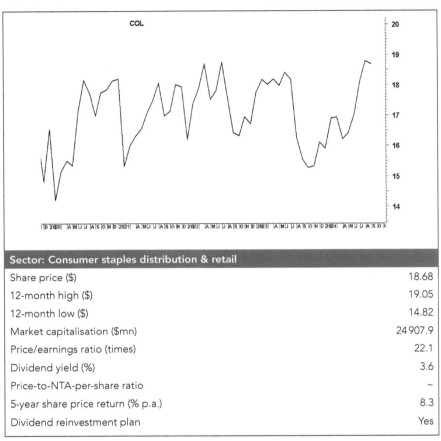

Sector: Consumer staples distribution & retail	
Share price ($)	18.68
12-month high ($)	19.05
12-month low ($)	14.82
Market capitalisation ($mn)	24 907.9
Price/earnings ratio (times)	22.1
Dividend yield (%)	3.6
Price-to-NTA-per-share ratio	~
5-year share price return (% p.a.)	8.3
Dividend reinvestment plan	Yes

Melbourne-based Coles Group dates back to 1914 and the opening of the first Coles store in the Melbourne suburb of Collingwood. Over many years it evolved from a single variety store to a chain of supermarkets, then expanded further with the acquisition of the Myer department store business. In 2006 the company sold Myer and in 2007 Coles was acquired by Wesfarmers. In 2018 it was demerged from Wesfarmers as, once again, an independent company. At June 2024 it operated 856 supermarkets nationwide and 992 liquor stores, the latter under the Liquorland, Vintage Cellars and First Choice banners. It is a 50 per cent shareholder of the Flybuys loyalty program.

Latest business results (June 2024, full year)

In another difficult year, with Australian households facing rising cost of living pressures, Coles saw revenues and profits higher. The Supermarkets division achieved sales growth of 6.2 per cent, or 4.3 per cent on a normalised basis, as the June 2024 year comprised 53 weeks, compared to 52 weeks for June 2023. The company's eCommerce sales were particularly strong, up by a normalised 30.1 per cent, and Coles exclusive products showed 6.6 per cent growth. Supermarkets EBIT rose 14.3 per cent, or 9.6 per cent normalised. Liquor division sales rose 2.3 per cent, or 0.5 per cent on a normalised basis, but with a notable slowdown in the second half as customers reduced spending, and EBIT recorded a double-digit decline. During the year Coles opened 12 new supermarkets and 45 new liquor stores.

Outlook

The big supermarket chains are generally immune to declines in discretionary consumer spending, apart from liquor sales. However, it is noteworthy that consumers are trading down to cheaper home brands. Coles has made a substantial investment in these products over many years and has become a beneficiary of this move, with 1100 new own-brand items introduced in the June 2024 year. It expects that the steady expansion of Australia's population will underpin its long-term growth, although it is also facing political pressures over pricing policies and its treatment of suppliers and smaller competitors. In July 2024 the company commenced operations at its customer fulfillment centres in New South Wales and Victoria, and expects these to deliver a significant improvement in customer service, along with a reduction in supply chain costs. It has developed major new automated distribution centres to service stores in NSW and Queensland. It has also invested in technology aimed at reducing stock loss, particularly from a rising wave of shoplifting.

Year to 30 June*	2023	2024
Revenues ($mn)	40483.0	43571.0
Supermarkets (%)	91	90
Liquor (%)	9	8
EBIT ($mn)	1859.0	2057.0
EBIT margin (%)	4.6	4.7
Gross margin (%)	25.8	24.3
Profit before tax ($mn)	1465.0	1615.0
Profit after tax ($mn)	1098.0	1128.0
Earnings per share (c)	82.31	84.56
Cash flow per share (c)	196.48	204.65
Dividend (c)	66	68
Percentage franked	100	100
Net tangible assets per share ($)	~	~
Interest cover (times)	4.7	4.7
Return on equity (%)	33.9	32.4
Debt-to-equity ratio (%)	15.5	27.0
Current ratio	0.6	0.6

*25 June 2023

Collins Foods Limited

ASX code: CKF www.collinsfoods.com

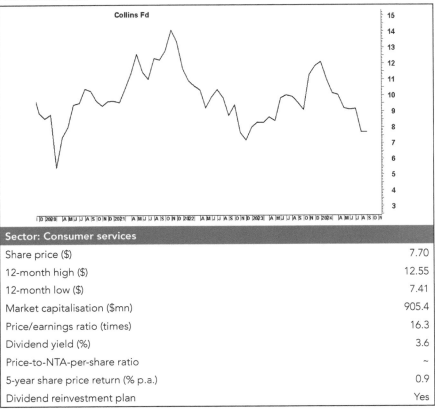

Sector: Consumer services	
Share price ($)	7.70
12-month high ($)	12.55
12-month low ($)	7.41
Market capitalisation ($mn)	905.4
Price/earnings ratio (times)	16.3
Dividend yield (%)	3.6
Price-to-NTA-per-share ratio	~
5-year share price return (% p.a.)	0.9
Dividend reinvestment plan	Yes

Collins Foods, based in Brisbane, dates back to 1968 when it obtained the KFC fried chicken franchise for Queensland. Today it operates KFC outlets across Australia, and is the country's largest KFC franchisee. It also manages the Taco Bell Mexican restaurant brand in Australia. It operates KFC stores in Germany and the Netherlands.

Latest business results (April 2024, full year)

Profits rebounded, despite continuing challenges from rising costs. Domestic KFC operations achieved a 6.6 per cent increase in sales, with the opening of a net seven new stores and same-store growth of 3.8 per cent. Profits rose at a faster pace, thanks to cost controls and some price rises. European operations enjoyed another excellent year, with sales up 26.1 per cent. This reflected same-store growth of 4.9 per cent and the opening of 11 new restaurants. However, European profit margins remained below those of Australia. Taco Bell revenues were up 11.7 per cent, thanks to a new agreement with Uber Eats and some buoyant demand in Victoria, but this business remained in the red. At the end of the period the company operated 279 franchised KFC restaurants in Australia, up from 272 a year earlier, with a further 59 in the

Netherlands, up from 48, and 16 in Germany, unchanged from the previous year. It also ran 27 Taco Bell restaurants in Australia, down from 28.

Outlook

KFC has a strong image in Australia and continues to grow. In the quick-service restaurant category it is the second-largest brand, after McDonald's. However, Collins, which manages around one third of Australia's KFC outlets in an agreement with the franchisor Yum Brands, is wary about the near-term outlook. While commodity costs have been stabilising, labour and energy expenses continue to rise. At the same time, consumer sentiment appears to be weakening. In response, it is placing a particular focus on product innovation. It is also working to add new digital sales channels, which already generate about 30 per cent of customer business. It expects to open nine new restaurants domestically in the April 2025 year and is also exploring the possibility of acquisitions. It faces similar challenges and opportunities in Europe. It has become the largest KFC franchisee in the Netherlands and expects to launch as many as 130 new restaurants in that country over 10 years. It has paused the roll-out of new Taco Bell outlets in Australia while it works to move this underperforming business into profit.

Year to 28 April*	2023	2024
Revenues ($mn)	1348.6	1488.9
KFC restaurants Australia (%)	78	75
KFC restaurants Europe (%)	18	21
Taco Bell restaurants (%)	4	4
EBIT ($mn)	110.9	122.2
EBIT margin (%)	8.2	8.2
Gross margin (%)	50.1	50.4
Profit before tax ($mn)	77.5	81.3
Profit after tax ($mn)	51.9	55.6
Earnings per share (c)	44.29	47.35
Cash flow per share (c)	128.06	137.30
Dividend (c)	27	28
Percentage franked	100	100
Net tangible assets per share ($)	~	~
Interest cover (times)	3.4	3.2
Return on equity (%)	13.3	13.7
Debt-to-equity ratio (%)	55.0	38.7
Current ratio	0.7	0.5

* 30 April 2023

Commonwealth Bank of Australia

ASX code: CBA　　　　　　　　　　　　　www.commbank.com.au

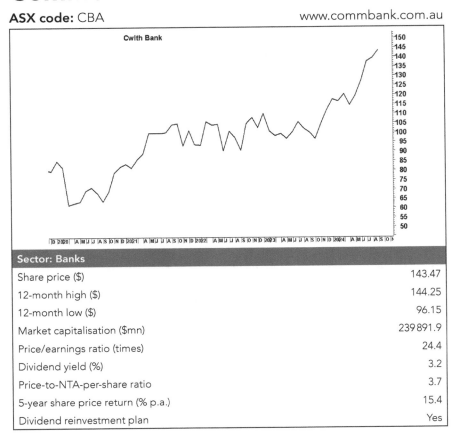

Sector: Banks	
Share price ($)	143.47
12-month high ($)	144.25
12-month low ($)	96.15
Market capitalisation ($mn)	239891.9
Price/earnings ratio (times)	24.4
Dividend yield (%)	3.2
Price-to-NTA-per-share ratio	3.7
5-year share price return (% p.a.)	15.4
Dividend reinvestment plan	Yes

The Commonwealth Bank, based in Sydney, was founded in 1911 as a state-owned institution. Privatised during the 1990s, it is today Australia's largest bank, and one of the country's top providers of home loans, personal loans and credit cards, as well as the largest holder of deposits, while its Commonwealth Securities business is a prominent online stockbroker. It has significant interests in New Zealand, through ASB Bank. It owns Bankwest in Western Australia.

Latest business results (June 2024, full year)

Profits edged down, after three straight years of increases, as a competitive home loans market sent the net interest margin down by eight basis points to 1.99 per cent. Inflationary pressures and additional technology spending also affected the result. The core Retail Banking Services division saw profits down by 4 per cent. By contrast, the Business Banking division achieved a 4 per cent rise in profits, with improved deposit margins and continued lending volume growth, offsetting an increase in expenses. The smaller Institutional Banking and Markets division recorded a 5 per cent profit increase, thanks to higher earnings on deposits and increased volumes in fixed income. New Zealand earnings fell by 10 per cent, with income down and costs rising.

Outlook

Commonwealth Bank occupies a powerful position in the domestic economy as well as in the local banking industry, and it is optimistic about the medium-term outlook. It views the Australian economy as generally strong, but with downside risks that include productivity, housing affordability and ongoing global uncertainty. It is also wary about renewed signs of mortgage competition and deposit customers shopping for better deals. Nevertheless, thanks to a large branch network, offering many cross-selling opportunities, it has pricing power that has generally enabled it to maintain a cost advantage over some of its rivals. In recent years it has been boosting market share, and now claims more than a third of the retail banking market and a quarter share of business banking. Thanks to this strength, it relies less on mortgage brokers for its home loans business than some rival banks, boosting margins. It continues to invest for future growth. Its CommBank Yello loyalty program, launched in November 2023, has attracted five million customers and is to be extended to business customers. A novel travel booking app was launched in June 2024, with plans for another app that enables property agents and tenants to manage rental payments. It continues to work to simplify the home loans process.

Year to 30 June	2023	2024
Operating income ($mn)	27428.0	26921.0
Net interest income ($mn)	23056.0	22824.0
Operating expenses ($mn)	12079.0	12337.0
Profit before tax ($mn)	14169.0	14154.0
Profit after tax ($mn)	10072.0	9836.0
Earnings per share (c)	595.98	587.93
Dividend (c)	450	465
Percentage franked	100	100
Non-interest income to total income (%)	15.9	15.2
Net tangible assets per share ($)	38.58	39.17
Cost-to-income ratio (%)	44.0	45.8
Return on equity (%)	13.9	13.6
Return on assets (%)	0.8	0.8

Computershare Limited

ASX code: CPU   www.computershare.com

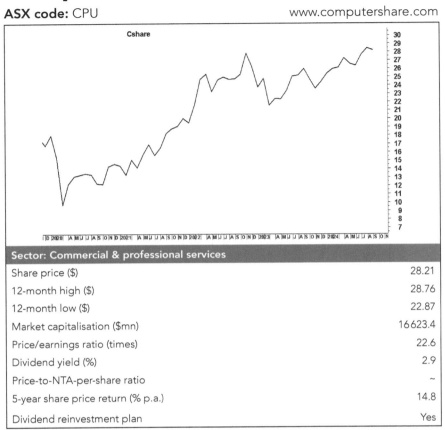

Sector: Commercial & professional services	
Share price ($)	28.21
12-month high ($)	28.76
12-month low ($)	22.87
Market capitalisation ($mn)	16 623.4
Price/earnings ratio (times)	22.6
Dividend yield (%)	2.9
Price-to-NTA-per-share ratio	~
5-year share price return (% p.a.)	14.8
Dividend reinvestment plan	Yes

Melbourne-based Computershare, established in 1978, is one of the world's leading financial services and technology providers for the global securities industry, offering services to listed companies, investors, employees, exchanges and other financial institutions. These offerings include share registration, employee equity plans, corporate governance, class action administration and other specialised financial, governance and stakeholder communication services. Its global corporate trust business helps administer debt securities in the US. The company manages more than 75 million customer records for more than 25 000 clients across all major financial markets, with significant market shares in many countries. More than 90 per cent of revenues come from abroad, including more than 60 per cent from the US.

Latest business results (June 2024, full year)

Revenues and profits rose in a solid result, bolstered by client fee growth and higher interest rates in the first half. The core Issuer Services division, which includes register maintenance, stakeholder relationship management and corporate governance services, recorded growth in all product lines and double-digit profit growth.

The Employee Share Plans division was also strong, thanks to higher trading activity and new client wins. By contrast, the Global Corporate Trust division experienced weakness, due largely to the cessation of document custody activities for the US Government National Mortgage Association. In May 2024 Computershare sold its low-margin US mortgage services operation, and the results in the table have been adjusted to exclude this business. Note that Computershare reports its results in US dollars. The Australian dollar figures in this book have been converted at prevailing exchange rates.

Outlook

Computershare is a beneficiary of robust worldwide equity markets and can suffer in periods of volatility. It is also hurt by rising inflation. Nevertheless, it continues to gain market share in its issuer services operation, and it is actively working on many new technological innovations. It notes that companies are increasingly using employee share plans to attract and reward staff. Thanks to the continuing roll-out of its EquatePlus technology, Computershare is achieving success in drawing new clients to its employee share plan business. It holds a considerable amount of clients' funds in various forms and is a beneficiary of rising interest rates. The sale of the mortgage services business is intended to reduce complexity within the company's operations and boost profitability. Computershare believes that growth initiatives will offset reduced earnings from lower interest rates, and its early forecast is EPS growth for the June 2025 year of 7.5 per cent.

Year to 30 June	2023	2024
Revenues ($mn)	4146.4	4421.0
Issuer services ($)	39	41
Global corporate trust (%)	34	32
Employee share plans (%)	12	15
EBIT ($mn)	1155.4	1256.2
EBIT margin (%)	27.9	28.4
Profit before tax ($mn)	1002.6	1052.2
Profit after tax ($mn)	721.3	747.2
Earnings per share (c)	119.47	124.82
Cash flow per share (c)	165.60	159.70
Dividend (c)	70	82
Percentage franked	0	10
Net tangible assets per share ($)	~	~
Interest cover (times)	10.6	10.2
Return on equity (%)	22.6	24.1
Debt-to-equity ratio (%)	56.8	23.7
Current ratio	1.7	2.9

Credit Corp Group Limited

ASX code: CCP   www.creditcorpgroup.com.au

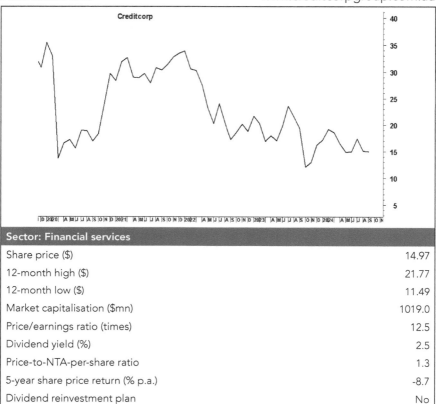

Sector: Financial services	
Share price ($)	14.97
12-month high ($)	21.77
12-month low ($)	11.49
Market capitalisation ($mn)	1019.0
Price/earnings ratio (times)	12.5
Dividend yield (%)	2.5
Price-to-NTA-per-share ratio	1.3
5-year share price return (% p.a.)	-8.7
Dividend reinvestment plan	No

Sydney-based Credit Corp was formed in 1992, although it has its origins in companies that started in the early 1970s. It engages in debt collection activity through the acquisition of defaulted consumer debt for companies in numerous industries, notably the banking, finance, telecommunications and utility sectors. It has operations in Australia, New Zealand and the United States, as well as a large call centre in the Philippines. It maintains an agency collection service under the brands National Credit Management, Baycorp and Collection House, for clients who wish to outsource debt collections without actually selling the debt. It also operates a fast-growing consumer lending business with brands that include CarStart and Wallet Wizard.

Latest business results (June 2024, full year)

Revenues rose but profits fell for the second straight year, as the company was hit by a low level of debt buying sales volumes in Australia and New Zealand and a contraction in collections. Efforts to reduce costs could not offset the deterioration, and profits fell sharply. US profits were also hurt by worsening market conditions. By contrast, the company's high-margin consumer lending operation was again the stand-out performer, with solid gains in revenues and profits, and continuing strong demand for the Wallet Wizard unsecured cash loan product. Consumer lending, representing about a third of total company turnover, contributed more than half the year's after-tax profit, and at June 2024 the company's loan book stood at $445 million, up from $358 million a year earlier. Credit Corp also reported two large non-cash adjustments, including a $65 million pre-tax impairment charge against its US operations, and the statutory profit after tax was $50.7 million.

Outlook

Credit Corp's main business effectively involves buying consumer debt at a discount to its face value, and then seeking to recover an amount in excess of the purchase price. Often this recovery takes the form of phased payments over an extended period, and Credit Corp thus has substantial recurring income. Setting an appropriate price for the acquisition of parcels of debt is one of the keys to success, and Credit Corp has acquired considerable expertise in this. It has reported that late in the June 2024 year it was experiencing a turn-around in its US operations and a pick-up in its domestic debt-buying business. In addition, it expects continuing strong earnings growth from consumer lending. Consequently, the company's early forecast is for an after-tax profit in the June 2025 year of between $90 million and $100 million.

Year to 30 June	2023	2024
Revenues ($mn)	473.4	519.6
EBIT ($mn)	145.3	142.1
EBIT margin (%)	30.7	27.4
Profit before tax ($mn)	128.4	116.2
Profit after tax ($mn)	91.3	81.2
Earnings per share (c)	134.22	119.29
Cash flow per share (c)	150.64	133.70
Dividend (c)	70	38
Percentage franked	100	100
Net tangible assets per share ($)	11.43	11.55
Interest cover (times)	9.0	5.7
Return on equity (%)	11.7	10.0
Debt-to-equity ratio (%)	30.4	42.4
Current ratio	5.7	6.1

CSL Limited

ASX code: CSL

investors.csl.com

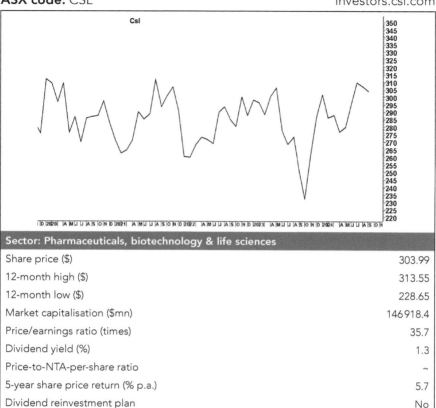

Sector: Pharmaceuticals, biotechnology & life sciences	
Share price ($)	303.99
12-month high ($)	313.55
12-month low ($)	228.65
Market capitalisation ($mn)	146918.4
Price/earnings ratio (times)	35.7
Dividend yield (%)	1.3
Price-to-NTA-per-share ratio	~
5-year share price return (% p.a.)	5.7
Dividend reinvestment plan	No

Melbourne-based CSL, formerly the state-owned Commonwealth Serum Laboratories, was founded in 1916. It has grown organically and through acquisition to become a major global biotechnology company, with operations in numerous countries — with particular strength in the US, Australia, Germany, the UK, China and Switzerland — and more than 90 per cent of revenues derive from outside Australia. Its principal business, through its CSL Behring division, is the provision of plasma-derived coagulation therapies for the treatment of a range of medical conditions. The CSL Seqirus division is one of the world's largest influenza vaccine companies and a producer of other prescription medicines and pharmaceutical products. The CSL Vifor division, based on the 2022 acquisition of Swiss biotech company Vifor Pharma, makes products for renal therapy and iron deficiency. CSL is Australia's largest healthcare company and enjoys high margins and high market shares for many of its products.

Latest business results (June 2024, full year)

Revenues and profits rose in another solid performance. The core CSL Behring division was particularly strong, with double-digit growth in sales and earnings, thanks especially to significant patient demand across all regions for immunoglobulin products. In addition, the company achieved further success in reducing plasma collection costs. The CSL Seqirus division reported a 4 per cent increase in revenues, driven by strong demand for the company's Fluad Quadrivalent influenza vaccine. CSL Vifor results were largely in line with the previous year, although the company reported progress in rationalising this new business. Note that CSL reports its results in US dollars. The figures in this book have been converted to Australian dollars based on prevailing exchange rates.

Outlook

CSL remains a powerhouse biotechnology company, with an impressive research and development capability and a solid pipeline of potential new products, and it believes that over the medium term it can deliver annualised double-digit earnings growth. It continues its work on driving down plasma collection costs, including new digital initiatives and a novel plasma collection system that extracts blood faster, and it expects this to boost margins. CSL Seqirus is well positioned in the global flu vaccine market, and is also developing next-generation COVID vaccines. The CSL Vifor division faces growing competition, but CSL believes the long-term outlook is promising as its markets expand and evolve. The company's early June 2025 forecast, on a constant currency basis, is for revenue growth of 5 per cent to 7 per cent, with rising margins delivering after-profit growth of 10 per cent to 13 per cent.

Year to 30 June	2023	2024
Revenues ($mn)	19865.7	22424.2
CSL Behring (%)	70	72
CSL Seqirus (%)	15	14
CSL Vifor (%)	15	14
EBIT ($mn)	5514.9	5834.8
EBIT margin (%)	27.8	26.0
Gross margin (%)	51.4	51.8
Profit before tax ($mn)	4852.2	5113.6
Profit after tax ($mn)	3895.5	4112.1
Earnings per share (c)	807.91	851.35
Cash flow per share (c)	1065.14	1145.59
Dividend (c)	362.92	397.35
Percentage franked	6	0
Net tangible assets per share ($)	~	~
Interest cover (times)	9.1	8.8
Return on equity (%)	17.3	16.4
Debt-to-equity ratio (%)	59.9	54.3
Current ratio	2.0	2.2

Data#3 Limited

ASX code: DTL   investor.data3.com

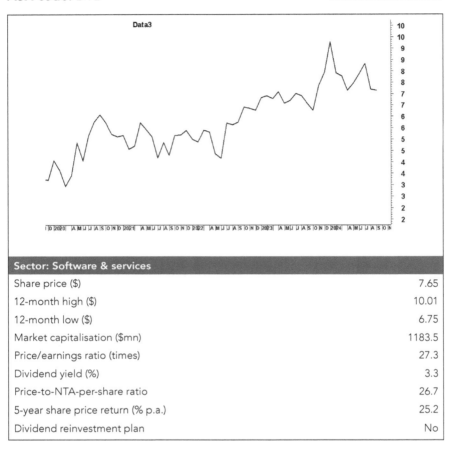

Sector: Software & services	
Share price ($)	7.65
12-month high ($)	10.01
12-month low ($)	6.75
Market capitalisation ($mn)	1183.5
Price/earnings ratio (times)	27.3
Dividend yield (%)	3.3
Price-to-NTA-per-share ratio	26.7
5-year share price return (% p.a.)	25.2
Dividend reinvestment plan	No

Brisbane-based IT consultant Data#3 was formed in 1984 from the merger of computer software consultancy Powell, Clark and Associates with IBM typewriter dealer Albrand Typewriters and Office Machines. Today it operates from offices around Australia and in Fiji, providing information and communication technology services to a wide range of sectors that include banking and finance, mining, tourism and leisure, legal, health care, manufacturing, distribution, government and utilities.

Latest business results (June 2024, full year)

In a subdued economic environment, revenues marked time but Data3 achieved its sixth straight year of higher profits, with growth across most customer sectors. Note that new accounting policies mean the revenue figures presented in this edition of *Top Stocks* are substantially less than in previous editions. Data#3 divides its activities into three broad divisions. Infrastructure Solutions helps clients maximise returns from infrastructure investments in servers, storage, networks and devices. A decline in sales of networking hardware meant sales for this business fell 3.6 per cent from the previous year. By contrast, the Software Solutions business, which helps customers maximise business value from software investments, achieved 11 per cent sales growth, and with the company reporting market share gains. The small Services division also enjoyed a good year, with sales up 9.6 per cent and particular strength in maintenance services, as customers moved from traditional software support to broader enterprise agreements.

Outlook

Technology investment continues to grow in Australia, and Data#3 expects IT, and particularly digital transformation, to play a leading role in the country's economic future. A key competitive advantage is the strength of its partnerships with major vendors, notably Microsoft, Cisco and Hewlett Packard, with each of whom it is the leading Australian partner. It sees particular potential in the evolution of artificial intelligence (AI). Thanks to its partnership with Microsoft it is in a strong position to sell Microsoft Copilot AI-enabled products, together with related services. The company has also begun carrying out audits of customers to determine their AI readiness and it expects AI to be introduced into its range of product offerings. Another growth sector is cybersecurity, which has become the leading priority for many customers. In July 2024 Data#3 opened its own Security Operations Centre to help protect customers. Thanks to its expertise in the design and implementation of networking projects at large sites, the company, which is based in Brisbane, expects to benefit from a series of major infrastructure developments in advance of the 2032 Brisbane Olympics.

Year to 30 June	2023	2024
Revenues ($mn)	808.6	805.7
EBIT ($mn)	54.5	63.2
EBIT margin (%)	6.7	7.8
Profit before tax ($mn)	53.2	62.1
Profit after tax ($mn)	37.0	43.3
Earnings per share (c)	23.96	28.00
Cash flow per share (c)	28.59	32.56
Dividend (c)	21.9	25.5
Percentage franked	100	100
Net tangible assets per share ($)	0.21	0.29
Interest cover (times)	~	~
Return on equity (%)	57.0	60.5
Debt-to-equity ratio (%)	~	~
Current ratio	1.1	1.1

Elders Limited

ASX code: ELD

www.elders.com.au

Sector: Food, beverage & tobacco

Share price ($)	9.04
12-month high ($)	9.96
12-month low ($)	5.45
Market capitalisation ($mn)	1422.6
Price/earnings ratio (times)	14.0
Dividend yield (%)	5.1
Price-to-NTA-per-share ratio	11.1
5-year share price return (% p.a.)	9.8
Dividend reinvestment plan	Yes

Adelaide-based agribusiness giant Elders dates back to 1839, when Scotsman Alexander Elder established a store in South Australia. It has expanded and undergone many transformations, until today it is a leader in a range of businesses serving rural Australia. It is a prominent supplier of agricultural products, including seeds, fertilisers, chemicals and animal health products. It is a leading agent for the sale of wool, grain and livestock. It is also a major provider of financial and real estate services to the rural sector.

Latest business results (March 2024, half year)

In a subdued rural environment Elders experienced another sharp decline in interim profits, with revenues this time also down, due especially to falling fertiliser and livestock prices. The company was also hurt by rising expenses, although this largely reflected acquisition costs and growth-related initiatives. The core Retail Products division achieved volume growth across its product range, but lower prices sent profits lower. The Agency Services division also experienced volume growth, offset by falling prices and profits. Other divisions were generally positive, with the Financial Services division benefiting from the Elders Insurance and Elders Home Loans businesses.

The Real Estate Services division experienced growth in both property sales and property management.

Outlook

As one of Australia's agribusiness leaders, Elders is heavily geared to the rural economy, which can be volatile. The weather, interest rates, supply chains and commodity prices are all important influences, along with trends in the domestic and global economies. Nevertheless, the Australian farm costs market is worth an estimated $48 billion annually, and Elders sees significant scope for expansion. In the near term it believes a return to average seasonal conditions, particularly in livestock markets, will boost its September 2024 results. For the longer term it has developed an ambitious eight-point growth plan aimed at winning market share across all its products and services, along with higher profits and moves into new product lines, notably in crop protection and animal health. It is also working to deepen its customer relationships, streamline its supply chains and upgrade its technological systems. The company is particularly interested in growing through acquisition, and recent staff recruitment efforts have partially been aimed at facilitating this. It sees a strong pipeline of potential bolt-on acquisitions. The May 2024 acquisition of the Knight Frank real estate business is expected to generate a significant boost to business in Tasmania. The company is also exploring greenfield locations where it sees opportunities for boosting market shares.

Year to 30 September	2022	2023
Revenues ($mn)	3445.3	3321.4
EBIT ($mn)	246.3	161.9
EBIT margin (%)	7.1	4.9
Gross margin (%)	18.6	18.2
Profit before tax ($mn)	237.7	138.9
Profit after tax ($mn)	162.9	100.8
Earnings per share (c)	104.08	64.44
Cash flow per share (c)	134.27	101.26
Dividend (c)	56	46
Percentage franked	30	30
Interest cover (times)	34.8	7.0
Return on equity (%)	20.0	11.7
Half year to 31 March	2023	2024
Revenues ($mn)	1657.3	1341.8
Profit before tax ($mn)	70.3	17.6
Profit after tax ($mn)	48.8	11.6
Earnings per share (c)	31.20	7.40
Dividend (c)	23	18
Percentage franked	30	50
Net tangible assets per share ($)	1.94	0.82
Debt-to-equity ratio (%)	49.6	42.8
Current ratio	1.2	1.1

Evolution Mining Limited

ASX code: EVN   www.evolutionmining.com.au

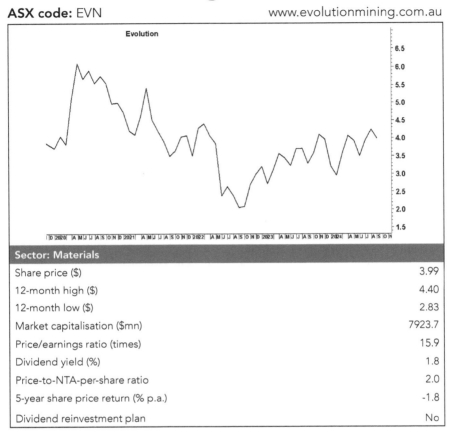

Sector: Materials	
Share price ($)	3.99
12-month high ($)	4.40
12-month low ($)	2.83
Market capitalisation ($mn)	7923.7
Price/earnings ratio (times)	15.9
Dividend yield (%)	1.8
Price-to-NTA-per-share ratio	2.0
5-year share price return (% p.a.)	-1.8
Dividend reinvestment plan	No

Gold and copper mining company Evolution Mining, based in Sydney, was formed in 2011 from the merger of Catalpa Resources and Conquest Mining and the acquisition of two mines from Newcrest Mining. It now operates five fully owned mines — Cowal in New South Wales, Ernest Henry and Mt Rawdon in Queensland, Mungari in Western Australia and Red Lake in Ontario, Canada — as well as an 80 per cent holding in the Northparkes mine in New South Wales. In addition, it maintains an active exploration program.

Latest business results (June 2024, full year)

Increased production and rising gold and copper prices sent profits surging. Total gold production for the year of 716 700 ounces was up 10 per cent from the previous year, with copper production of 47 348 tonnes up 43 per cent. The average production cost of $1477 per ounce was 2 per cent down from the previous year, despite rising labour and consumables expenses. The average gold price received by the company of $3190 per ounce was up 23 per cent from the previous year, with the average copper price of $13 657 per tonne up 9 per cent.

Outlook

Evolution's strategy is to build its gold reserves through developing or acquiring new assets, while also improving the quality of its portfolio and driving down expenses in order to remain a low-cost producer. In particular, it has aimed at delivering operational stability and predictability through the ownership of a number of similar-sized mines, rather than holding just a single mine or a dominant mine. Its target is to own six to eight mines and has said it is continually looking for additional long-life, low-cost assets to add to its portfolio. It continues work at Cowal, its largest-producing asset, with the aim of boosting production and extending the mine life. It is also working to expand the Mungari mine and has initiated development work on its new Northparkes holding. It continues to work at driving down operating costs at its Red Lake mine, which it acquired in 2020. It expects mining activity at Mt Rawdon to cease by the end of 2024. It is also actively seeking new gold and copper deposits at its existing operations as well as at sites in Australia, the US and Canada. Evolution has set a gold production target of 710 000 ounces to 780 000 ounces for the June 2025 year, with copper production of 70 000 to 80 000 tonnes. It expects an average cost of $1475 to $1575 per ounce.

Year to 30 June	2023	2024
Revenues ($mn)	2226.9	3215.8
Cowal (%)	32	31
Ernest Henry (%)	32	28
Mungari (%)	16	12
Red Lake (%)	13	11
Northparkes (%)	0	9
EBIT ($mn)	383.8	853.3
EBIT margin (%)	17.2	26.5
Gross margin (%)	19.3	28.7
Profit before tax ($mn)	293.1	704.8
Profit after tax ($mn)	205.0	481.8
Earnings per share (c)	11.17	25.12
Cash flow per share (c)	39.67	59.80
Dividend (c)	4	7
Percentage franked	100	100
Net tangible assets per share ($)	1.77	2.04
Interest cover (times)	4.6	5.9
Return on equity (%)	6.3	13.0
Debt-to-equity ratio (%)	52.1	36.7
Current ratio	0.6	1.1

Fiducian Group Limited

ASX code: FID
www.fiducian.com.au

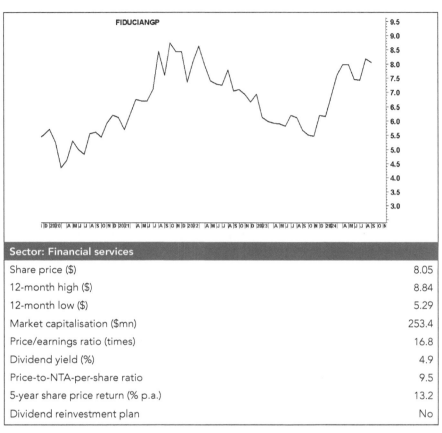

Sector: Financial services	
Share price ($)	8.05
12-month high ($)	8.84
12-month low ($)	5.29
Market capitalisation ($mn)	253.4
Price/earnings ratio (times)	16.8
Dividend yield (%)	4.9
Price-to-NTA-per-share ratio	9.5
5-year share price return (% p.a.)	13.2
Dividend reinvestment plan	No

Sydney financial services company Fiducian Group was founded in 1996 by executive chairman Indy Singh, who owns more than a third of the company equity. Initially it specialised in the provision of masterfund, client administration and financial planning services to financial advisory groups. It has since expanded and is now a holding company with five divisions — Fiducian Portfolio Services is in charge of trustee and superannuation services; Fiducian Investment Management Services operates the company's managed funds; Fiducian Services is the administration service provider for all the company's products; Fiducian Financial Services manages the company's financial planning businesses; and Fiducian Business Services provides accounting and business services.

Latest business results (June 2024, full year)

Rising financial markets helped revenues rise again, and profits rebounded from the previous year's decline, with strength across all activities. For reporting purposes the company divides its operations into broad segments. The largest of these is now the funds management business, which enjoyed solid growth in a buoyant market environment. Financial planning achieved moderate gains in revenues and profits as the company opened three new offices and continued to work at building this business. Funds under advice rose to $4.8 billion, from $4.6 billion in June 2023. However, profit margins for this business remained substantially below those for other activities. The third key segment, platform administration, which offers portfolio wrap administration services to financial planners, was also strong, thanks to continuing inflows from the company's advisers. At June 2024 the total funds under management, advice and administration of $13.5 billion was up from $12.3 billion a year earlier.

Outlook

Fiducian managed 48 financial planning offices across Australia at June 2024, both company-owned and franchised, with a total of 80 financial advisers. It is continually seeking new offices to join the group, and it has also been achieving solid organic growth. At the same time, Fiducian itself has been named as a possible takeover target for a larger financial institution. The funds management business offers a suite of funds from various asset managers, and the company believes that its method of choosing managers with differing investment styles offers the ability to deliver above-average returns with greater diversification and reduced risk. Fiducian management have stated that, thanks especially to the 2022 acquisition of People's Choice Credit Union of South Australia, they see excellent growth prospects. However, the company is vulnerable to any major downturn in financial markets. At June 2024 it had no debt and cash holdings of more than $26 million.

Year to 30 June	2023	2024
Revenues ($mn)	72.4	79.3
Funds management (%)	36	37
Financial planning (%)	38	36
Platform administration (%)	26	27
EBIT ($mn)	17.7	21.4
EBIT margin (%)	24.4	27.0
Profit before tax ($mn)	17.7	21.4
Profit after tax ($mn)	12.3	15.0
Earnings per share (c)	39.14	47.78
Cash flow per share (c)	54.31	62.45
Dividend (c)	30.3	39.3
Percentage franked	100	100
Net tangible assets per share ($)	0.60	0.84
Interest cover (times)	~	~
Return on equity (%)	25.1	28.5
Debt-to-equity ratio (%)	~	~
Current ratio	2.5	2.7

Fortescue Limited

ASX code: FMG

www.fortescue.com

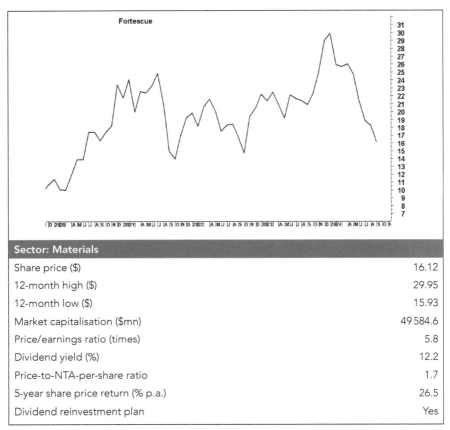

Sector: Materials	
Share price ($)	16.12
12-month high ($)	29.95
12-month low ($)	15.93
Market capitalisation ($mn)	49 584.6
Price/earnings ratio (times)	5.8
Dividend yield (%)	12.2
Price-to-NTA-per-share ratio	1.7
5-year share price return (% p.a.)	26.5
Dividend reinvestment plan	Yes

Perth-based Fortescue was founded in 2003. It has been responsible for discovering and developing some of the largest iron ore mines in the world and is today one of the world's largest iron ore producers, with operations at the Chichester Hub, the Western Hub and Iron Bridge, all in the Pilbara region. It operates its own heavy-haul railway between its mines and Port Hedland. In addition, it is involved in the Belinga Iron Ore Project in Gabon. It is engaged in exploration work at sites across Australia, with other ventures in South America, Europe and Canada. It is also involved in a variety of green energy projects. Some 85 per cent to 90 per cent of its iron ore sales are to China.

Latest business results (June 2024, full year)

Revenues and profits rebounded for Fortescue, thanks to higher iron ore prices. Sales of 191.3 million tonnes were slightly down from 192.4 million tonnes in the previous year, but the average price received of US$103 per tonne was up from US$95. Inflationary pressures pushed up average production costs to US$18.24 per tonne from US$17.54 in June 2023. The company's relatively tiny Energy division contributed US$91 million in revenues, down from US$107 million in the previous year, and was in the red. Note that Fortescue reports its results in US dollars. The Australian dollar figures in this book — converted at prevailing exchange rates — are for guidance only.

Outlook

Fortescue is responsible for major iron ore developments. Its primary production hubs of Chichester and Western have a combined annual production capacity of up to 200 million tonnes. Its US$4 billion Iron Bridge Magnetite Project, a joint venture with Formosa Steel, signifies Fortescue's entry into the high-grade segment of the iron ore market. It has begun production, with the first concentrate shipped in July 2023, and with forecast output of some 22 million tonnes annually. It has also shipped its first ore from Belinga in Gabon, and has reported that the project has the potential to be of significant scale. With its Energy division the company is involved in a diverse flurry of green energy projects in many countries. Among these are an ammonia project in Norway costing more than US$1 billion, with construction expected from 2025. The company has also initiated a range of green hydrogen projects, including a US$150 million green hydrogen project in Queensland, though in July 2024 it abandoned its goal of producing 15 million tonnes of green hydrogen by 2030.

Year to 30 June	2023	2024
Revenues ($mn)	25180.6	27606.1
EBIT ($mn)	10688.1	13160.6
EBIT margin (%)	42.4	47.7
Gross margin (%)	53.7	52.4
Profit before tax ($mn)	10277.6	12575.8
Profit after tax ($mn)	7161.2	8610.6
Earnings per share (c)	232.82	279.93
Cash flow per share (c)	317.44	385.54
Dividend (c)	175	197
Percentage franked	100	100
Net tangible assets per share ($)	8.71	9.44
Interest cover (times)	56.8	51.7
Return on equity (%)	27.3	30.3
Debt-to-equity ratio (%)	5.7	2.5
Current ratio	2.5	2.7

Gold Road Resources Limited

ASX code: GOR

www.goldroad.com.au

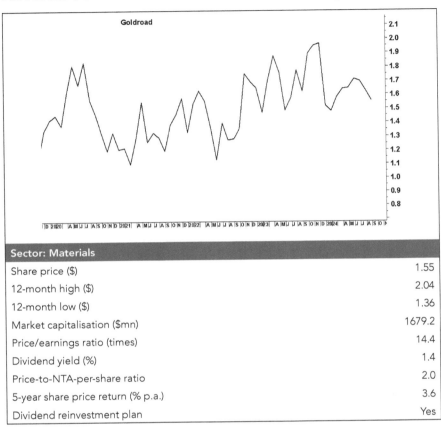

Sector: Materials	
Share price ($)	1.55
12-month high ($)	2.04
12-month low ($)	1.36
Market capitalisation ($mn)	1679.2
Price/earnings ratio (times)	14.4
Dividend yield (%)	1.4
Price-to-NTA-per-share ratio	2.0
5-year share price return (% p.a.)	3.6
Dividend reinvestment plan	Yes

Perth gold explorer and producer Gold Road Resources started in 2004 as Faulkner Resources. It changed its name to Eleckra Mines in 2006 and to Gold Road Resources in 2010. Its initial projects were in the Yamarna Greenstone Belt, 200 kilometres east of Laverton in Western Australia. Today it is engaged in production at the 50-per-cent-owned Gruyere Gold Mine, within the Yamarna Belt, together with South African company Gold Fields, the operator of the mine. The company also maintains an active exploration program at a large portfolio of sites across Western Australia, South Australia and Queensland.

Latest business results (June 2024, half year)

Severe rainfall hit production, and company revenues and profits fell, despite a rising gold price. The protracted rainfall during March 2024 caused extensive flooding in the Eastern Goldfields region and the closure of the main access road to Gruyere for seven weeks. Consequently, processing and mining activities operated at reduced capacity for much of March and were then suspended until mid April. A total of 126 858 ounces of gold were produced during the period — with half for Gold Road — compared to

158 657 ounces in the June 2023 half. Inflationary pressures and the rainfall forced production costs substantially higher. The average All-In Sustaining Cost (AISC) — the normal measure for evaluating the total cost of producing an ounce of gold — jumped from $1504 per ounce in June 2023 to $2316. The company sold 63 542 ounces of gold during the period at an average price of $3331 per ounce, compared to 80 115 ounces sold in the June 2023 period at an average $2858 per ounce.

Outlook

Gold Road discovered the Gruyere Gold Mine in 2013 and funded its development through the sale of a 50 per cent share to Gold Fields. Initial production came in 2019, and the company estimates it has a mine life that will extend at least to 2032. It maintains an active exploration program. It has had promising results at the Golden Highway Project, 25 kilometres from the Gruyere mine, and has started feasibility studies in preparation for mining operations from 2026. It plans test drilling at the Greenvale project in northern Queensland from late 2024. At June 2024 Gold Road had no debt and cash holdings of more than $79 million. It also held an investment portfolio valued at more than $478 million. The company expects total 2024 production of 290 000 ounces to 305 000 ounces, at an average AISC of $2050 to $2200 per ounce.

Year to 31 December	2022	2023
Revenues ($mn)	382.9	472.1
EBIT ($mn)	98.9	175.4
EBIT margin (%)	25.8	37.2
Gross margin (%)	38.8	46.8
Profit before tax ($mn)	90.8	167.1
Profit after tax ($mn)	63.7	115.7
Earnings per share (c)	6.45	10.73
Cash flow per share (c)	14.71	17.97
Dividend (c)	1.5	2.2
Percentage franked	100	100
Interest cover (times)	14.8	59.3
Return on equity (%)	10.0	13.0
Half year to 30 June	2023	2024
Revenues ($mn)	229.0	211.7
Profit before tax ($mn)	80.8	61.3
Profit after tax ($mn)	55.7	43.1
Earnings per share (c)	5.17	3.98
Dividend (c)	1.2	0.5
Percentage franked	100	100
Net tangible assets per share ($)	0.72	0.77
Debt-to-equity ratio (%)	~	~
Current ratio	3.0	2.3

Grange Resources Limited

ASX code: GRR   www.grangeresources.com.au

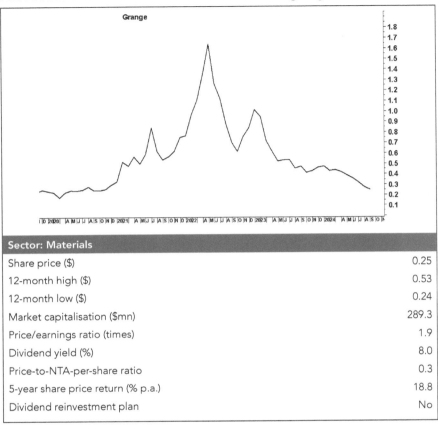

Sector: Materials	
Share price ($)	0.25
12-month high ($)	0.53
12-month low ($)	0.24
Market capitalisation ($mn)	289.3
Price/earnings ratio (times)	1.9
Dividend yield (%)	8.0
Price-to-NTA-per-share ratio	0.3
5-year share price return (% p.a.)	18.8
Dividend reinvestment plan	No

Based in Burnie, Tasmania, Grange Resources is an iron ore producer. It dates back to the 1980s when it was a Western Australian gold-copper miner with the name Sabminco. It is today involved in three major projects — the Savage River magnetite iron ore mine and the Port Latta pellet plant and port facility, both in Tasmania, and the Southdown Magnetite Project in Western Australia's Great Southern region.

Latest business results (June 2024, half year)

A weakened iron ore price and rising costs once again sent revenues and profits down. The company produced 1.22 million tonnes of iron ore pellets, up from 1.19 million tonnes in the June 2023 period, and sold 1.05 million tonnes, down from 1.21 million tonnes. Lower iron ore prices meant the company received an average price of $184.60 per tonne, down from $198.14 in the June 2023 half, which compares to $241.59 in June 2022 and $339.21 in June 2021. Production costs of an average $152.79 per tonne were up from $137.41, which the company attributed to rising wages and higher costs for major components and mechanical consumables.

Outlook

Grange's fortunes are quite dependent on movements in the iron ore market, which in turn have become fairly reliant on Chinese economic trends. The company's business involves the mining of magnetite from its Savage River mine and then refining it at the Port Latta plant into an iron ore concentrate that can be used for steel production. Its output is sold through a combination of long-term supply contracts and a spot sales process. Following a feasibility study at Savage River, completed in February 2024, it believes it can develop its North Pit ore body through a new underground mine, with annual production of six million to seven million tonnes of ore and a mine life of 15 years. It believes operating costs would be 30 per cent less than its current open pit mining expenses. The company expects to decide late in 2024 whether to proceed with this development, which it estimates could cost at least $890 million. It is carrying out a feasibility study regarding its Southdown Magnetite Project in Western Australia, with a view to initiating mining operations. It believes the mine could be capable of an annual output of 5 million tonnes of high-quality magnetite concentrate. It is seeking strategic partners to join it in the development of the mine. At June 2024 Grange had no debt and cash holdings of more than $119 million.

Year to 31 December	2022	2023
Revenues ($mn)	594.6	614.7
EBIT ($mn)	252.3	219.2
EBIT margin (%)	42.4	35.7
Gross margin (%)	43.8	35.8
Profit before tax ($mn)	248.8	215.1
Profit after tax ($mn)	171.7	150.1
Earnings per share (c)	14.84	12.97
Cash flow per share (c)	19.64	23.53
Dividend (c)	4	2
Percentage franked	100	100
Interest cover (times)	~	~
Return on equity (%)	19.3	15.5
Half year to 30 June	2023	2024
Revenues ($mn)	278.4	234.0
Profit before tax ($mn)	101.0	32.4
Profit after tax ($mn)	70.4	26.5
Earnings per share (c)	6.08	2.29
Dividend (c)	0	0.5
Percentage franked	~	100
Net tangible assets per share ($)	0.82	0.89
Debt-to-equity ratio (%)	~	~
Current ratio	7.8	7.8

GWA Group Limited

ASX code: GWA   www.gwagroup.com.au

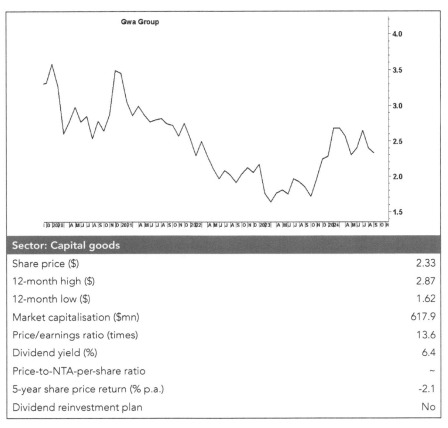

Sector: Capital goods	
Share price ($)	2.33
12-month high ($)	2.87
12-month low ($)	1.62
Market capitalisation ($mn)	617.9
Price/earnings ratio (times)	13.6
Dividend yield (%)	6.4
Price-to-NTA-per-share ratio	~
5-year share price return (% p.a.)	-2.1
Dividend reinvestment plan	No

Brisbane-based GWA is a prominent designer, importer and distributor of residential and commercial bathroom, laundry and kitchen products, marketed under brands that include Caroma, Dorf, Methven and Clark. About 9 per cent of its sales are in New Zealand, with a further 8.5 per cent in other countries, primarily the United Kingdom.

Latest business results (June 2024, full year)

Sales and profits edged up in a subdued housing market. Revenues in Australia rose by 1.8 per cent, reversing the 1.2 per cent decline of the previous year, with solid demand for new products for the detached housing market and for maintenance plumbers. Price increases from February 2024 helped the result. The best performance came from British operations, with a strong second half helping boost total revenues by 8.6 per cent. By contrast, New Zealand was again weak, with revenues falling 16.5 per cent in a troubled economic environment. Thanks to disciplined cost management, the company's cost of sales figure edged down, even as sales rose.

Outlook

GWA is almost completely exposed to a bathroom, laundry and kitchen fixtures market that in Australia is worth more than $2 billion annually. It claims market shares as high as 50 per cent for some of its products. Around 56 per cent of its Australian sales go to the residential repair and renovation market, and demand is expected to remain flat as households cut back on discretionary spending. The commercial segment represents a further 21 per cent of Australian sales, and the company forecasts declining overall demand, despite increased sales to the healthcare and aged care sectors. Residential detached housing is around 17 per cent of Australian sales, with demand easing. In this weak business environment GWA has a variety of strategies aimed at maintaining sales. It is placing an emphasis on the development of new products, and these now represent more than 10 per cent of total sales. It has launched a new range of entry-level sanitaryware for the affordable housing market and plans the launch of its CleanFlush Urinal technology and its smart connected tapware, both aimed at the commercial market. The company is placing a particular focus on developing strong relations with the plumbing industry, including the provision of specialist technical services and training to plumbers, to help them meet their continuing professional development requirements. New client wins in the UK are boosting business there. GWA is working to cut costs in New Zealand in the face of continuing economic weakness.

Year to 30 June	2023	2024
Revenues ($mn)	411.8	413.5
EBIT ($mn)	70.4	74.2
EBIT margin (%)	17.1	17.9
Gross margin (%)	38.4	39.3
Profit before tax ($mn)	61.6	65.1
Profit after tax ($mn)	44.1	45.6
Earnings per share (c)	16.63	17.19
Cash flow per share (c)	23.66	24.52
Dividend (c)	13	15
Percentage franked	100	100
Net tangible assets per share ($)	~	~
Interest cover (times)	8.7	9.6
Return on equity (%)	14.5	14.9
Debt-to-equity ratio (%)	37.9	31.4
Current ratio	1.8	1.6

IDP Education Limited

ASX code: IEL

investors.idp.com

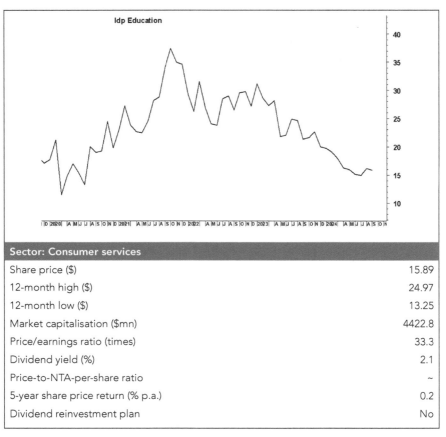

Sector: Consumer services	
Share price ($)	15.89
12-month high ($)	24.97
12-month low ($)	13.25
Market capitalisation ($mn)	4422.8
Price/earnings ratio (times)	33.3
Dividend yield (%)	2.1
Price-to-NTA-per-share ratio	~
5-year share price return (% p.a.)	0.2
Dividend reinvestment plan	No

Melbourne-based IDP Education dates back to 1969 and the launch of the Australian Asian Universities Cooperation Scheme, aimed at helping Asian students study in Australia. In 1981 it changed its name to the International Development Program (IDP) and opened a series of offices throughout Asia. It has since expanded through acquisition and organic growth, and today helps students from around the world find placements in higher education programs in English-speaking countries. It also works with University of Cambridge ESOL Examinations and the British Council to administer worldwide testing for the International English Language Testing System (IELTS). About 25 per cent of IDP's equity is held by 38 Australian universities.

Latest business results (June 2024, full year)

Revenues continued to rise but profits fell as IDP was hit by a sharp second-half slowdown in the international education industry. This resulted especially from moves by governments in Australia, Canada and the UK to limit international student numbers in their countries. The company's language testing business was affected especially badly, with an 18 per cent decline in testing volumes, including a 42 per cent plunge in the key Indian market. Despite a 9 per cent increase in average testing fees, testing revenues were down 11 per cent. By contrast, student placement revenues rose 28 per cent, thanks to both fee increases and rising student numbers. IDP also reports its results on a geographical basis, with Asian revenues up 2 per cent, Australasia jumping by nearly 24 per cent and the Rest of the World segment rising 14 per cent.

Outlook

IDP estimates that the number of new international students beginning their studies in the major markets will decline by as much as 20 per cent to 25 per cent in the June 2025 year. Consequently, the company expects its own business to fall, although it believes its strengths mean it will not decline as much as rival companies. With a focus on quality, it believes it can gain market share during a period of weakness and will recover quickly when conditions improve. A cost reduction program initiated in 2024 will help mitigate the financial impact. It has completed the roll-out of its new English language testing platform, which allows additional flexibility for future product delivery. Its new FastLane app allows students to get an indicative placement offer from an institution instantly; it facilitated more than 32 000 offers in the June 2024 year, an 83 per cent increase from the year before.

Year to 30 June	2023	2024
Revenues ($mn)	981.9	1037.2
Asia (%)	74	72
Rest of World (%)	21	23
Australasia (%)	5	5
EBIT ($mn)	223.5	213.7
EBIT margin (%)	22.8	20.6
Profit before tax ($mn)	207.3	188.8
Profit after tax ($mn)	148.5	132.7
Earnings per share (c)	53.36	47.69
Cash flow per share (c)	71.49	67.61
Dividend (c)	41	34
Percentage franked	21	73
Net tangible assets per share ($)	~	~
Interest cover (times)	16.7	9.9
Return on equity (%)	30.5	25.5
Debt-to-equity ratio (%)	8.2	32.5
Current ratio	1.3	1.6

Iluka Resources Limited

ASX code: ILU www.iluka.com

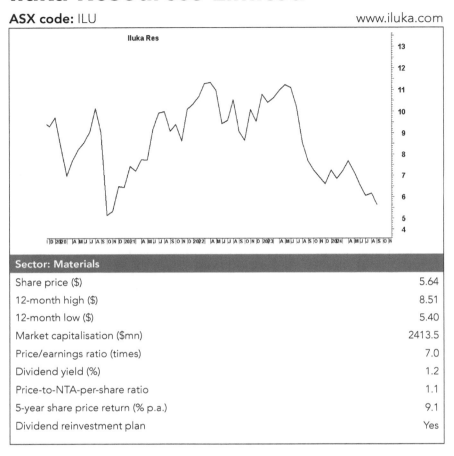

Sector: Materials	
Share price ($)	5.64
12-month high ($)	8.51
12-month low ($)	5.40
Market capitalisation ($mn)	2413.5
Price/earnings ratio (times)	7.0
Dividend yield (%)	1.2
Price-to-NTA-per-share ratio	1.1
5-year share price return (% p.a.)	9.1
Dividend reinvestment plan	Yes

Perth resources company Iluka started in 1954 as Westralian Sands, before merging in 1998 with the titanium mineral business of RGC and subsequently taking its present name. It is today a global leader in the mining and processing of mineral sands and rare earths. It has four operations in Western Australia: it manages the Cataby mine, a large ilmenite deposit with associated zircon and rutile; its Eneabba development involves the reclaiming and processing of a strategic stockpile high in monazite; its Narngulu mineral separation plant produces zircon, rutile and ilmenite products; and the Capel operation incorporates two synthetic rutile kilns. In South Australia it operates the world's largest zircon mine, Jacinth-Ambrosia, and it is involved in exploration and development work in other states. It holds a 20 per cent holding in ASX-listed Deterra Royalties, a company that receives royalties from certain BHP iron ore tenements.

Latest business results (June 2024, half year)

Weakening demand and some lower prices saw revenues and profits drop again. The company arranges its sales profile into four products. Zircon volume sales fell just 1 per cent from the June 2023 half, but with average prices down about 9 per cent.

Synthetic rutile sales fell 27 per cent, with average prices a little lower. Ilmenite sales dropped 13 per cent, with rutile sales down 12 per cent. Profits were hurt by rising production costs, particularly for fuel, consumables and labour, although these started to ease during the period. The company benefited from a weaker dollar.

Outlook

Rare earth minerals are a key component for a growing number of high-tech industries. They are essential for the creation of powerful magnets for wind turbines and electric vehicles. They are also needed in vehicle emission control units and in modern rechargeable batteries, as well as for many defence industry applications, including jet engines and drones. Consequently, they are in growing demand globally. However, with some 80 per cent of the world's supply now coming from China, countries in the West have been urging Australia, which has large-scale reserves of rare earths, to boost output. In 2022 Iluka received a $1.25 billion loan from the government to build Australia's first rare earth refinery at its Eneabba operation, although Iluka is now asking for increased funding. Its rutile-rich critical minerals development at Balranald in New South Wales is on track for commissioning in late 2025. It is investigating a possible new rare earths and zircon development at Wimmera in Victoria.

Year to 31 December	2022	2023
Revenues ($mn)	1611.3	1291.0
EBIT ($mn)	736.1	479.3
EBIT margin (%)	45.7	37.1
Profit before tax ($mn)	730.1	471.5
Profit after tax ($mn)	517.3	342.6
Earnings per share (c)	122.48	80.50
Cash flow per share (c)	155.89	119.22
Dividend (c)	45	7
Percentage franked	100	100
Interest cover (times)	~	~
Return on equity (%)	29.7	16.9
Half year to 30 June	2023	2024
Revenues ($mn)	745.4	629.7
Profit before tax ($mn)	291.4	187.0
Profit after tax ($mn)	203.8	133.7
Earnings per share (c)	48.30	31.30
Dividend (c)	3	4
Percentage franked	100	100
Net tangible assets per share ($)	4.69	5.30
Debt-to-equity ratio (%)	~	~
Current ratio	5.0	4.9

Insurance Australia Group Limited

ASX code: IAG   www.iag.com.au

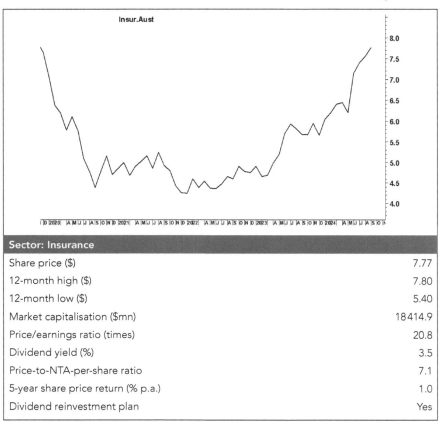

Sector: Insurance	
Share price ($)	7.77
12-month high ($)	7.80
12-month low ($)	5.40
Market capitalisation ($mn)	18414.9
Price/earnings ratio (times)	20.8
Dividend yield (%)	3.5
Price-to-NTA-per-share ratio	7.1
5-year share price return (% p.a.)	1.0
Dividend reinvestment plan	Yes

Sydney-based Insurance Australia Group (IAG), formerly NRMA Insurance, dates back to 1925, when the National Roads and Motorists' Association began providing insurance to its members in New South Wales and the Australian Capital Territory. It subsequently demutualised and listed on the ASX. It has grown through acquisition, and is now the largest general insurance group in Australia and New Zealand. Its brands include NRMA Insurance, CGU, WFI, ROLLiN' and Swann Insurance, all in Australia, as well as NZI, State, AMI and Lumley Insurance in New Zealand. In Victoria it provides general insurance products under the RACV brand through a distribution and underwriting relationship with RACV, and it underwrites the Coles Insurance brand nationally through a distribution agreement with Coles. It operates a reinsurance partnership with Berkshire Hathaway, the American company associated with famed investor Warren Buffett.

Latest business results (June 2024, full year)

Rising premiums and a good investment performance generated a further solid increase in revenues and profits. There was gross written premium growth of 11.3 per cent to $16.4 billion as the company steadily raised premiums. Buoyant markets meant the company's investment portfolio added $286 million to income. The insurance profit of $1.438 billion generated an insurance margin — insurance and investment profits as a percentage of premiums, a key measure of profitability — of 15.6 per cent, up from 9.6 per cent in the previous year. New Zealand operations benefited significantly from a sharp reduction in claims. In the June 2023 year the insurer was hit badly by flooding in Auckland and the impact of Cyclone Gabrielle.

Outlook

IAG occupies a strong position in the Australian and New Zealand general insurance business, giving it considerable pricing power. But the insurance business is inherently volatile, and any unforeseen major natural disaster has the capacity to take a big chunk from company earnings. It is benefiting from moves taken in 2021 to reset its business, with a simpler operating model and a greater focus on its core activities. It expects to continue raising its insurance premiums in order to meet rising costs involved in house and car repairs. Anticipating more frequent extreme weather events, it has also lifted its natural peril allowance by 17 per cent to $1.28 billion. It believes it can achieve gross written premium growth in the mid to high single digits in the June 2025 year, with an insurance profit of $1.4 billion to $1.6 billion and an insurance margin of 13.5 per cent to 15.5 per cent.

Year to 30 June	2023	2024
Revenues ($mn)	13838.0	15425.0
Profit before tax ($mn)	1354.0	1491.0
Profit after tax ($mn)	832.0	898.0
Earnings per share (c)	33.92	37.31
Cash flow per share (c)	41.46	45.45
Dividend (c)	15	27
Percentage franked	30	46
Net tangible assets per share ($)	1.09	1.09
Return on equity (%)	13.0	13.5
Debt-to-equity ratio (%)	23.6	26.2

IPH Limited

ASX code: IPH   www.iphltd.com.au

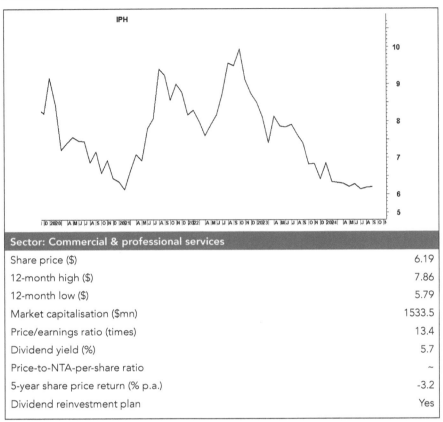

Sector: Commercial & professional services	
Share price ($)	6.19
12-month high ($)	7.86
12-month low ($)	5.79
Market capitalisation ($mn)	1533.5
Price/earnings ratio (times)	13.4
Dividend yield (%)	5.7
Price-to-NTA-per-share ratio	~
5-year share price return (% p.a.)	-3.2
Dividend reinvestment plan	Yes

Sydney-based IPH, formed in 2014 but with roots that stretch back to 1887, is a holding company for a group of businesses offering a wide range of intellectual property services and products. These include the filing, prosecution, enforcement and management of patents, designs, trademarks and other intellectual property. IPH incorporates seven brands: AJ Park, Griffith Hack, Smart & Biggar, Spruson & Ferguson, Pizzeys, ROBIC and Applied Marks. It operates in more than 25 countries, with offices in Australia, Canada, China, Hong Kong, Indonesia, Malaysia, New Zealand, the Philippines, Singapore and Thailand. In August 2024 it announced the acquisition of the Canadian intellectual property firm Bereskin & Parr.

Latest business results (June 2024, full year)

Revenues and underlying profits continued to grow, with a positive domestic performance and the continuing growth of Canadian operations more than offsetting Asian weakness. Australian and New Zealand businesses achieved a single-digit rise in revenues and profits, despite fewer patent filings and a decline in the company's market share. Canadian business, based on the October 2022 acquisition of Smart & Biggar, was bolstered by two further Canadian acquisitions late in 2023 — Ridout & Maybee and ROBIC — and achieved revenue and profit growth. Asian businesses reported single-digit declines in revenues and profits, with Singapore patent filings down by more than 8 per cent. The company also reported one-off business acquisition and restructuring costs that are not included in the table, and on a statutory basis profits fell.

Outlook

IPH has established itself as one of the leaders in Australia, New Zealand, Canada and South-East Asia in the intellectual property business. It has expanded steadily, through organic growth and acquisition. As it grows it achieves economies of scale that boost margins. It is achieving success with its strategy of leveraging its network of companies, with a growing number of referrals between member companies in different regions. It has targeted Canada as a market with great potential and is rapidly expanding operations there. Its $90 million acquisition of Bereskin & Parr will be its fourth in that country and will further consolidate its position as Canadian market leader. In addition to boosting business, the acquired operations deliver considerable cost synergies, helping the company reduce its cost base. In 2023 it opened its first office in the Philippines and it continues to seek out further acquisition opportunities, with the stated goal of becoming the leading intellectual property services group in markets outside the US, EU or Japan.

Year to 30 June	2023	2024
Revenues ($mn)	490.1	605.6
Australia & New Zealand (%)	57	48
Canada (%)	19	32
Asia (%)	24	20
EBIT ($mn)	155.5	184.3
EBIT margin (%)	31.7	30.4
Profit before tax ($mn)	135.3	149.5
Profit after tax ($mn)	99.0	112.4
Earnings per share (c)	43.90	46.37
Cash flow per share (c)	51.22	53.46
Dividend (c)	33	35
Percentage franked	37	32
Net tangible assets per share ($)	~	~
Interest cover (times)	8.5	6.4
Return on equity (%)	19.7	18.6
Debt-to-equity ratio (%)	51.0	56.5
Current ratio	3.2	2.8

JB Hi-Fi Limited

ASX code: JBH   investors.jbhifi.com.au

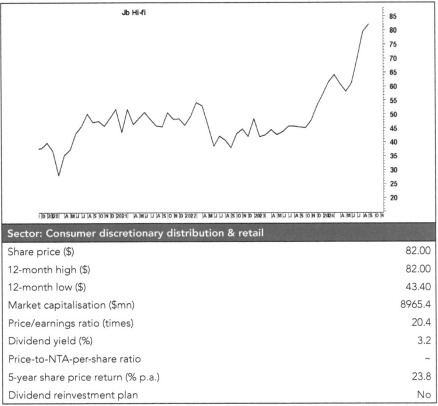

Sector: Consumer discretionary distribution & retail	
Share price ($)	82.00
12-month high ($)	82.00
12-month low ($)	43.40
Market capitalisation ($mn)	8965.4
Price/earnings ratio (times)	20.4
Dividend yield (%)	3.2
Price-to-NTA-per-share ratio	~
5-year share price return (% p.a.)	23.8
Dividend reinvestment plan	No

Melbourne-based JB Hi-Fi dates back to the opening in 1974 of a single recorded music store in the Melbourne suburb of East Keilor. It has since grown into a nationwide chain of home electronics and home appliance products outlets, and it has also expanded to New Zealand. In Australia it operates The Good Guys chain of home appliance stores, as well as specialised divisions that sell to the commercial and educational sectors. The company also maintains an online presence. At June 2024 it operated 205 JB Hi-Fi and JB Hi-Fi Home stores in Australia, 19 JB Hi-Fi stores in New Zealand and 106 The Good Guys stores in Australia. In September 2024 it acquired a 75 per cent stake in home appliance retailer E&S Trading.

Latest business results (June 2024, full year)

In a volatile and competitive consumer goods market JB Hi-Fi saw profits fall for a second straight year. The company's JB Hi-Fi stores in Australia recorded a small increase in sales, but with EBIT down 11 per cent as inflationary pressures and competitive forces hurt profit margins. The Good Guys business, subject to the same stresses, suffered a 4.8 per cent decline in sales, with EBIT plunging by 25.8 per cent.

The opening of five new stores in New Zealand helped boost sales there by 12.3 per cent, but this business fell into the red. Total online sales bounced back, having fallen in the previous year.

Outlook

JB Hi-Fi has a strong brand image throughout Australia and great customer loyalty. It has shown an impressive ability to contain costs. It continues to open new stores, though at a slower pace than in previous years. It is boosting floor space at its stores for growth categories such as mobile phones, gaming and connected technology. It is also working to strengthen its membership program and its online activities. It plans to open a further five new stores in New Zealand during the June 2025 year, and is working to strengthen operations in that country. However, as long as Australian consumer spending remains subdued, the company could be forced to discount more in order to maintain sales, cutting into profit margins. The $47.8 million acquisition of 75 per cent of E&S Trading delivers to JB Hi-Fi 10 Victorian stores and one in the ACT, and provides it with enhanced exposure to the premium home appliance and bathroom categories as well as to commercial construction customers.

Year to 30 June	2023	2024
Revenues ($mn)	9626.4	9592.4
JB Australia (%)	68	69
The Good Guys (%)	29	28
JB New Zealand (%)	3	3
EBIT ($mn)	773.4	658.4
EBIT margin (%)	8.0	6.9
Gross margin (%)	22.7	22.3
Profit before tax ($mn)	747.1	627.4
Profit after tax ($mn)	524.6	438.8
Earnings per share (c)	479.96	401.46
Cash flow per share (c)	683.35	616.65
Dividend (c)	312	261
Percentage franked	100	100
Net tangible assets per share ($)	~	~
Interest cover (times)	35.3	33.3
Return on equity (%)	38.9	29.5
Debt-to-equity ratio (%)	~	~
Current ratio	1.2	1.2

Johns Lyng Group Limited

ASX code: JLG   investors.johnslyng.com.au

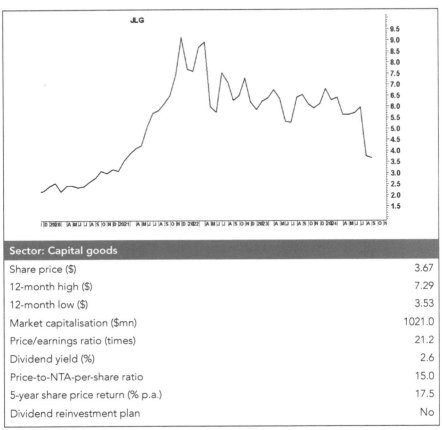

Sector: Capital goods	
Share price ($)	3.67
12-month high ($)	7.29
12-month low ($)	3.53
Market capitalisation ($mn)	1021.0
Price/earnings ratio (times)	21.2
Dividend yield (%)	2.6
Price-to-NTA-per-share ratio	15.0
5-year share price return (% p.a.)	17.5
Dividend reinvestment plan	No

Specialist Melbourne building company Johns Lyng Group was established in 1953 as Johns & Lyng Builders. It has a particular specialty in building and restoration work for insurance claims, with operations nationwide under various brands, and its clients include most of Australia's leading insurance companies. It also undertakes a range of commercial construction work and operates a fast-growing strata services business. The company has grown substantially through acquisition and at June 2024 operated from 106 offices in Australia under the Johns Lyng, Steamatic and Bright & Duggan brands and from 54 offices in the United States under the Johns Lyng USA and Steamatic brands.

Latest business results (June 2024, full year)

A sharp decline in demand for the company's disaster-related services sent revenues down, with a mixed result for profits. The core Insurance Building and Restoration Services division recorded an 8 per cent decline in revenues, with EBITDA edging up by less than 1 per cent. In the previous year this division reported revenues up

53 per cent and EBITDA jumping 61 per cent. Johns Lyng has a specialty in repair work related to major weather disasters, mainly storms and floods, and revenues for this business fell by nearly 45 per cent to $205.6 million. The small Commercial Building Services division, which is engaged in flooring work, emergency repairs, retail shop fitting and heating and air conditioning services, enjoyed another year of double-digit growth in revenues and profits. But the Commercial Construction division remained in the red. American revenues rose 1 per cent to represent 21.6 per cent of the total.

Outlook

Johns Lyng has developed a high reputation for its insurance-related work and it continues to expand. It also sees particular potential in its strata management activities, with substantial cross-selling opportunities for its building work. Thanks to a series of acquisitions in this highly fragmented sector, it now manages some 101 000 strata lots at around 4099 properties. It believes that the US can become a key pillar of long-term future growth, and has been introducing a comprehensive range of services. Following successful work with insurers and government authorities in the aftermath of Florida's devastating Hurricane Ian, the company has the opportunity to help provide emergency services to customers of US insurance giant Allstate. The 2023 acquisitions of two prominent smoke alarm and fire safety specialist companies have laid the foundation for a new Essential Home Services division, which the company believes can become another growth pillar.

Year to 30 June	2023	2024
Revenues ($mn)	1281.3	1158.9
Insurance building & restoration (%)	89	91
Commercial building services (%)	6	7
Commercial construction (%)	5	2
EBIT ($mn)	97.2	97.8
EBIT margin (%)	7.6	8.4
Gross margin (%)	21.5	25.0
Profit before tax ($mn)	93.4	92.3
Profit after tax ($mn)	46.8	48.0
Earnings per share (c)	17.94	17.34
Cash flow per share (c)	26.05	28.29
Dividend (c)	9	9.4
Percentage franked	100	100
Net tangible assets per share ($)	0.20	0.24
Interest cover (times)	80.1	50.5
Return on equity (%)	13.8	11.9
Debt-to-equity ratio (%)	~	~
Current ratio	1.3	1.3

Jumbo Interactive Limited

ASX code: JIN   www.jumbointeractive.com

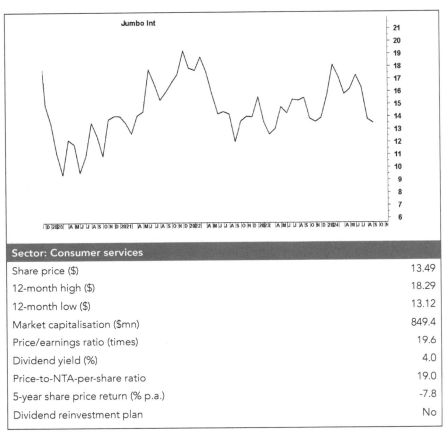

Sector: Consumer services

Share price ($)	13.49
12-month high ($)	18.29
12-month low ($)	13.12
Market capitalisation ($mn)	849.4
Price/earnings ratio (times)	19.6
Dividend yield (%)	4.0
Price-to-NTA-per-share ratio	19.0
5-year share price return (% p.a.)	-7.8
Dividend reinvestment plan	No

Jumbo Interactive was founded in Brisbane in 1995 as an internet service provider, but has since evolved into a major operator of internet services for lotteries. Its core business, Oz Lotteries, involves the provision of lottery services for The Lottery Corporation at its ozlotteries.com website. These lotteries include OzLotto, Powerball, Lotto Strike and Lucky Lotteries. Its Powered by Jumbo software platform manages lotteries for charitable organisations and other institutions. It also runs a Managed Services division to provide lottery management services to charities and other organisations, with operations in the United Kingdom and Canada.

Latest business results (June 2024, full year)

Some massive Powerball jackpots generated a substantial boost to lottery ticket sales and helped deliver a significant boost to company revenues and profits. The average OzLotto/Powerball Division 1 jackpot rose from $36.9 million in the June 2023 year to $43 million, with 55 large jackpots — defined as any Division 1 jackpot worth more than $15 million — compared to 42 in the previous year, including one record

$200 million jackpot in February 2024. Consequently, total lottery transaction value for the company of $543.8 million was up 21.1 per cent from the year before. The number of active online lottery customers rose 19.3 per cent to 1.1 million, with an average spend per active lottery customer of $498.37, up 6.9 per cent. The Managed Services division now represents 16 per cent of total company turnover, and continued to grow strongly. The Powered by Jumbo business, representing 6 per cent of income, achieved double-digit gains in revenues and profits. Corporate expenses — particularly for salaries and marketing — rose at a slightly faster pace than revenue growth, and profit margins edged down.

Outlook

Jumbo is a significant beneficiary of the Australian love of gambling. Its growth slowed after the ending of the COVID pandemic, but has since revived, although much depends on the level of lottery jackpots. It regards active customer numbers as the foundation for future expansion and spends heavily on promotional activities aimed at attracting new customers. Its new loyalty program, Daily Winners, was initiated in September 2023 with the aim of boosting spending by existing customers and increasing customer retention rates. It continues to attract new charities to its Powered by Jumbo platform. Following its entry to the British and Canadian markets it is seeking further acquisitions that enable access to new markets and new businesses. It is actively introducing artificial intelligence capabilities to its operations.

Year to 30 June	2023	2024
Revenues ($mn)	118.7	159.3
EBIT ($mn)	48.2	64.2
EBIT margin (%)	40.6	40.3
Profit before tax ($mn)	47.4	63.7
Profit after tax ($mn)	33.1	43.3
Earnings per share (c)	52.60	68.86
Cash flow per share (c)	70.55	88.49
Dividend (c)	43	54.5
Percentage franked	100	100
Net tangible assets per share ($)	0.43	0.71
Interest cover (times)	186.0	~
Return on equity (%)	34.3	40.3
Debt-to-equity ratio (%)	~	~
Current ratio	1.6	1.9

Lindsay Australia Limited

ASX code: LAU   www.lindsayaustralia.com.au

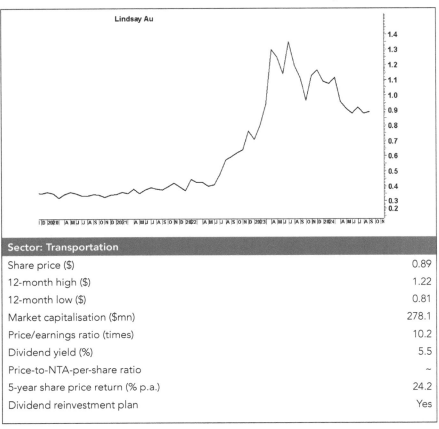

Sector: Transportation	
Share price ($)	0.89
12-month high ($)	1.22
12-month low ($)	0.81
Market capitalisation ($mn)	278.1
Price/earnings ratio (times)	10.2
Dividend yield (%)	5.5
Price-to-NTA-per-share ratio	~
5-year share price return (% p.a.)	24.2
Dividend reinvestment plan	Yes

Brisbane-based trucking company Lindsay Australia was established as Lindsay Brothers in 1953. It quickly developed a specialty in the transportation of fruit and vegetables and became a pioneer in the use of refrigerated trailers. It is today a fully integrated transport, logistics and rural supply company, servicing customers in the food processing, food services, rural and horticultural sectors, mainly in the eastern states. It operates from 24 branches, with a fleet of more than 1000 vehicles. Its Lindsay Rural business operates from 22 stores, supplying more than 1500 farmers with an extensive range of agricultural services and products. In August 2023 it acquired rural merchandise retailer W.B. Hunter.

Latest business results (June 2024, full year)

Revenues rose but profits fell after the company experienced significant disruptions from adverse weather, rail stoppages and sluggish economic conditions. Most of the revenue increase was due to an 11-month contribution from the $35 million Hunter acquisition, although on a like-for-like basis company sales rose 6 per cent. The

Transport division actually saw profits edge up at the EBITDA level as it enlarged its customer base, though a big jump in depreciation and amortisation charges meant that the division's EBIT and after-tax profit fell. The Rural division saw sales and profits down, hit by adverse weather in northern Queensland and subdued customer sentiment. The new Hunter business suffered from inflationary pressures, heightened competition and reduced consumer confidence and reported a small after-tax loss.

Outlook

Lindsay occupies a strong position in the transportation and rural supplies sectors within its regions of operation. It has a particular strength in the delivery of fresh fruit and vegetables. It has benefited from consolidation within the industry. It continues to invest in the growth of its road fleet, including the acquisition of larger new trailer combinations that will boost operational performance. Its rail business also continues to grow in importance, and rail revenues now represent more than a quarter of total transport income. Lindsay Rural uses its branch network of stores — most of them in Queensland — to supply its customer base with a wide diversity of agricultural products and services. W.B. Hunter, based in Victoria's Goulburn Valley, operates eight rural supplies stores in Victoria and New South Wales. Lindsay views the acquisition as an opportunity to expand its operations, and is seeking further acquisition opportunities. With the company facing inflationary pressures and a competitive labour market it has initiated a comprehensive transformation program aimed at boosting productivity and reducing costs.

Year to 30 June	2023	2024
Revenues ($mn)	676.2	804.4
Transport (%)	76	70
Rural (%)	24	19
Hunter (%)	0	11
EBIT ($mn)	59.2	53.6
EBIT margin (%)	8.8	6.7
Profit before tax ($mn)	49.4	39.8
Profit after tax ($mn)	34.5	27.3
Earnings per share (c)	11.40	8.75
Cash flow per share (c)	25.55	26.55
Dividend (c)	4.9	4.9
Percentage franked	61	100
Net tangible assets per share ($)	~	~
Interest cover (times)	6.8	4.7
Return on equity (%)	30.0	19.7
Debt-to-equity ratio (%)	~	~
Current ratio	1.4	1.0

Lovisa Holdings Limited

ASX code: LOV   www.lovisa.com.au

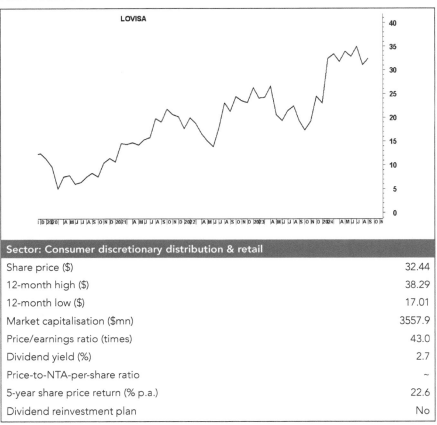

Sector: Consumer discretionary distribution & retail	
Share price ($)	32.44
12-month high ($)	38.29
12-month low ($)	17.01
Market capitalisation ($mn)	3557.9
Price/earnings ratio (times)	43.0
Dividend yield (%)	2.7
Price-to-NTA-per-share ratio	~
5-year share price return (% p.a.)	22.6
Dividend reinvestment plan	No

Melbourne-based jewellery and accessories retailer Lovisa Holdings was established in 2010. It specialises in lower-cost but up-to-date fashion pieces. It has grown significantly since its launch, and at June 2024 operated 168 stores in Australia and a further 732 in some 45 other countries globally, including 190 stores in the US, now its largest single market.

Latest business results (June 2024, full year)

Revenues and profits rose strongly again in another good result. However, the growth came from the company's continuing global expansion, with sales down 2 per cent on a same-store basis, despite a second-half recovery. Tight cost control helped offset inflationary pressures, especially for wages, and profit margins were up. Finance costs and depreciation expenses rose as the store network expanded. Once again the strongest growth came from abroad. Australia/New Zealand sales were up less than 1 per cent to $200 million, European sales rose 27 per cent to $230 million and American sales jumped 38 per cent to $177 million. During the year the company opened 128 new stores, including 50 in Europe and 27 in the

Americas, and closed 28. It entered seven new markets — China, Vietnam, Ireland, Ecuador, Senegal, Guadeloupe and Gabon.

Outlook

Lovisa remains optimistic about the outlook, despite a slowdown in discretionary consumer spending in many countries, as it continues to build its store network. It locates its stores within high-foot-traffic areas of high-performing shopping centres, and aims to develop some 100 new fashion jewellery lines every week for a younger demographic. It views digital media as an important part of its marketing strategy, and operates dedicated e-commerce sites across all its key markets. It also maintains a presence on popular online marketplaces, including WeChat and others in China, which it regards as a highly promising growth market. Product innovation is a key component of what Lovisa believes to be its competitive advantage, and the company employs large product development teams in several cities to ensure the company meets market demand. It is working to streamline and optimise its supply base in Asia while also ensuring it can speedily deliver new products to its stores. It operates a warehouse in China to support its Asian and African stores, another in Australia for its Australia/New Zealand business and one in Poland for the European market. In August 2024 it opened a new warehouse in Ohio to service the growing Americas region. With its business largely transacted in US dollars, it is affected by currency rate trends.

Year to 30 June*	2023	2024
Revenues ($mn)	596.5	698.7
Europe (%)	31	33
Australia/New Zealand (%)	33	29
Americas (%)	21	25
Africa/Middle East (%)	8	8
Asia (%)	6	5
EBIT ($mn)	106.0	128.4
EBIT margin (%)	17.8	18.4
Profit before tax ($mn)	92.9	110.6
Profit after tax ($mn)	68.2	82.4
Earnings per share (c)	63.25	75.38
Cash flow per share (c)	132.13	160.56
Dividend (c)	69	87
Percentage franked	87	17
Net tangible assets per share ($)	~	~
Interest cover (times)	8.3	7.3
Return on equity (%)	94.5	102.8
Debt-to-equity ratio (%)	41.7	29.2
Current ratio	1.0	0.9

*2 July 2023

Lycopodium Limited

ASX code: LYL   www.lycopodium.com

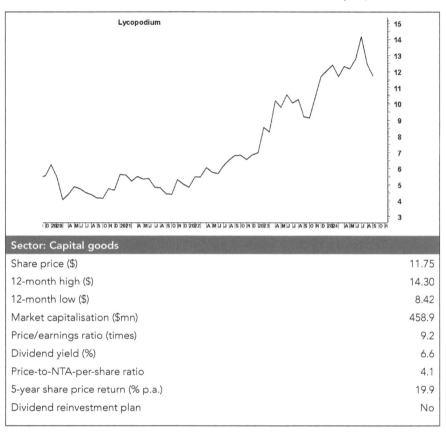

Sector: Capital goods	
Share price ($)	11.75
12-month high ($)	14.30
12-month low ($)	8.42
Market capitalisation ($mn)	458.9
Price/earnings ratio (times)	9.2
Dividend yield (%)	6.6
Price-to-NTA-per-share ratio	4.1
5-year share price return (% p.a.)	19.9
Dividend reinvestment plan	No

Founded in 1992, Perth-based Lycopodium is an engineering and project management company with activities around the world. Its particular specialty is the evaluation and development of projects for the resources, rail infrastructure and industrial processes sectors. It has operations in many countries and manages offices in Australia, South Africa, Canada, Peru, Ghana and the Philippines.

Latest business results (June 2024, full year)

Lycopodium reported another good result, with growth in revenues and profits, although not on the scale of the previous year. The company's successful resources operations generated the overwhelming bulk of revenues and profits, with sales up 9 per cent and profits rising 16 per cent. Major projects completed during the year included the Kathleen Valley Lithium Project in Western Australia, the Langer Heinrich Mine Restart Project in Namibia and the Mutamba Mineral Sands Pilot Project in Mozambique. Industrial processes revenues fell 6 per cent to $11.2 million with profits down 38 per cent as the company completed the detailed design for the

CSL Seqirus influenza vaccine manufacturing facility in Melbourne. Rail infrastructure revenues fell 38 per cent to $10.2 million, with profits down 49 per cent. Overseas operations were responsible for 64 per cent of total turnover.

Outlook

Despite economic weakness around the world, Lycopodium expects a significant level of investment to continue in the resources sector, related especially to the global energy transition, which is boosting demand for low-emission technologies. Thanks to many new development projects, especially for lithium, copper, graphite and nickel, it forecasts solid demand for its services. It also expects gold and iron ore production to continue to increase steadily, with the latter supported by increased infrastructure spending in China and India. Among the company's contracts are two for Barrick Gold, at the Reko Diq Project in Pakistan, one of the world's largest undeveloped copper–gold deposits, and the Lumwana Copper Project in Zambia, one of the world's largest copper deposits. Domestically, it is optimistic that a number of large, publicly funded infrastructure projects will ramp up across the country, including rail developments, in which Lycopodium already has a significant involvement. In the industrial processes sector it believes it will benefit from a slow return to domestic manufacturing, together with the rise of new markets in recycling, wastewater and hydrogen. Lycopodium is involved in two battery recycling schemes and is also working with government and academic bodies on the development of new energy storage technologies. It has developed new methods of reducing the carbon footprint of gold mining operations.

Year to 30 June	2023	2024
Revenues ($mn)	323.9	344.5
EBIT ($mn)	64.1	70.5
EBIT margin (%)	19.8	20.5
Profit before tax ($mn)	63.3	69.7
Profit after tax ($mn)	46.8	50.7
Earnings per share (c)	117.71	127.61
Cash flow per share (c)	133.73	144.15
Dividend (c)	81	77
Percentage franked	100	100
Net tangible assets per share ($)	2.41	2.85
Interest cover (times)	~	~
Return on equity (%)	43.5	41.8
Debt-to-equity ratio (%)	~	~
Current ratio	1.9	2.3

Macmahon Holdings Limited

ASX code: MAH   www.macmahon.com.au

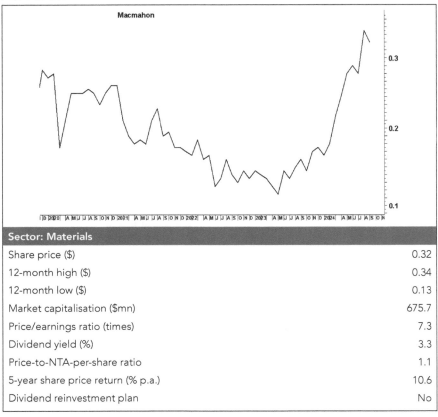

Sector: Materials

Share price ($)	0.32
12-month high ($)	0.34
12-month low ($)	0.13
Market capitalisation ($mn)	675.7
Price/earnings ratio (times)	7.3
Dividend yield (%)	3.3
Price-to-NTA-per-share ratio	1.1
5-year share price return (% p.a.)	10.6
Dividend reinvestment plan	No

Perth-based contracting group Macmahon Holdings, established in 1963, has a specialty in mining operations. In surface mining it offers a broad array of services, including mine planning, drill and blast, crushing and screening, water management, and equipment operation and maintenance, with operations in Australia and Asia. In underground mining it provides development and production services as well as services to facilitate ventilation and access to underground mines, including shaft sinking, raise drilling and shaft lining. Other activities include civil engineering, and in August 2024 it acquired civil engineer Decmil Group.

Latest business results (June 2024, full year)

Macmahon overcame commodity price volatility and labour shortages to post a solid rise in revenues and profits. Surface mining represented 66 per cent of revenues, with projects that included a five-year contract with Red 5 to provide mining services at the King of the Hills Gold Mine and a seven-year contract with Talison Lithium at the Greenbushes Lithium Mine. Underground mining provided a further 25 per cent of revenues. Projects included work for Genesis Minerals at the Gwalia Gold Mine and the new Ulysses Gold Mine. Gold projects contributed more than half of total turnover, with metallurgical coal a further quarter. Overseas work, mainly in Indonesia, was responsible for 7 per cent of revenues. At June 2024 the company held a $4.6 billion order backlog, which was down from $5.1 billion a year earlier.

Outlook

Macmahon has a solid reputation and provides contracting services to many of Australia's mining companies. Levels of activity in the mining sector remain strong and the company sees ahead a tender pipeline of some $21.4 billion of projects. It is working to reduce capital intensity in its operations, with a particular aim of a further expansion in underground mining operations. It has a goal of boosting underground mining revenues by 50 per cent over the coming two to three years. It sees great potential in its $127 million acquisition of Decmil. It allows the company to diversify its operations and provides a natural hedge to the cyclicality of contract mining. Decmil has a strong presence in government infrastructure and renewables projects, and will help Macmahon pursue its ambition of $1 billion in annual civil infrastructure revenues. It also allows Macmahon to expand its presence in Victoria and New South Wales, where it is relatively weak. Macmahon's early forecast is for revenues of $2.4 billion to $2.5 billion in the June 2025 year, with underlying profits up at least 14 per cent.

Year to 30 June	2023	2024
Revenues ($mn)	1906.2	2031.3
EBIT ($mn)	118.0	142.0
EBIT margin (%)	6.2	7.0
Profit before tax ($mn)	92.3	113.5
Profit after tax ($mn)	67.6	91.9
Earnings per share (c)	3.22	4.36
Cash flow per share (c)	12.60	14.41
Dividend (c)	0.75	1.05
Percentage franked	0	57
Net tangible assets per share ($)	0.28	0.30
Interest cover (times)	4.9	5.3
Return on equity (%)	11.6	14.8
Debt-to-equity ratio (%)	33.2	23.1
Current ratio	1.2	1.3

Macquarie Group Limited

ASX code: MQG   www.macquarie.com

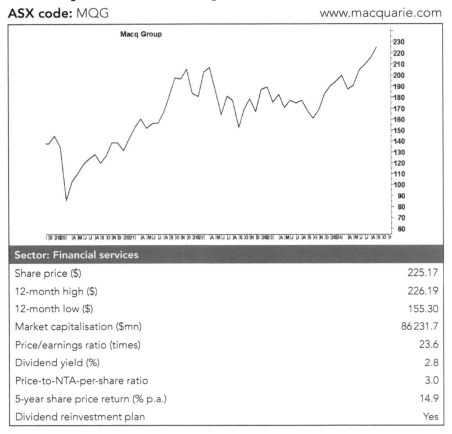

Sector: Financial services	
Share price ($)	225.17
12-month high ($)	226.19
12-month low ($)	155.30
Market capitalisation ($mn)	86 231.7
Price/earnings ratio (times)	23.6
Dividend yield (%)	2.8
Price-to-NTA-per-share ratio	3.0
5-year share price return (% p.a.)	14.9
Dividend reinvestment plan	Yes

Sydney-based Macquarie Group was established in 1969 as Hill Samuel Australia, a subsidiary of a British merchant bank. It is now Australia's leading locally owned investment bank, with a wide spread of activities and boasting special expertise in specific industries that include finance, resources and commodities, energy, infrastructure and real estate. It operates in 34 markets around the world, and international business accounts for around 70 per cent of total company revenue.

Latest business results (March 2024, full year)

A three-year run of fast-growing profits came to an end, as subdued markets in many parts of the world sent revenues and earnings down. The largest of the bank's four broad operating segments, Commodities and Global Markets, saw profits tumble by 47 per cent. This was a sharp reversal after three straight annual gains in profits of more than 50 per cent, when the bank had been able to take advantage of market volatility. Macquarie Asset Management also experienced a sharp 48 per cent fall, its second straight earnings decline, driven by lower asset realisations in green investments and rising expenses. By contrast, Macquarie Capital recovered from weakness in the previous year to post a 31 per cent jump in profits, thanks to higher investment-related income and growth in the private credit portfolio. The Banking and Financial Services segment was again firm, with profits edging up 3 per cent, as the bank benefited from a growing loan portfolio and rising bank deposits.

Outlook

Though cautious about the near-term outlook, Macquarie believes it is well placed to deliver a superior medium-term performance as it builds on its existing businesses and steadily moves into new products and new markets. It has been placing a strong emphasis on building a portfolio of decarbonisation assets, through its Green Investment Group, with green energy projects in hand across more than 25 markets. It believes that investments totalling some US$4 trillion will be needed by 2030 for governments around the world to meet their net-zero emission targets, and it has become a leader in the wind and solar industries. It is also expanding its involvement in emerging technologies, including utility-scale energy storage, hydrogen fuel and zero-emission transport. In addition, Macquarie is a major investor in global infrastructure assets, at a time when governments in both Europe and the US are expected to boost spending on essential infrastructure renewal projects. The Banking and Financial Services division continues to grow, although it has been facing some competitive pressures on margins.

Year to 31 March	2023	2024
Operating income ($mn)	19122.0	16887.0
Net interest income ($mn)	3028.0	3459.0
Operating expenses ($mn)	12130.0	12061.0
Profit before tax ($mn)	6992.0	4826.0
Profit after tax ($mn)	5182.0	3522.0
Earnings per share (c)	1398.75	953.66
Dividend (c)	750	640
Percentage franked	40	40
Non-interest income to total income (%)	84.2	79.5
Net tangible assets per share ($)	74.34	74.15
Cost-to-income ratio (%)	63.4	71.4
Return on equity (%)	16.8	10.6
Return on assets (%)	1.3	0.9

Mader Group Limited

ASX code: MAD   www.madergroup.com.au

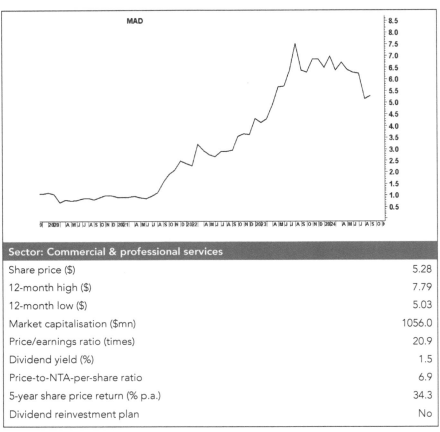

Sector: Commercial & professional services	
Share price ($)	5.28
12-month high ($)	7.79
12-month low ($)	5.03
Market capitalisation ($mn)	1056.0
Price/earnings ratio (times)	20.9
Dividend yield (%)	1.5
Price-to-NTA-per-share ratio	6.9
5-year share price return (% p.a.)	34.3
Dividend reinvestment plan	No

Perth-based contractor Mader was founded in 2005 and is a specialist in mobile and fixed plant equipment maintenance and support. Its key business is the supply of trades people for the maintenance of heavy mobile equipment in the resources and energy sectors. However, it has grown rapidly to provide support services of many kinds to a wide range of industries. It works throughout Australia and has also expanded abroad, with 23 per cent of revenues derived from North America. It is also moving into the Asia-Pacific region.

Latest business results (June 2024, full year)

Mader recorded double-digit growth in sales and profits, with strength across most businesses. Australian revenues rose 25 per cent to $585.7 million, with particularly strong demand for core mechanical and ancillary services. North American revenues rose 34 per cent to $177.8 million, despite second-half weakness in US business as softer coal prices and political uncertainty resulted in site closures and the delay of some investment decisions. By contrast, Canadian operations continued to grow strongly. Revenues of $11 million from four Asia-Pacific countries were 36 per cent higher than the previous year. At June 2024 the company was servicing some 430 customers at more than 570 locations.

Outlook

Mader is a beneficiary of the continuing strength of the Australian and North American resources and energy sectors. It maintains an ambitious growth program, based on service and geographical expansion and sector diversification. In Australia it has moved from its resources base to the provision of services to a range of sectors that include infrastructure, rail, road transport, power generation and marine, and it continues to seek out new growth opportunities. However, it sees its best near-term prospects in the large North American market. In the US it has operations in multiple commodities across 37 states, and despite some market consolidation during the June 2024 year it believes the growth potential remains excellent. It entered the Canadian market in 2022 and continues to grow strongly, with services now extended to eight provinces and territories. Its Mader Energy business unit is targeting field maintenance support service opportunities for customers in the natural gas compression industry. Mader is also working to extend its services to customers in other countries. The company's early forecast for June 2025 is for continuing strength across all markets, delivering revenues of at least $870 million and an after-tax profit of at least $57 million. The longer-term target is for annual revenues of at least $1 billion.

Year to 30 June	2023	2024
Revenues ($mn)	608.8	774.5
Australia (%)	77	76
North America (%)	22	23
EBIT ($mn)	58.1	74.7
EBIT margin (%)	9.5	9.6
Gross margin (%)	22.3	20.9
Profit before tax ($mn)	54.6	70.5
Profit after tax ($mn)	38.5	50.4
Earnings per share (c)	19.25	25.21
Cash flow per share (c)	27.73	37.47
Dividend (c)	5.8	7.8
Percentage franked	100	100
Net tangible assets per share ($)	0.56	0.76
Interest cover (times)	16.4	19.0
Return on equity (%)	37.6	36.0
Debt-to-equity ratio (%)	35.7	19.4
Current ratio	1.9	1.7

Magellan Financial Group Limited

ASX code: MFG
www.magellangroup.com.au

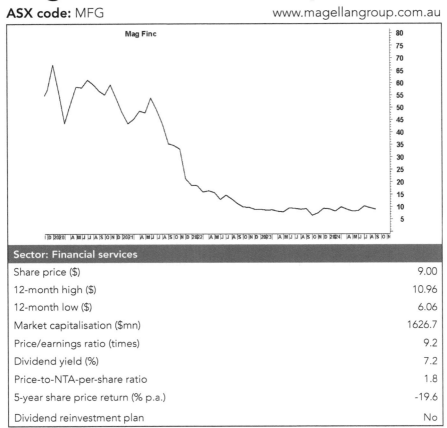

Sector: Financial services	
Share price ($)	9.00
12-month high ($)	10.96
12-month low ($)	6.06
Market capitalisation ($mn)	1626.7
Price/earnings ratio (times)	9.2
Dividend yield (%)	7.2
Price-to-NTA-per-share ratio	1.8
5-year share price return (% p.a.)	-19.6
Dividend reinvestment plan	No

Sydney-based Magellan is a specialist investment management company that evolved in 2006 from the ASX-listed Pengana Hedgefunds Limited. Its main business is Magellan Asset Management, which offers managed funds to retail and institutional investors, with particular specialties in global equities, in global listed infrastructure and, through Airlie Funds Management, in Australian equities. In August 2024 it acquired a 29.5 per cent equity stake in global funds management firm Vinva Investment Management.

Latest business results (June 2024, full year)

Revenues and underlying profits fell again as the company continued to suffer client outflows from its funds, although payments from associates generated a small increase in the after-tax profit. Funds under management, which in June 2021 had risen to $113.9 billion, declined again, reaching $36.6 billion at June 2024, down from $39.7 billion in June 2023. Management and services fees also fell again, down 22 per cent to $257.9 million, although performance fees jumped 67 per cent to $19.2 million as Magellan achieved some success in global equities. The company continued to work at cutting costs, with employee expenses down 20 per cent and fund administration and operational costs falling by 10 per cent.

Outlook

Magellan has been through a torrid period, as the continuing underperformance of its main global funds sparked a chain of client withdrawals and management departures. Now, under new management, it is seeking to rebuild. The $138.5 million acquisition of a stake in Vinva Investment Management is seen as part of this strategy. Vinva runs a series of funds that have delivered excellent returns since 2010 and it boasts a strong distribution team, providing a boost to Magellan's own investment capabilities and its distribution channels. Meanwhile, Magellan has reported that net flows, both retail and institutional, have at last stabilised, with significant client wins. This follows success in achieving some strong investment performances for its key global funds during the June 2024 year. Magellan has also seen client wins for its infrastructure funds, which are based on an investment strategy that it believes is well placed to deliver strong returns over the long term. In addition, its successful Australian equities business continues to see fund inflows. It has appointed new leadership to its US distribution platform, laying the foundation for future growth. Magellan is also benefiting from its 36 per cent holding in the financial services firm Barrenjoey Capital Partners, which is growing strongly. At the end of August 2024 Magellan funds under management were $37.8 billion.

Year to 30 June	2023	2024
Revenues ($mn)	343.0	278.3
EBIT ($mn)	254.1	239.8
EBIT margin (%)	74.1	86.2
Profit before tax ($mn)	252.6	238.8
Profit after tax ($mn)	174.3	177.9
Earnings per share (c)	95.43	98.24
Cash flow per share (c)	98.73	100.43
Dividend (c)	86.7	65.1
Percentage franked	85	50
Net tangible assets per share ($)	4.66	5.02
Interest cover (times)	~	~
Return on equity (%)	17.5	18.0
Debt-to-equity ratio (%)	~	~
Current ratio	2.0	7.2

Medibank Private Limited

ASX code: MPL   www.medibank.com.au

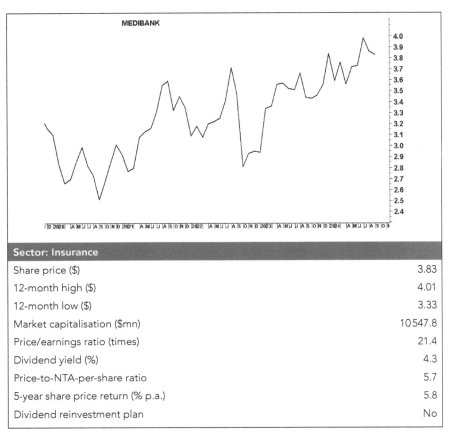

Sector: Insurance	
Share price ($)	3.83
12-month high ($)	4.01
12-month low ($)	3.33
Market capitalisation ($mn)	10547.8
Price/earnings ratio (times)	21.4
Dividend yield (%)	4.3
Price-to-NTA-per-share ratio	5.7
5-year share price return (% p.a.)	5.8
Dividend reinvestment plan	No

Melbourne-based Medibank Private was established by the Australian government in 1976 as a not-for-profit private health insurer. It was privatised and listed on the ASX in 2014. Today it is Australia's largest private health insurer, with a market share of around 27 per cent, operating under the Medibank and ahm brands. It has also branched into other areas, including travel insurance, pet insurance, life insurance, income protection and funeral insurance. Its Medibank Health division specialises in the provision of a diverse mix of healthcare services.

Latest business results (June 2024, full year)
Rising policyholder numbers and higher premium revenues helped generate another good result for Medibank, bolstered by a $43.6 million increase in net investment income to $182.2 million. The company reported that its underlying after-tax profit, which has been adjusted for movement in the COVID equity reserve and for the normalisation of investment returns, rose 14.1 per cent to $570.4 million. Accounting changes meant the company restated its June 2023 figures. Policyholder numbers

grew by 0.7 per cent, with 3.4 per cent growth for the budget ahm health insurance brand, which is aimed at younger customers, and a 0.2 per cent decline for the Medibank brand. Total premium revenue rose 4 per cent, outstripping the net claims expense, which was up 3.4 per cent. The very small Medibank Health division — representing around 3 per cent of company turnover — achieved double-digit increases in revenues and profits.

Outlook

Medibank occupies a central role in the national health sector. Nevertheless, its business is heavily regulated, and it is difficult to achieve significant growth. Intense competition means it failed to achieve growth targets in the June 2024 year and its market share edged down. It is under pressure from the private hospital sector for help in meeting fast-rising costs and declining patient numbers. In addition, with many households facing cost of living pressures, private health insurance growth rates could start to decline. It is experiencing very strong growth for its non-resident health insurance operations, particularly in the foreign student market. It also expects continuing strong growth for its Medibank Health division, which provides online and telehealth services, home care support and a variety of prevention and health management services. It is targeting acquisitions to further strengthen this business. It forecasts modest health insurance industry growth in the June 2025 year, and it aims to grow in line with the market. It has a further goal of boosting market share in the June 2026 year.

Year to 30 June	2023	2024
Revenues ($mn)	7086.4	7623.1
EBIT ($mn)	439.7	715.5
EBIT margin (%)	6.2	9.4
Profit before tax ($mn)	437.9	711.7
Profit after tax ($mn)	308.6	492.5
Earnings per share (c)	11.21	17.88
Cash flow per share (c)	13.88	20.99
Dividend (c)	14.6	16.6
Percentage franked	100	100
Net tangible assets per share ($)	0.70	0.67
Interest cover (times)	~	~
Return on equity (%)	13.6	21.7
Debt-to-equity ratio (%)	~	~
Current ratio	2.2	1.9

Metcash Limited

ASX code: MTS

www.metcash.com

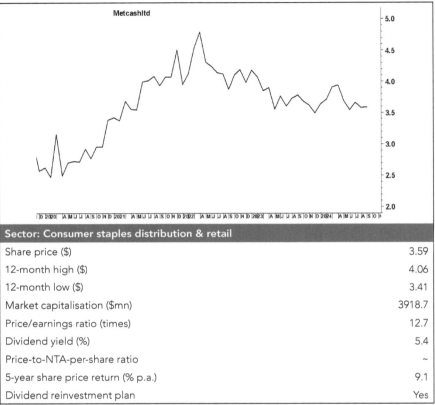

Sector: Consumer staples distribution & retail	
Share price ($)	3.59
12-month high ($)	4.06
12-month low ($)	3.41
Market capitalisation ($mn)	3918.7
Price/earnings ratio (times)	12.7
Dividend yield (%)	5.4
Price-to-NTA-per-share ratio	~
5-year share price return (% p.a.)	9.1
Dividend reinvestment plan	Yes

Sydney-based Metcash, with a history dating back to the 1920s, is a leading food and liquor wholesaler. Its Food division supports a network of more than 1600 independently owned grocery stores and supermarkets, mainly under the IGA and Foodland brands. The Liquor division is Australia's largest supplier of liquor to independently owned liquor retailers, with more than 12 000 customers. These include the Independent Brands Australia network of Cellarbrations, Bottle-O, IGA Liquor and Porters. The Hardware division operates the Independent Hardware Group, which supplies more than 700 stores, including the Mitre 10, Home Timber & Hardware and Total Tools chains.

Latest business results (April 2024, full year)

Sales edged up, with continuing growth in the Hardware and Liquor divisions more than offsetting a dip in the Food division, which was caused by a decline in tobacco sales. However, rising costs and a challenging construction environment hurt the hardware business, and total profits fell. The company's food sales actually rose by 4.6 per cent, but tobacco sales slumped by nearly 14 per cent, which Metcash attributed to an acceleration in illicit trade and a move to alternatives. Nevertheless, Food division EBIT was up by 3 per cent, with enhanced margins. Liquor division sales and profits grew modestly. However, the Hardware division, which in earlier years had been growing strongly, was affected by rapidly slowing builder confidence and reduced market activity, generating significantly increased competition. Sales rose, thanks to the opening of new stores, but EBIT fell by 3.8 per cent. Nevertheless, though just 16 per cent of total turnover, the Hardware division delivered around 40 per cent of company EBIT.

Outlook

Metcash maintains its efficiency drive, with $15 million in additional annualised cost savings expected in 2025. It also continues to expand. In March 2024 it boosted its exposure to the construction industry in South Australia and the Northern Territory with the $82 million acquisition of Bianco Construction Supplies, a prominent supplier of building materials. Also in March 2024 it acquired Victorian company Alpine Truss for $64 million, providing Metcash with access to new frame and truss markets in Victoria and the ACT. In June 2024 it completed the $412 million acquisition of Superior Foods, a leading food service company that supplies some 20 000 cafes, restaurants, hotels and canteens from 23 branches across Australia. The acquisition is expected to generate some $14 million in annual cost synergies as well as providing Metcash with significant further consolidation opportunities in the fragmented $21 billion food service market.

Year to 30 April	2023	2024
Revenues ($mn)	15 803.4	15 912.4
Food (%)	53	52
Liquor (%)	32	32
Hardware (%)	15	16
EBIT ($mn)	461.4	445.9
EBIT margin (%)	2.9	2.8
Gross margin (%)	11.7	12.2
Profit before tax ($mn)	436.1	403.7
Profit after tax ($mn)	307.5	282.3
Earnings per share (c)	31.85	28.31
Cash flow per share (c)	49.97	47.57
Dividend (c)	22.5	19.5
Percentage franked	100	100
Net tangible assets per share ($)	~	~
Interest cover (times)	20.0	11.3
Return on equity (%)	28.6	21.8
Debt-to-equity ratio (%)	32.2	16.5
Current ratio	1.1	1.1

Monadelphous Group Limited

ASX code: MND   www.monadelphous.com.au

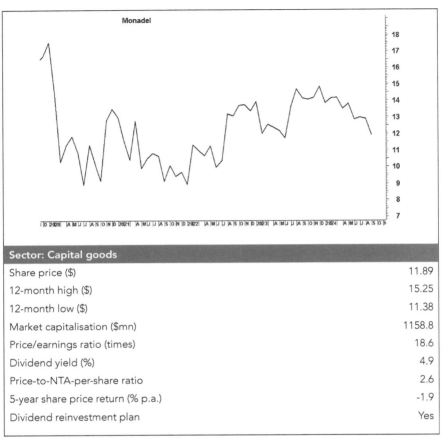

Sector: Capital goods	
Share price ($)	11.89
12-month high ($)	15.25
12-month low ($)	11.38
Market capitalisation ($mn)	1158.8
Price/earnings ratio (times)	18.6
Dividend yield (%)	4.9
Price-to-NTA-per-share ratio	2.6
5-year share price return (% p.a.)	-1.9
Dividend reinvestment plan	Yes

Perth-based Monadelphous, established in 1972, is an engineering company that provides a wide range of construction, maintenance, project management and support services to the minerals, energy and infrastructure industries. It operates from branches throughout Australia, with a client base that includes most of the country's resource majors. It has also established a presence in overseas markets that include China, Mongolia, Papua New Guinea and the Philippines. Its Zenviron joint venture is involved in large-scale renewable energy projects and its Mondium joint venture is involved in minerals processing.

Latest business results (June 2024, full year)

Revenues and profits rose in a good year for the company. Monadelphous classifies its activities into two broad segments. The best result came from the Engineering Construction division, with a 32 per cent jump in revenues to $713 million, after two years of double-digit declines. Around 38 per cent of business came from what the company terms as energy transition metals, with a further 35 per cent from iron ore.

The Maintenance and Industrial Services division recorded a 2 per cent increase in revenues, with energy projects responsible for 44 per cent of income and iron ore a further 22 per cent.

Outlook

Monadelphous plays an important role in the Australian minerals, energy and infrastructure industries, and it stands to benefit from growing demand for its services. It enjoys particular strength in the energy sector, with projects that include a long-term services agreement with Woodside, valued at some $180 million per year, for onshore and offshore gas production facilities in Western Australia. A new $200 million contract is for modifications to Woodside's Pluto facility. The company has also secured a significant amount of new construction work for lithium projects in Western Australia. However, it has also suffered the termination of one of these contracts, Albermarle's Kemerton Expansion Project, with a hit to June 2025 revenues of $75 million to $85 million. The iron ore sector remains buoyant, despite concerns about a possible slump in prices, and Monadelphous continues to experience strong demand from long-term customers Rio Tinto, BHP and Fortescue. It is increasing its exposure to decarbonisation projects, and hopes to benefit from the significant capital investment it believes will be needed to meet the rapidly growing demand for copper. Its Zenviron joint venture is a beneficiary of a growing number of renewable energy projects. Monadelphous is working to address skills shortages, which are driving labour costs higher and leading to delays in completing projects.

Year to 30 June	2023	2024
Revenues ($mn)	1721.0	2015.9
Maintenance & industrial services (%)	71	66
Engineering construction (%)	29	34
EBIT ($mn)	76.9	95.7
EBIT margin (%)	4.5	4.7
Gross margin (%)	6.9	7.1
Profit before tax ($mn)	73.4	91.9
Profit after tax ($mn)	53.5	62.2
Earnings per share (c)	55.85	64.08
Cash flow per share (c)	90.43	103.71
Dividend (c)	49	58
Percentage franked	100	100
Net tangible assets per share ($)	4.37	4.59
Interest cover (times)	~	~
Return on equity (%)	12.6	13.8
Debt-to-equity ratio (%)	~	~
Current ratio	2.0	1.6

Monash IVF Group Limited

ASX code: MVF　　　　　　　　　www.monashivfgroup.com.au

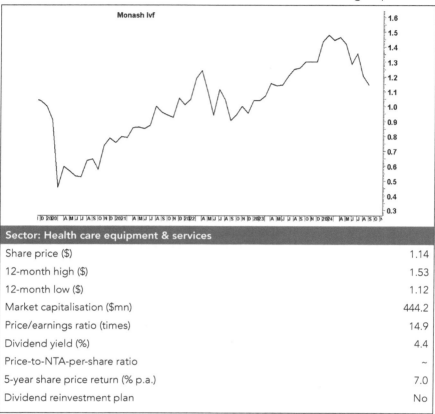

Sector: Health care equipment & services

Share price ($)	1.14
12-month high ($)	1.53
12-month low ($)	1.12
Market capitalisation ($mn)	444.2
Price/earnings ratio (times)	14.9
Dividend yield (%)	4.4
Price-to-NTA-per-share ratio	~
5-year share price return (% p.a.)	7.0
Dividend reinvestment plan	No

Melbourne-based Monash IVF traces its origins to the start of in-vitro fertilisation research at Monash University in 1971, and it has become a global pioneer in a wide range of assisted reproductive technology services. These include frozen embryo births, birth from donor eggs, surgically removed sperm, sperm micro-injection technology, surrogate births and vitrified egg pregnancy. The company is also a provider of specialised women's imaging services. It operates clinics throughout Australia and has expanded to Malaysia, Singapore and Indonesia.

Latest business results (June 2024, full year)

Monash IVF reported a strong result, with double-digit gains in revenues and underlying profits. Australian operations saw revenues up by nearly 19 per cent, thanks to a combination of industry growth, market share gains and price increases. The company also received a contribution from its acquisition in March 2024 of Western Australian business Fertility North. It said that it boosted its domestic share of the assisted reproductive market by 1.5 per cent to 21.7 per cent. International operations, representing 6 per cent of total turnover, recorded a 28 per cent increase in revenues, with the after-tax profit surging 85 per cent, thanks especially to volume growth across the company's clinics. Monash also reported a large one-off after-tax loss of $32.6 million — not included in the figures in the table — as settlement of a class action case initiated in 2020 in relation to its genetic testing business. Thus, on a statutory basis, the company's after-tax profit became a $6 million loss.

Outlook

It is estimated that one in six Australian couples experience infertility issues, with the fertility clinic market worth some $765 million in 2024. Demand continues to grow, driven by several factors, including the fact that more women wish to have children later in life, along with a growing success rate for fertility treatments. In addition, Australia offers substantial government funding, more than many other countries, for fertility treatments. Monash occupies a leading position in the provision of these services, and it continues to boost its market share. A four-year infrastructure program, with new flagship clinics in major cities, will be completed during the June 2025 year. It also continues to seek out new acquisition opportunities, as well as recruiting additional fertility specialists. Thanks to recent capacity expansion it is seeing growth in its specialised women's imaging services. An ongoing optimisation and efficiency program is boosting profit margins. Monash has said it expects further revenue and profit growth in the June 2025 year.

Year to 30 June	2023	2024
Revenues ($mn)	213.6	255.0
EBIT ($mn)	38.1	43.4
EBIT margin (%)	17.8	17.0
Profit before tax ($mn)	34.8	38.0
Profit after tax ($mn)	25.5	29.9
Earnings per share (c)	6.54	7.67
Cash flow per share (c)	10.48	12.44
Dividend (c)	4.4	5
Percentage franked	100	100
Net tangible assets per share ($)	~	~
Interest cover (times)	11.6	8.2
Return on equity (%)	9.4	11.6
Debt-to-equity ratio (%)	11.2	19.6
Current ratio	0.6	0.5

National Australia Bank Limited

ASX code: NAB   www.nab.com.au

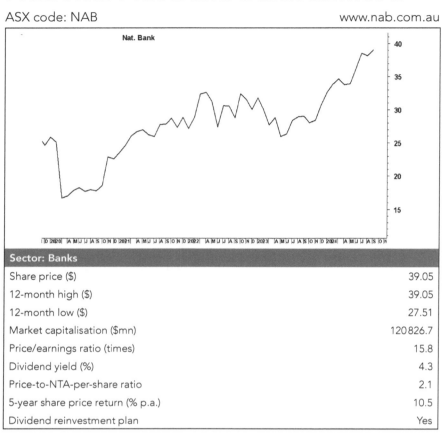

Sector: Banks	
Share price ($)	39.05
12-month high ($)	39.05
12-month low ($)	27.51
Market capitalisation ($mn)	120826.7
Price/earnings ratio (times)	15.8
Dividend yield (%)	4.3
Price-to-NTA-per-share ratio	2.1
5-year share price return (% p.a.)	10.5
Dividend reinvestment plan	Yes

National Australia Bank, based in Melbourne, has a history dating back to the establishment of the National Bank of Australasia in 1858. It is one of Australia's largest banks, with a wide spread of financial activities and particular strength in business banking. It owns the Bank of New Zealand, and also operates offices in several countries in Asia. It is involved in financial planning and wealth management, including with its long-established JBWere advisory service. Other activities include the nabtrade online broking service and the ubank online bank.

Latest business results (March 2024, half year)

Competitive pressures and a slowing economy pushed revenues and profits down. The bank was also affected by a 5.8 per cent increase in costs, reflecting an inflationary environment along with expanding investments in technology, with a particular focus on fraud and cyber-crime. The net interest margin fell five basis points to 1.72 per cent. All four key divisions experienced weakness. The Business and Private Banking division, representing more than 40 per cent of bank earnings, saw profits edge down, with strong volume growth offset by lower margins. However, the Personal Banking division was hit hard by intense competition in the home loans business, and profits tumbled by nearly 30 per cent. New Zealand operations, which a year earlier had recorded double-digit gains in revenues and profits, this time saw profits affected by rising expenses, including higher salary and technology-related costs and compliance obligations. The Corporate and Institutional Banking division reported a modest decline in earnings, with lower market income driving revenues down, only partially offset by stronger margins.

Outlook

A key focus for the bank in recent years has been to simplify, automate and digitise its businesses, while also increasing its use of data and analytics. This has helped it manage costs, although it continues to be hurt by inflationary and competitive pressures. However, it has reported signs that the strong competition in the home loans market is starting to ease. It is working to boost its Business and Private Banking division, where it is already a market leader. It is realising excellent growth in new business transaction accounts for small and medium-sized enterprises. Its business banking arm has also been performing well with home lending. A further area of growth is the ubank online bank, which has been recording strong new customer acquisition in the target segment of under-35-year-olds. In New Zealand, NAB is working to become a simpler, more digital bank.

Year to 30 September	2022	2023
Operating income ($mn)	18284.0	20654.0
Net interest income ($mn)	14840.0	16807.0
Operating expenses ($mn)	8274.0	9023.0
Profit before tax ($mn)	9897.0	10829.0
Profit after tax ($mn)	7104.0	7731.0
Earnings per share (c)	220.69	246.52
Dividend (c)	151	167
Percentage franked	100	100
Non-interest income to total income (%)	18.8	18.6
Cost-to-income ratio (%)	45.3	43.7
Return on equity (%)	11.7	12.9
Return on assets (%)	0.7	0.7
Half year to 31 March	2023	2024
Operating income ($mn)	10529.0	10138.0
Profit before tax ($mn)	5715.0	5098.0
Profit after tax ($mn)	4070.0	3548.0
Earnings per share (c)	129.50	114.00
Dividend (c)	83	84
Percentage franked	100	100
Net tangible assets per share ($)	18.09	18.21

Netwealth Group Limited

ASX code: NWL   www.netwealth.com.au

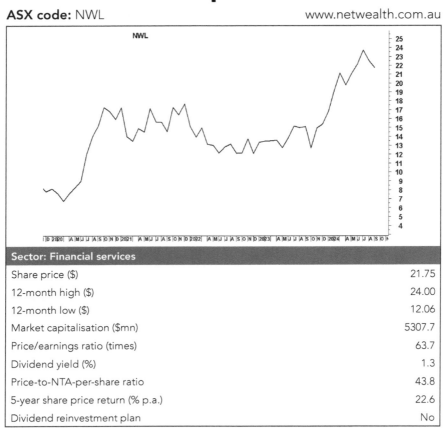

Sector: Financial services	
Share price ($)	21.75
12-month high ($)	24.00
12-month low ($)	12.06
Market capitalisation ($mn)	5307.7
Price/earnings ratio (times)	63.7
Dividend yield (%)	1.3
Price-to-NTA-per-share ratio	43.8
5-year share price return (% p.a.)	22.6
Dividend reinvestment plan	No

Melbourne-based financial services business Netwealth was founded in 1999. Through its wealth management platform it specialises in superannuation products, investor-directed portfolio services for self-managed superannuation, managed accounts and managed funds. The founding Heine family own more than half the company equity.

Latest business results (June 2024, full year)

Rebounding equity markets and easing bond rates helped generate another strong performance. During the year the company recorded inflows to its funds of $22 billion, up 18 per cent from the previous year, with outflows of $10.7 billion which was 21 per cent higher. Net inflows were up by nearly 14 per cent from the previous year. Total funds under administration at June 2024 of $88 billion were up 25 per cent from a year earlier and the number of client accounts was up 12 per cent to 143 251. Effective cost control during the year meant that company revenues grew at a faster pace than expenses, and margins rose.

Outlook

Netwealth runs a wealth management platform, which is a comprehensive software system that is designed to help financial advisers and others to track their investment portfolios, perform research on new investments and execute trades. It is estimated that more than $1 trillion in investor assets are currently being managed on such platforms in Australia and it is a highly competitive business. The leaders, with around 70 per cent of the market, are major financial institutions such as Insignia Financial, BT Panorama, AMP, Colonial First State and Macquarie Group. These are mostly losing market share, and catching up on them are several smaller and fast-growing firms like Netwealth, which have a particular strength in the development of user-friendly technology. Netwealth says that, based on industry analysis, it was again one of Australia's fastest-growing platform providers in the 12 months to March 2024, boosting its market share by 0.9 per cent to 7.7 per cent. It continues to invest heavily in its IT infrastructure and in personnel in order to promote continuing growth, with a particular target of increased business from high-net-worth individuals. Its August 2024 full acquisition of data management software house Xeppo means Netwealth can provide financial advisers with a specialist service that gives them the ability to connect and unify all their client data and systems. Several significant new client wins for the company are expected to boost fund inflows in the June 2025 year. At June 2024 Netwealth had no debt and more than $126 million in cash holdings.

Year to 30 June	2023	2024
Revenues ($mn)	211.5	249.5
EBIT ($mn)	97.5	121.0
EBIT margin (%)	46.1	48.5
Profit before tax ($mn)	97.0	120.4
Profit after tax ($mn)	67.2	83.4
Earnings per share (c)	27.54	34.16
Cash flow per share (c)	28.88	35.66
Dividend (c)	24	28
Percentage franked	100	100
Net tangible assets per share ($)	0.43	0.50
Interest cover (times)	~	~
Return on equity (%)	59.1	62.3
Debt-to-equity ratio (%)	~	~
Current ratio	5.3	5.1

NIB Holdings Limited

ASX code: NHF

www.nib.com.au

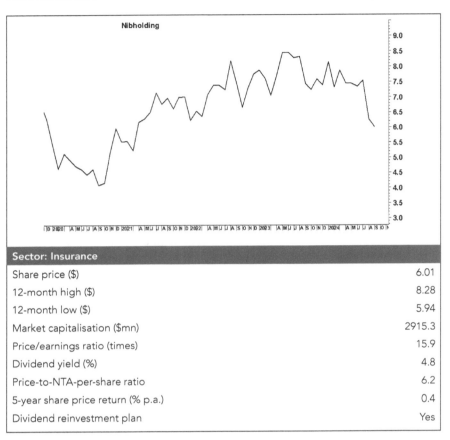

Sector: Insurance	
Share price ($)	6.01
12-month high ($)	8.28
12-month low ($)	5.94
Market capitalisation ($mn)	2915.3
Price/earnings ratio (times)	15.9
Dividend yield (%)	4.8
Price-to-NTA-per-share ratio	6.2
5-year share price return (% p.a.)	0.4
Dividend reinvestment plan	Yes

Newcastle private health insurer NIB Holdings was established as the Newcastle Industrial Benefits Hospital Fund in 1952 by workers at the BHP steelworks. It subsequently demutualised and became the first private health insurer to list on the ASX. It is also active in New Zealand. Other businesses are travel insurance and the provision of specialist insurance services to international students and workers in Australia. Through its new nib Thrive business it has entered the National Disability Insurance Scheme (NDIS) plan management sector.

Latest business results (June 2024, full year)

Revenues and profits rose strongly, although much of the apparent growth derived from accountancy changes that restated the June 2023 figures, as well as from gains to the company's investment portfolio. In an increasingly competitive market, the company's flagship Australian Residents Health Insurance, representing 82 per cent of company income, saw policyholder numbers grow by 2.5 per cent, compared to

4.7 per cent in the previous year. Premium revenues rose 8.5 per cent, bolstered by two price rises during the year. The total claims expense rose 4.9 per cent. New Zealand health insurance represents a further 11.5 per cent of company turnover. Premium revenues grew by 10.2 per cent with policyholder numbers up 3.1 per cent. However, claims inflation led to a 16.9 per cent jump in the claims expense, and NZ profits fell sharply. The company's health insurance program for international students and workers in Australia enjoyed double-digit gains in premium revenues, policyholder numbers and profits. The small but fast-growing nib Thrive business achieved substantial increases in revenues and profits.

Outlook

NIB believes a growing and ageing population in Australia will help deliver continued growth in policyholder numbers for its health insurance operations. However, this is a highly regulated business, with restrictions on health insurance premium price rises. At the same time the company faces twin problems of rising claims expenses and increased pricing demands from private hospitals, which are seeking to restore profitability after a period of low activity during the COVID pandemic. This is all occurring at a time when many households are facing severe cost of living pressures. NIB benefits from its New Zealand exposure, where it is the country's second-largest health insurer. It is working to branch into new areas of business, and sees particularly strong prospects for its moves into the NIDS plan management sector. Through its investments in healthcare support providers Midnight Health and Honeysuckle Health it also sees excellent potential in the field of obesity management.

Year to 30 June	2023	2024
Premium revenues ($mn)	3052.6	3337.7
EBIT ($mn)	180.5	283.4
EBIT margin (%)	5.9	8.5
Profit before tax ($mn)	166.5	265.8
Profit after tax ($mn)	109.1	182.6
Earnings per share (c)	22.94	37.71
Cash flow per share (c)	29.14	46.22
Dividend (c)	28	29
Percentage franked	100	100
Net tangible assets per share ($)	1.02	0.97
Interest cover (times)	13.1	16.3
Return on equity (%)	12.2	18.2
Debt-to-equity ratio (%)	0.3	~
Current ratio	2.1	2.1

Nick Scali Limited

ASX code: NCK   www.nickscali.com.au

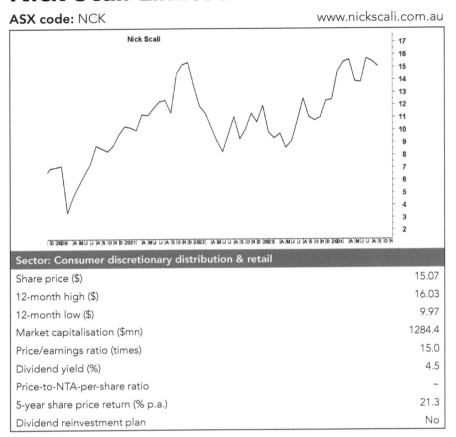

Sector: Consumer discretionary distribution & retail

Share price ($)	15.07
12-month high ($)	16.03
12-month low ($)	9.97
Market capitalisation ($mn)	1284.4
Price/earnings ratio (times)	15.0
Dividend yield (%)	4.5
Price-to-NTA-per-share ratio	~
5-year share price return (% p.a.)	21.3
Dividend reinvestment plan	No

Sydney-based Nick Scali is one of Australia's largest furniture importers and retailers, with a history dating back more than 60 years. It specialises in leather and fabric lounge suites along with dining room and bedroom furniture. It also owns Plush Sofas. In May 2024 it entered the British market with the acquisition of Anglia Home Furnishings.

Latest business results (June 2024, full year)

The company's operations were hit by higher interest rates and economic uncertainty, with rising costs also hurting the result, and sales and profits fell, reversing the strong gains of the previous year. Total Australia and New Zealand written sales orders of $447.4 million actually represented a small increase from the previous year. Enhancements to the company's digital marketing platforms drove a 17.8 per cent jump in online written sales orders to $34.8 million. The result included a seven-and-a-half-week contribution from the new British operations of $8.3 million in sales and $6.8 million in written sales orders, but a $1.4 million after-tax loss. During the year the company opened three new Plush stores and closed two, and at June 2024 it operated 59 Nick Scali Furniture stores in Australia, and five in New Zealand, the same as in the previous year, along with 44 Plush stores in Australia, one more than in June 2023.

Outlook

Nick Scali is directly affected by trends in consumer spending, interest rates, currency movements, housing sales, renovation activity and the general economy. Despite short-term volatility it is optimistic about the longer-term outlook. It has achieved success in boosting profit margins with its $102.5 million Plush acquisition of 2021, and its long-term target is for at least 86 Nick Scali stores and up to 100 Plush stores, across Australia and New Zealand. During the June 2025 year it expects to open two new Nick Scali stores and three to five Plush stores. It sees great potential in its acquisition of Anglia Home Furnishings, which operates 20 large-scale stores in out-of-town retail parks across the UK under the name Fabb Furniture. It plans major renovations across the entire British network, transitioning the stores to the existing Nick Scali lounge and dining product range, with a marketing campaign aimed at establishing the Nick Scali brand. It is also in advanced discussions for the establishment of a new British distribution centre. Its target is to restore British business to profitability within 18 months, and it then plans a steady expansion of the store network.

Year to 30 June	2023	2024
Revenues ($mn)	507.7	468.2
EBIT ($mn)	156.8	132.9
EBIT margin (%)	30.9	28.4
Gross margin (%)	63.5	65.5
Profit before tax ($mn)	143.5	117.8
Profit after tax ($mn)	101.1	82.0
Earnings per share (c)	124.79	100.43
Cash flow per share (c)	177.59	156.05
Dividend (c)	75	68
Percentage franked	100	100
Net tangible assets per share ($)	~	~
Interest cover (times)	14.5	11.4
Return on equity (%)	63.0	37.5
Debt-to-equity ratio (%)	1.4	~
Current ratio	1.1	1.1

Nine Entertainment Company Holdings Limited

ASX code: NEC

www.nineforbrands.com.au

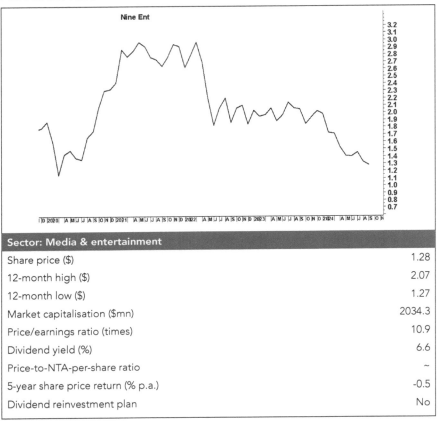

Sector: Media & entertainment	
Share price ($)	1.28
12-month high ($)	2.07
12-month low ($)	1.27
Market capitalisation ($mn)	2034.3
Price/earnings ratio (times)	10.9
Dividend yield (%)	6.6
Price-to-NTA-per-share ratio	~
5-year share price return (% p.a.)	-0.5
Dividend reinvestment plan	No

With roots that stretch back to the first edition of the *Sydney Herald* in 1831 and the launch of channel TCN-9 in 1956, Sydney-based Nine Entertainment is today one of Australia's media giants. It divides its activities into four broad segments. The Broadcasting division incorporates its free-to-air television activities, its 9Now streaming video service and its radio stations. Publishing comprises a portfolio of newspapers, including the *Sydney Morning Herald*, *The Age* and the *Australian Financial Review*, as well as magazines and online publications. The Stan division represents the Stan subscription video-on-demand service. The fourth segment, Domain Group, is an ASX-listed real estate media and services business in which Nine holds a 60 per cent interest.

Latest business results (June 2024, full year)

Revenues were down and profits fell for a second year as Nine was hit by weakness in its core broadcasting and publishing businesses. The prolonged advertising market downturn sent broadcasting revenues down 9 per cent and EBIT down 39 per cent, despite good audience numbers and reduced costs. Publishing revenues fell 3 per cent with profits down 11 per cent, despite subscriber growth. By contrast, the Domain Group division rebounded from the previous year's decline, thanks to a buoyant housing market, with sales up 12 per cent and profits surging by 52 per cent. Another excellent result came from the Stan division, with revenues up 5 per cent and profits jumping 47 per cent. Nevertheless, profit margins at Stan remained substantially below those at Nine's other divisions.

Outlook

Nine Entertainment occupies a central position in Australia's media landscape. In the past it benefited from a robust economy and from its own restructuring efforts. The challenge now is to maintain this momentum as the economy slows and inflationary pressures grow. A key strategy is an acceleration of the shift to digital platforms for its content. Its 9Now business continues to grow strongly and an increasing share of the company's radio audience is listening online or via apps. Price rises are helping offset cost inflation and the company also continues its cost-cutting drive. It believes that Stan is on a strong growth trajectory, thanks to investment in original programming, solid demand for Stan Sport and extensions to key strategic licensing deals. It expects that its $305 million contract for Olympic broadcasting rights, through to the 2032 Brisbane Olympics, will provide a strong growth opportunity. It is believed to be evaluating a sale of its Domain Group holding or a possible privatisation.

Year to 30 June	2023	2024
Revenues ($mn)	2704.4	2629.8
Broadcasting (%)	50	47
Publishing (%)	21	21
Stan (%)	16	17
Domain Group (%)	13	15
EBIT ($mn)	442.8	370.4
EBIT margin (%)	16.4	14.1
Profit before tax ($mn)	394.1	307.4
Profit after tax ($mn)	262.1	189.4
Earnings per share (c)	15.68	11.73
Cash flow per share (c)	24.99	21.40
Dividend (c)	11	8.5
Percentage franked	100	100
Net tangible assets per share ($)	~	~
Interest cover (times)	10.5	6.8
Return on equity (%)	14.7	11.6
Debt-to-equity ratio (%)	27.9	35.8
Current ratio	1.0	1.0

NRW Holdings Limited

ASX code: NWH   www.nrw.com.au

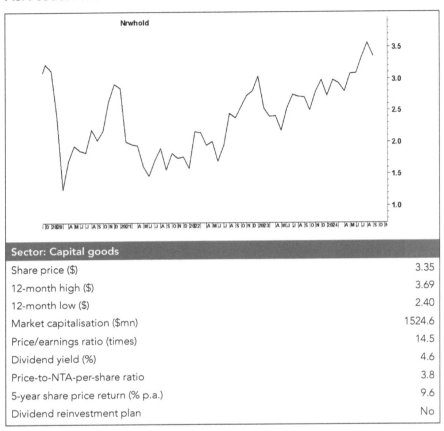

Sector: Capital goods	
Share price ($)	3.35
12-month high ($)	3.69
12-month low ($)	2.40
Market capitalisation ($mn)	1524.6
Price/earnings ratio (times)	14.5
Dividend yield (%)	4.6
Price-to-NTA-per-share ratio	3.8
5-year share price return (% p.a.)	9.6
Dividend reinvestment plan	No

Perth company NRW Holdings, a specialist provider of services to the mining and resources industries, was founded in 1994. It segments its operations into three divisions. The Mining division specialises in mine management, contract mining, drill and blast operations, and maintenance services. The Civil division is involved in the delivery of a wide range of private and public civil infrastructure projects, including roads, bridges and renewable energy facilities. The Minerals, Energy and Technologies division incorporates mining equipment manufacturer RCR Mining Technologies, specialist metals and mining engineer DIAB Engineering, resources and energy construction specialist Primero, and industrial electrical engineer OFI Group Holdings.

Latest business results (June 2024, full year)

In another good result, NRW achieved a solid increase in revenues and profits, with strength across all key businesses. The Minerals, Energy and Technologies division enjoyed particularly strong profit growth, thanks especially to some important contracts from the resources industry for the Primero and DIAB operations, offsetting another sluggish performance from RCR. The Civil division reported substantial increases in revenues and profits, with growing demand for its services from Western Australian resources companies. The Mining division achieved continuing growth, despite uncertainty in the lithium market, and with profit margins that remained significantly higher than for the other two divisions.

Outlook

NRW held an order book of $5.5 billion at June 2024, down from $5.9 billion a year earlier, with around $2.9 billion of this expected to be earned during the June 2025 year. It also sees some $16.4 billion of potential projects coming up for tender, and it is optimistic about the long-term outlook. The core Mining division continues to show particular strength, with a full order book, which allows NRW to selectively target those commodities and projects that deliver the best returns. The Minerals, Energy and Technologies division continues to diversify its operations across commodities, including iron ore, gold, rare earths and battery-critical minerals. It is also moving into the alternative energy, decarbonisation and defence sectors. It views its $973 million contract from Northern Star Resources, for a major gold development in Kalgoorlie, as providing a possible launching pad for further major contracts in the gold sector. The company believes that population growth and housing shortages will benefit its Civil division as demand builds for transport, utility and housing infrastructure projects. For June 2025 NRW forecasts revenues of around $3.1 billion and EBITA of $205 million to $215 million, compared to $195.1 million in June 2024.

Year to 30 June	2023	2024
Revenues ($mn)	2667.1	2913.0
Mining (%)	53	51
Minerals, energy & technologies (%)	27	27
Civil (%)	20	22
EBIT ($mn)	143.4	164.3
EBIT margin (%)	5.4	5.6
Profit before tax ($mn)	124.9	142.8
Profit after tax ($mn)	85.6	105.1
Earnings per share (c)	19.01	23.15
Cash flow per share (c)	47.52	55.22
Dividend (c)	16.5	15.5
Percentage franked	48	100
Net tangible assets per share ($)	0.78	0.89
Interest cover (times)	8.4	9.0
Return on equity (%)	14.3	16.6
Debt-to-equity ratio (%)	5.4	5.1
Current ratio	1.3	1.3

Objective Corporation Limited

ASX code: OCL www.objective.com.au

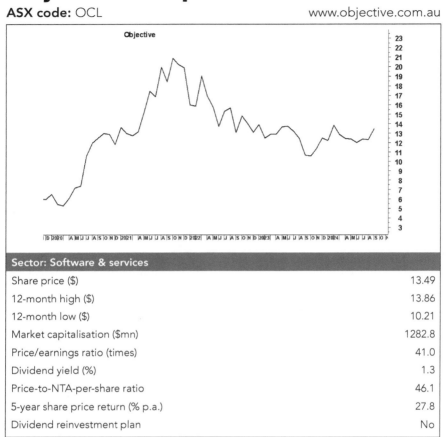

Sector: Software & services	
Share price ($)	13.49
12-month high ($)	13.86
12-month low ($)	10.21
Market capitalisation ($mn)	1282.8
Price/earnings ratio (times)	41.0
Dividend yield (%)	1.3
Price-to-NTA-per-share ratio	46.1
5-year share price return (% p.a.)	27.8
Dividend reinvestment plan	No

Sydney-based Objective, founded in 1987, provides information technology software and services. Its particular specialty is working with federal, state and local governments, as well as government agencies and regulated industries, and it has operations in Australia, New Zealand and the United Kingdom. It has grown substantially, organically and through acquisition, and now operates under numerous product categories.

Latest business results (June 2024, full year)

Revenues rose modestly, and profits rebounded strongly from the previous year's declines, with strength across all businesses. For reporting purposes the company divides its businesses into three broad segments, each of which reported 5 per cent growth in revenues. The largest segment, Content Solutions, incorporates the company's core software products, which allow customers to manage, process and publish information and collaborate with external organisations. Revenue growth would have been higher but for the strategic decision to discontinue the Perpetual

Right to Use licensing system. A second segment, Regulatory Solutions, comprising products that manage governmental safety and compliance regulatory processes, enjoyed success with its first UK customer, a $3.4 million, six-year contract with the British Gambling Commission for its Objective RegWorks software. The third segment, Planning and Building, digitally manages the development and construction planning consent process. It achieved significant success in winning new customers for its Objective Build product. Overseas sales, primarily in New Zealand and the UK, comprised 23 per cent of total company income.

Outlook

Objective is a small company working in niche businesses but with a solid reputation and a high level of profitability. The company's particular goal is to help customers digitalise and streamline the processes of compliance, accountability and governance. It is working to move its businesses, as much as possible, to a subscription model. It spends heavily on research and development, and this reached $28.2 million in the June 2024 year, up from $27.2 million a year earlier. It is steadily moving customers to its Objective Nexus next-generation Software-as-a-Service platform, introduced in mid 2023, presenting significant new marketing opportunities. Customer numbers for Objective Nexus more than doubled during the June 2024 year. The Objective Keystone document creation software is achieving success in the financial services sector, with 17 of Australia's 25 largest superannuation funds now among its customers. Following a considerable investment in the Objective RegWorks regulatory compliance software, and its adoption by the Gambling Commission, the company sees great potential for this product. At June 2024 Objective had no debt and $96 million in cash holdings.

Year to 30 June	2023	2024
Revenues ($mn)	110.4	117.5
Content solutions (%)	70	70
Regulatory solutions (%)	19	19
Planning & building (%)	11	11
EBIT ($mn)	22.5	39.0
EBIT margin (%)	20.4	33.2
Profit before tax ($mn)	22.0	38.4
Profit after tax ($mn)	21.1	31.3
Earnings per share (c)	22.20	32.92
Cash flow per share (c)	27.39	39.20
Dividend (c)	13.5	17
Percentage franked	0	47
Net tangible assets per share ($)	0.20	0.29
Interest cover (times)	~	~
Return on equity (%)	31.1	37.8
Debt-to-equity ratio (%)	~	~
Current ratio	1.4	1.6

Origin Energy Limited

ASX code: ORG www.originenergy.com.au

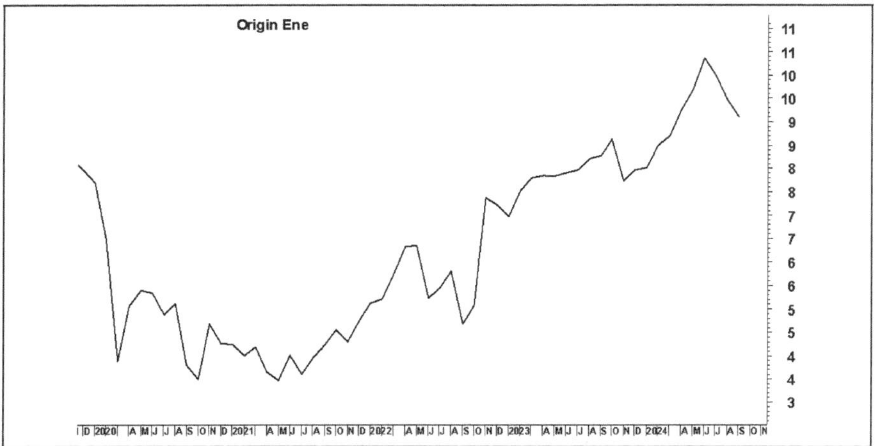

Origin Ene

Sector: Utilities

Share price ($)	9.61
12-month high ($)	11.06
12-month low ($)	7.77
Market capitalisation ($mn)	16 507.7
Price/earnings ratio (times)	14.0
Dividend yield (%)	5.7
Price-to-NTA-per-share ratio	2.4
5-year share price return (% p.a.)	8.1
Dividend reinvestment plan	No

Sydney-based Origin Energy, formerly the energy arm of the Boral group, was de-merged in 2000 and is today one of Australia's leading energy companies. It operates the Eraring coal-fired power station in New South Wales, Australia's largest power station, as well as gas-fired power stations in Queensland, New South Wales, Victoria and South Australia. It is also involved in a range of renewable energy projects throughout Australia. Through its joint venture Australia Pacific LNG (APLNG) it supplies 30 per cent of east coast gas demand and also exports LNG to customers in Asia. Its retailing arm supplies electricity, gas and broadband internet to some 4.7 million residential and business customers. It owns 23 per cent of the United Kingdom renewable energy retailer Octopus Energy.

Latest business results (June 2024, full year)

Rising electricity prices and reduced fuel costs — the latter due to a government cap on coal prices — helped deliver a big increase in profits. Around 45 per cent of Origin's profits at the EBITDA level derive from its core energy business, and this figure soared 59 per cent to $1.66 billion. More than half of EBITDA derives from the company's 27.5 per cent holding in APLNG, and this fell 14 per cent from the previous year to $1.94 billion, with increased production and hedging gains offset by lower commodity prices. The investment in Britain's Octopus Energy generated EBITDA of $55 million, a sharp fall from $240 million in the previous year, as that company was hit by rising costs and a decline in earnings for its UK retail business.

Outlook

Origin expects that higher coal costs and reduced retail margins are set to hit profits, and it expects EBITDA for its core energy business to fall from $1.66 billion in June 2024 to between $1.1 billion and $1.4 billion in the June 2025 year. For the longer term it has a pipeline of renewable energy projects, in line with government plans to reduce carbon emissions. It manages a series of wind and solar energy developments with a combined total output of around 2.6 gigawatts, including the 1.5-gigawatt Yanco Delta Wind Farm in New South Wales, acquired in April 2024. It is also involved in 1.5 gigawatts of battery projects for energy storage. It had intended to close its giant Eraring power station in 2025. However, to support the security of electricity supplies, it has agreed with the New South Wales government to delay this closure for at least two years.

Year to 30 June	2023	2024
Revenues ($mn)	16481.0	16138.0
Electricity (%)	48	56
Gas (%)	34	29
Pool revenue (%)	17	13
EBIT ($mn)	1477.0	1987.0
EBIT margin (%)	9.0	12.3
Gross margin (%)	12.1	20.5
Profit before tax ($mn)	1283.0	1818.0
Profit after tax ($mn)	747.0	1183.0
Earnings per share (c)	43.42	68.69
Cash flow per share (c)	74.05	98.94
Dividend (c)	36.5	55
Percentage franked	100	100
Net tangible assets per share ($)	3.72	4.05
Interest cover (times)	10.3	16.2
Return on equity (%)	7.9	12.9
Debt-to-equity ratio (%)	31.4	29.0
Current ratio	1.0	1.1

Perpetual Limited

ASX code: PPT

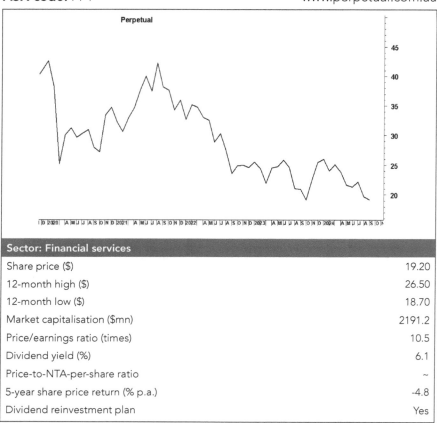

Sector: Financial services	
Share price ($)	19.20
12-month high ($)	26.50
12-month low ($)	18.70
Market capitalisation ($mn)	2191.2
Price/earnings ratio (times)	10.5
Dividend yield (%)	6.1
Price-to-NTA-per-share ratio	~
5-year share price return (% p.a.)	-4.8
Dividend reinvestment plan	Yes

Sydney-based financial services company Perpetual was established in 1886 as Perpetual Trustees. Following several major acquisitions, Perpetual divides its operations into three broad areas. Asset Management offers an extensive range of specialist investment capabilities through six boutique businesses and seven brands in key regions around the world. Wealth Management provides advisory and trustee services to individuals, families, companies and not-for-profit organisations. The Corporate Trust division is a prominent provider of fiduciary and digital services to the banking and financial services industry in Australia and Singapore. Perpetual has announced plans to sell its Wealth Management and Corporate Trust divisions.

Latest business results (June 2024, full year)

Revenues and profits rose, with strength across all divisions. Asset Management provided the biggest gains, though this in large part reflected a full year's contribution from the January 2023 acquisition of the Pendal Group funds management company.

In a buoyant market environment, the company also benefited from a rise in funds under management, although it also suffered from higher-than-expected fund outflows. The Wealth Management division achieved a 15 per cent rise in profits on a 4 per cent increase in revenues, thanks especially to rising equity markets and a strong performance from the Fordham specialist wealth advisory business. The Corporate Trust division reported single-digit gains in revenues and profits, with a particularly good performance from the commercial property arm of its managed funds services operation. Roughly half of all income derived from Australia, with a third from the US and 10 per cent from the UK. Perpetual also announced a $547 million asset write-down related to its Pendal acquisition, and on a statutory basis the company reported a large loss.

Outlook

Perpetual is set to be transformed with the sale of its Wealth Management and Corporate Trust divisions to global investment company Kohlberg Kravis Roberts for $2.175 billion, with net proceeds to be returned to shareholders. The transaction is expected to occur in February 2025, following a shareholder vote on the scheme. Perpetual will then become purely a global multi-boutique asset management business operating under seven brands: Perpetual, Pendal, Barrow Hanley, J O Hambro, Trillium, Regnan, and Thompson, Siegel and Walmsley. It will have strength in major markets around the world, and with no debt will have opportunities for significant organic expansion. At June 2024 these businesses held total funds under management of $215 billion. Perpetual has announced a simplification program for its asset management activities, aimed at reducing annual costs by up to $35 million.

Year to 30 June	2023	2024
Revenues ($mn)	1034.1	1357.5
Asset management (%)	60	68
Wealth management (%)	22	17
Corporate trust (%)	18	14
EBIT ($mn)	264.0	353.9
EBIT margin (%)	25.5	26.1
Profit before tax ($mn)	219.2	283.6
Profit after tax ($mn)	163.2	206.1
Earnings per share (c)	202.57	183.66
Cash flow per share (c)	354.50	329.00
Dividend (c)	120	118
Percentage franked	40	42
Net tangible assets per share ($)	~	~
Interest cover (times)	6.7	6.7
Return on equity (%)	10.1	10.2
Debt-to-equity ratio (%)	27.4	35.4
Current ratio	1.5	0.5

Pinnacle Investment Management Group Limited

ASX code: PNI   www.pinnacleinvestment.com

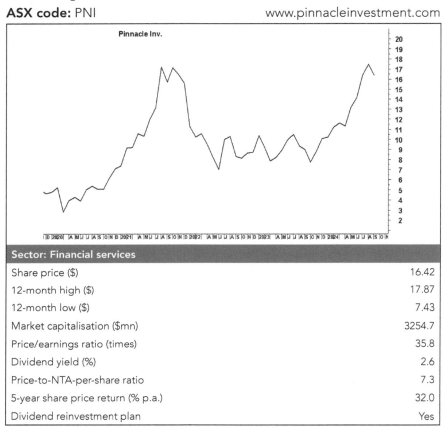

Sector: Financial services	
Share price ($)	16.42
12-month high ($)	17.87
12-month low ($)	7.43
Market capitalisation ($mn)	3254.7
Price/earnings ratio (times)	35.8
Dividend yield (%)	2.6
Price-to-NTA-per-share ratio	7.3
5-year share price return (% p.a.)	32.0
Dividend reinvestment plan	Yes

Sydney-based Pinnacle Investment Management started life in 2006 as a boutique funds management company that was majority-owned by Wilson HTM Investment Group. In 2016 it was fully acquired by Wilson Group, with Wilson Group changing its own name to Pinnacle. Today it is a prominent adviser to small funds management groups, providing them with distribution services, business support and responsible entity services, while also holding an equity stake in these companies.

Latest business results (June 2024, full year)

Profits rose in an excellent year for Pinnacle as its funds overcame market volatility to benefit from a solid investment performance and strong fund inflows. At June 2024 the company comprised 15 fund management affiliates, collectively managing investments across a diverse range of asset classes. Pinnacle held shareholdings in these affiliates that ranged from 23.9 per cent to 49.9 per cent. Total revenues during the year for the 15 fund managers of $663.4 million was up from $511.6 million in the previous year, and this included $109.8 million in performance fees, an 89 per cent surge from a year before. Total funds under management rose to $110.1 billion at

June 2024, up from $91.9 billion a year earlier, thanks to market movements and a strong investment performance, together with net inflows during the year of $9.9 billion.

Outlook

Pinnacle's initial role is to provide its fund manager affiliates with equity, seed capital and working capital. It then allows its managers to focus on investment performance by providing them with marketing and other support services. Pinnacle's own revenues and profits derive from the revenues it receives from its affiliates for its services, together with its share of their profits, and performance is important. It has achieved significant success with the fund management companies it has chosen to join its group, reporting that 85 per cent of funds with a five-year track record had by June 2024 outperformed their relevant benchmarks during this period. The company is confident about its long-term evolution, and has a variety of strategies for growth, including investment in high-margin retail channels and moves into new asset classes. It is also working to attract more investment from abroad, and funds under management sourced from non-Australian clients have risen sharply to represent nearly 17 per cent of total funds. Nevertheless, Pinnacle recognises that, at least in the short term, global economic conditions remain uncertain, with continuing geopolitical tensions exerting a significant impact on financial markets.

Year to 30 June	2023	2024
Revenues ($mn)	112.9	139.8
EBIT ($mn)	82.5	97.7
EBIT margin (%)	73.1	69.9
Profit before tax ($mn)	76.5	90.4
Profit after tax ($mn)	76.5	90.4
Earnings per share (c)	39.35	45.81
Cash flow per share (c)	39.51	45.87
Dividend (c)	36	42
Percentage franked	100	82
Net tangible assets per share ($)	2.16	2.25
Interest cover (times)	15.5	16.1
Return on equity (%)	18.5	20.6
Debt-to-equity ratio (%)	21.9	14.8
Current ratio	7.2	11.5

Platinum Asset Management Limited

ASX code: PTM   www.platinum.com.au

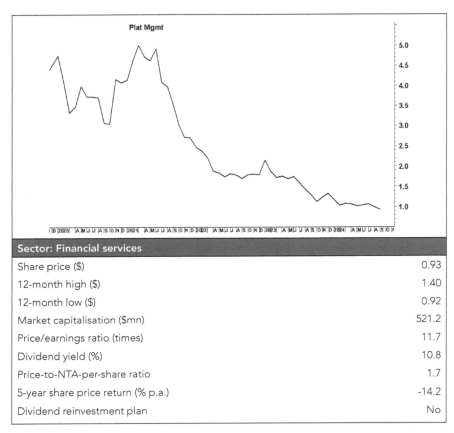

Sector: Financial services	
Share price ($)	0.93
12-month high ($)	1.40
12-month low ($)	0.92
Market capitalisation ($mn)	521.2
Price/earnings ratio (times)	11.7
Dividend yield (%)	10.8
Price-to-NTA-per-share ratio	1.7
5-year share price return (% p.a.)	-14.2
Dividend reinvestment plan	No

Sydney funds management company Platinum Asset Management was established in 1994. It has a specialty in managing portfolios of international equities. Its flagship product is the Platinum International Fund. Other funds specialise in Europe, Asia, Japan, healthcare, technology and international brands.

Latest business results (June 2024, full year)

Revenues and profits experienced more double-digit declines as the company's funds suffered from further outflows. Management fees of $174.3 million were down from $201.4 million in the previous year as average funds under management during the year fell from $18.1 billion to $15.3 billion. Underlying expenses fell 10 per cent, reflecting reduced staffing costs and a cut in marketing activities. The company also incurred one-off costs of $20 million for what it has billed as a turnaround program.

At June 2024 Platinum held funds under management of $13 billion, down from $17.3 billion in June 2023, driven by a positive investment performance of $0.7 billion, net fund outflows of $4.9 billion and $0.1 billion in net distributions to investors.

Outlook

Platinum gained a degree of renown among Australian investors for an impressive long-term period of outperformance for its international equity funds, thanks to its stock-picking skills, and this sparked some solid growth in funds under management. However, in recent years the performance has often been weak, with most funds underperforming their benchmarks in the June 2024 year. The company has attributed this to its preference for value stocks, at a time when growth stocks were leading global markets higher. In addition, strong markets have caused many investors to choose passive investment products over actively managed investments. In February 2024 Platinum announced its turnaround program, designed to revitalise the company. This began with a reset phase, which involved the alignment of its expense base to actual revenue conditions, and it expects substantial reductions to costs during 2025 and 2026. It has also undertaken an extensive review of product offerings and distribution channels, and is closing its Platinum Global Transition Fund. Further measures include a renewal of client communication strategies, a deep examination of the firm's investment platform and a review of its remuneration framework. The company has now entered what it calls the growth phase of its turnaround program, though it recognises that investment performance is the key to turning around fund flows. It is working to build a portfolio of new investment products and is also seeking partnerships with global fund managers who wish to access the Australian market. In September 2024 it announced that the investment management firm Regal Partners was proposing a friendly takeover of Platinum.

Year to 30 June	2023	2024
Revenues ($mn)	202.7	174.3
EBIT ($mn)	116.8	73.1
EBIT margin (%)	57.6	42.0
Profit before tax ($mn)	116.8	73.1
Profit after tax ($mn)	80.9	45.0
Earnings per share (c)	14.10	7.95
Cash flow per share (c)	14.57	8.50
Dividend (c)	14	10
Percentage franked	100	100
Net tangible assets per share ($)	0.57	0.54
Interest cover (times)	~	~
Return on equity (%)	24.8	14.0
Debt-to-equity ratio (%)	~	~
Current ratio	12.9	16.4

Premier Investments Limited

ASX code: PMV   www.premierinvestments.com.au

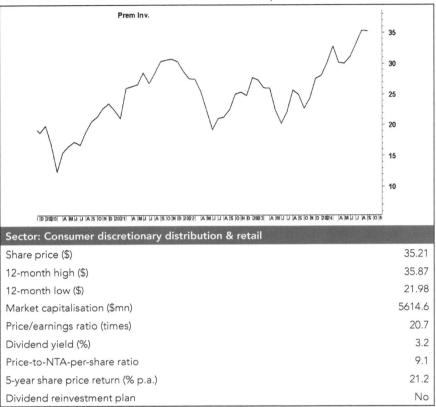

Sector: Consumer discretionary distribution & retail	
Share price ($)	35.21
12-month high ($)	35.87
12-month low ($)	21.98
Market capitalisation ($mn)	5614.6
Price/earnings ratio (times)	20.7
Dividend yield (%)	3.2
Price-to-NTA-per-share ratio	9.1
5-year share price return (% p.a.)	21.2
Dividend reinvestment plan	No

Melbourne-based Premier was founded in 1987 and operates as an investment company. Its main holding is a 100 per cent stake in the retailer Just Group, which was founded in 1970. The Just Group incorporates the brands Just Jeans, Smiggle, Peter Alexander, Jay Jays, Portmans, Jacqui E and Dotti, with more than 1100 stores in six countries. Premier also holds 28 per cent of the equity in home appliance specialist Breville Group and a 31 per cent stake in department store chain Myer Holdings. Premier's chairman Solomon Lew owns more than 40 per cent of the company's equity.

Latest business results (January 2024, half year)

Sales and profits fell in a subdued retail environment, although a reduced tax bill meant that the after-tax profit and EPS figures were up. The Peter Alexander sleepwear chain was again an excellent performer, with revenues of $279.3 million, up 6.7 per cent from the January 2023 half. However, the company's other leading driver of growth, Smiggle, which specialises in colourful school stationery and other products for children, saw sales fall 3.6 per cent to $183.9 million. In the January 2023 period its sales had soared by more than 30 per cent from January 2022. The other five apparel brands experienced a total sales decline of 8.1 per cent to $416.3 million. Online sales of $171.2 million were little changed from a year before.

Outlook

In the face of rising costs and weakness in consumer spending, Premier has a variety of strategies for growth. It plans to open new Peter Alexander stores, and in 2025 will launch the brand in the United Kingdom. It also plans new Smiggle outlets, domestically and abroad. It has opened seven Smiggle stores in the Middle East, and plans 60 stores in the region within 10 years. In addition, it plans to enter the Indonesian market, with an agreement to open more than 100 stores within 10 years. Premier is also involved in a review process that could see the company radically transformed. Following a strategic review initiated in August 2023, the company will explore the possibility of creating two new listed companies from its Smiggle and its Peter Alexander businesses. Further, in June 2024 Myer Holdings proposed the acquisition of the remaining five brands, Just Jeans, Jay Jays, Portmans, Jacqui E and Dotti, with payment in Myer shares, which would be distributed to Premier shareholders. This proposal remains under consideration.

Year to 29 July*	2022	2023
Revenues ($mn)	1497.5	1643.5
EBIT ($mn)	401.5	398.7
EBIT margin (%)	26.8	24.3
Profit before tax ($mn)	392.7	382.1
Profit after tax ($mn)	285.2	271.1
Earnings per share (c)	179.40	170.31
Cash flow per share (c)	283.94	270.97
Dividend (c)	100	114
Percentage franked	100	100
Interest cover (times)	53.2	169.6
Return on equity (%)	17.8	15.9
Half year to 27 January**	2023	2024
Revenues ($mn)	905.2	879.5
Profit before tax ($mn)	242.9	238.3
Profit after tax ($mn)	174.3	177.2
Earnings per share (c)	109.58	111.22
Dividend (c)	54	63
Percentage franked	100	100
Net tangible assets per share ($)	4.82	3.88
Debt-to-equity ratio (%)	~	~
Current ratio	1.9	2.1

* 30 July 2022
** 28 January 2023

Pro Medicus Limited

ASX code: PME

www.promed.com.au

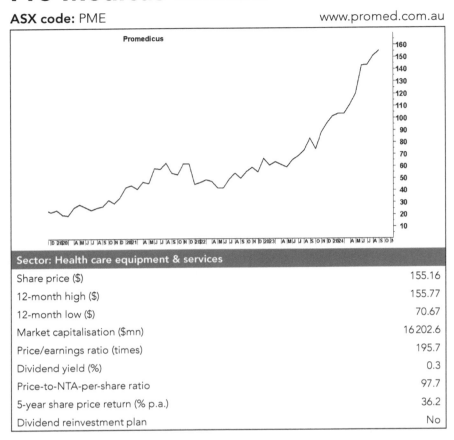

Sector: Health care equipment & services	
Share price ($)	155.16
12-month high ($)	155.77
12-month low ($)	70.67
Market capitalisation ($mn)	16 202.6
Price/earnings ratio (times)	195.7
Dividend yield (%)	0.3
Price-to-NTA-per-share ratio	97.7
5-year share price return (% p.a.)	36.2
Dividend reinvestment plan	No

Melbourne-based Pro Medicus, established in 1983, provides a range of medical imaging software and services to the medical profession. Its Visage 7 medical imaging software provides radiologists and clinicians with advanced visualisation capability for the rapid viewing of medical images. Its Radiology Information Systems (RIS) product provides proprietary medical software for practice management. In Australia it operates the Promedicus.net online network for doctors. It has extensive business operations throughout Australia, the US and Germany, with offices in Melbourne, Berlin and San Diego, and overseas sales represent nearly 90 per cent of total turnover.

Latest business results (June 2024, full year)

Pro Medicus enjoyed another successful year of strong double-digit revenue and profit growth. America is by far the company's largest market, accounting for more than 85 per cent of sales, and revenues there jumped 34 per cent, with the signing of nine new contracts. The relatively small German operation saw sales down 7 per cent, as a hospital contract extension in the previous year was not replicated in the latest year.

Australian sales rose 6 per cent, again due especially to RIS contracts with Healius, along with additional licence revenue from private radiology groups.

Outlook

Pro Medicus continues to enjoy some outstanding success in America for its Visage 7 software, which has the speed, functionality and versatility to meet the requirements of many different kinds of users. The company is now a market leader in this business, and says that 11 of the 20 leading American hospitals are using its products. A global shortage of radiologists is helping boost demand. It is making a substantial investment in research and development activities aimed at new products and enhancements to existing products, including artificial intelligence–based products. It is benefiting from moves to cloud-based systems. It has established an R&D centre in New York in order to collaborate with customer research projects. It has introduced a cardiology application to its existing imaging platform, and together with Yale New Haven Health has developed a promising breast density algorithm based on artificial intelligence. It has also released Visage Ease VP for Apple Vision Pro. Most of the company's revenue is recurring in nature, and, with nine new contract signings in the June 2024 year, with a combined minimum total value of $245 million, the outlook remains very positive. With no debt and cash holdings of more than $60 million at June 2024 it is seeking out acquisition opportunities offering access to new technologies.

Year to 30 June	2023	2024
Revenues ($mn)	124.9	161.5
EBIT ($mn)	86.1	116.5
EBIT margin (%)	69.0	72.1
Profit before tax ($mn)	86.1	116.5
Profit after tax ($mn)	60.6	82.8
Earnings per share (c)	58.09	79.27
Cash flow per share (c)	65.68	87.42
Dividend (c)	30	40
Percentage franked	100	100
Net tangible assets per share ($)	1.11	1.59
Interest cover (times)	~	~
Return on equity (%)	50.4	50.7
Debt-to-equity ratio (%)	~	~
Current ratio	5.3	6.0

PWR Holdings Limited

ASX code: PWH   www.pwr.com.au

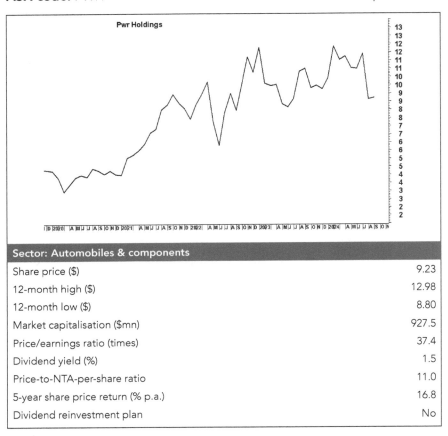

Sector: Automobiles & components	
Share price ($)	9.23
12-month high ($)	12.98
12-month low ($)	8.80
Market capitalisation ($mn)	927.5
Price/earnings ratio (times)	37.4
Dividend yield (%)	1.5
Price-to-NTA-per-share ratio	11.0
5-year share price return (% p.a.)	16.8
Dividend reinvestment plan	No

Based on the Gold Coast, automotive products company PWR got its start in 1987. It specialises in cooling systems, including aluminium radiators, intercoolers and oil coolers. It has a particular specialty in the supply of cooling systems to racing car teams. Other customers include the automotive original equipment manufacturing (OEM) sector and the automotive aftermarket sector, along with the aerospace, defence and renewable energy industries. It operates from manufacturing and distribution facilities in Australia, the United States and the United Kingdom. More than 90 per cent of company sales are to customers overseas, mainly in Europe and North America.

Latest business results (June 2024, full year)

Sales and profits rose again, with strength across all key markets. Of particular note was a doubling of revenues for aerospace and defence applications, from $10.5 million to $21 million, as the company continued to boost its expertise in this sector. It has leveraged its motorsports technology with an expansion to two-wheel categories, and motorsports revenues rose 8 per cent to $67.3 million. Automotive OEM and automotive aftermarket sales each grew 9 per cent, to $28 million and $19.5 million respectively. The company's research and development spending rose to $11 million, from $10.1 million in the previous year.

Outlook

PWR supplies its cooling systems to all Formula One racing teams, as well as to teams in other motor sports around the world, including Nascar and Indycar. It sees opportunities in new F1 regulations requiring upgraded cooling from 2026. It also supplies bespoke cooling systems to a range of high-performance automobile companies such as Aston Martin. It spends heavily on research and development in order to maintain its market-leading position, and it is working to move into other market areas with high growth prospects. It sees aerospace and defence as offering particularly strong potential and is investing heavily in this business. It is working with several aircraft manufacturers, and with the completion of pre-production program certifications is progressing towards long-term production supply contracts. In March 2024 it received a grant from the Australian Space Agency to develop its thermal management technology for space applications. It is expanding its American manufacturing facility and is moving into new global headquarters at Stapylton, on Queensland's Gold Coast, more than doubling its Australian factory space. It sees particular potential in the advance of electric vehicles, and it is working with several electric car manufacturers for the supply of sophisticated cooling technology. Other applications include helicopters, drones and storage batteries for alternative energy systems.

Year to 30 June	2023	2024
Revenues ($mn)	118.3	139.4
Motorsports (%)	53	48
Automotive OEM (%)	22	20
Aerospace & defence (%)	9	15
Automotive aftermarket (%)	15	14
EBIT ($mn)	30.8	35.4
EBIT margin (%)	26.0	25.4
Profit before tax ($mn)	30.2	34.8
Profit after tax ($mn)	21.8	24.8
Earnings per share (c)	21.67	24.69
Cash flow per share (c)	30.12	34.78
Dividend (c)	12.5	14
Percentage franked	100	100
Net tangible assets per share ($)	0.72	0.84
Interest cover (times)	92.4	122.2
Return on equity (%)	26.4	26.3
Debt-to-equity ratio (%)	~	~
Current ratio	3.3	3.0

Ramelius Resources Limited

ASX code: RMS   www.rameliusresources.com.au

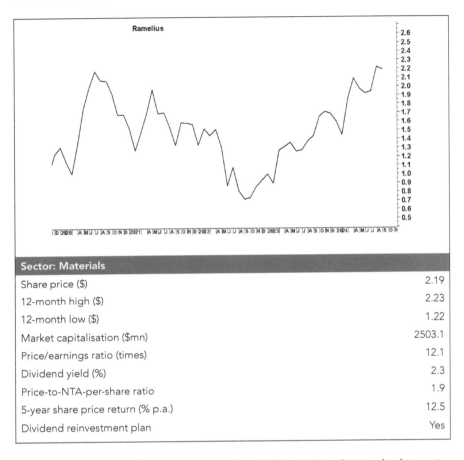

Sector: Materials	
Share price ($)	2.19
12-month high ($)	2.23
12-month low ($)	1.22
Market capitalisation ($mn)	2503.1
Price/earnings ratio (times)	12.1
Dividend yield (%)	2.3
Price-to-NTA-per-share ratio	1.9
5-year share price return (% p.a.)	12.5
Dividend reinvestment plan	Yes

Perth gold miner Ramelius Resources was founded in 1979 and is involved in major gold mining projects around Western Australia. It owns mines and processing centres at Mt Magnet and Edna May. It is also involved in operations at the Penny, Tampia, Marda and Symes gold mines. It maintains an active exploration program. In 2023 it acquired Musgrave Minerals, with its primary asset the Cue Gold Project.

Latest business results (June 2024, full year)

A rising gold price, strong sales and lower costs generated soaring revenues and profits for Ramelius. Production of 293 033 ounces was up from 240 996 ounces in the June 2023 year. Sales of 293 966 ounces rose from 243 263 ounces, with the average price of $2995 per ounce up from $2591. The average All-In Sustaining Cost (AISC) — the normal measure for evaluating the total cost of producing an ounce of gold — was $1583 per ounce, down 16 per cent from the previous year, which the company attributed to a combination of improved mill feed grades, an increasing contribution from the Penny mine, the extension of the Edna May underground mine and the introduction of higher-grade ore from the Symes mine.

Outlook

The Mt Magnet Gold Project dates back to the discovery of gold in the region in 1891 and today comprises numerous open pit and underground mines, as well as exploration targets, over a wide area. Ramelius maintains a major program of resource development and exploration at Mt Magnet in order to extend its life. In March 2024 it announced a 10-year plan for further development, with an annual production target of approximately 150 000 ounces of gold. The company also plans a boost to production at the Penny mine. In addition, following the acquisition of Musgrave Minerals, it plans the further development of the Cue Gold Project. Underground mining helped extend the life of Edna May, but the company has suspended proposals for a major new project at the site, and production activities ended in May 2024. Ramelius has also ended production at the Marda and Symes mines. In mid 2024 it acquired 18.35 per cent of the equity of Spartan Resources, which operates the Dalgaranga Gold Project, 65 kilometres from Mt Magnet. Ramelius has a production target for the June 2025 year of 270 000 ounces to 300 000 ounces of gold, with an AISC of an average $1500 to $1700 per ounce. At June 2024 the company had no debt and cash holdings of more than $424 million.

Year to 30 June	2023	2024
Revenues ($mn)	631.3	882.6
Mt Magnet (%)	53	55
Edna May (%)	47	45
EBIT ($mn)	115.8	277.2
EBIT margin (%)	18.3	31.4
Gross margin (%)	21.6	35.5
Profit before tax ($mn)	109.9	271.9
Profit after tax ($mn)	75.3	200.3
Earnings per share (c)	8.50	18.06
Cash flow per share (c)	26.98	34.42
Dividend (c)	2	5
Percentage franked	100	100
Net tangible assets per share ($)	0.95	1.16
Interest cover (times)	59.9	~
Return on equity (%)	9.1	17.7
Debt-to-equity ratio (%)	~	~
Current ratio	3.7	3.4

REA Group Limited

ASX code: REA

www.rea-group.com

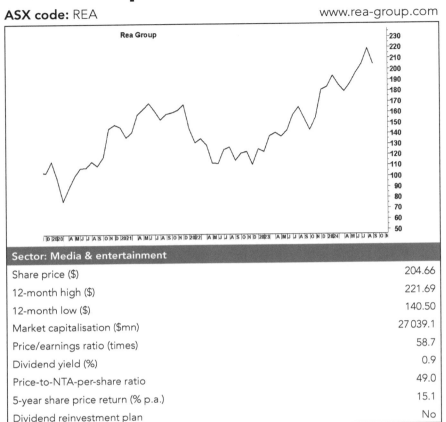

Rea Group

Sector: Media & entertainment	
Share price ($)	204.66
12-month high ($)	221.69
12-month low ($)	140.50
Market capitalisation ($mn)	27 039.1
Price/earnings ratio (times)	58.7
Dividend yield (%)	0.9
Price-to-NTA-per-share ratio	49.0
5-year share price return (% p.a.)	15.1
Dividend reinvestment plan	No

Melbourne-based REA was founded in 1995. Through its websites realestate.com.au and realcommercial.com.au it is the leader in the provision of online real estate advertising services in Australia. It also operates the share property website flatmates.com.au and the property research website property.com.au. In addition, it owns the mortgage broking franchise group Mortgage Choice, the property data company PropTrack and the advertising and home preparation finance platform Campaign Agent. It has interests in property websites in Asia, and holds a 20 per cent shareholding in the Move online property marketing company in the US. News Australia owns more than 60 per cent of REA's equity.

Latest business results (June 2024, full year)

Profits rebounded strongly from the decline of the previous year in a buoyant housing environment, and with particular strength in the two key markets of Sydney and Melbourne. Price rises and moves by customers to premium products helped boost the good result. Residential revenues rose 24 per cent to $996 million, with commercial and developer revenues up 12 per cent to $159 million despite a decline in new project commencements. The company's media, data and other segment achieved a 25 per cent jump in revenues to $122 million, although this mainly reflected the full acquisition in mid 2023 of Campaign Agent. The financial services businesses saw revenues up 8 per cent to $74 million. Indian revenues — about 7 per cent of total turnover — grew 31 per cent, but this business remained in the red. American activities, represented by the 20 per cent shareholding in Move, were again hit by lower transaction volumes, and reported another loss.

Outlook

REA is heavily geared to trends in the domestic housing market, and it expects continuing growth, thanks to high levels of demand and generally rising property prices. Underlying fundamentals are also positive, with low unemployment, wages growth, increasing migration and a possible peaking of interest rates. The company has noted that properties recently have been selling at a faster pace than the six-year average. REA will also benefit from price increases and planned new product launches. It holds more than 5 per cent of the Australian mortgage market and its long-term target is to double this share. In June 2024 it acquired a full interest in the property sales platform Realtair. Continuing growth in the huge Indian market is expected to lead to a steady reduction in operating losses there. In August 2024 REA announced that it was selling its holding in the Asian property listing business PropertyGuru. In September 2024 it announced a takeover bid for Rightmove, the UK's largest property listing website.

Year to 30 June	2023	2024
Revenues ($mn)	1183.2	1430.0
EBIT ($mn)	551.7	697.1
EBIT margin (%)	46.6	48.7
Profit before tax ($mn)	534.2	670.8
Profit after tax ($mn)	372.2	460.5
Earnings per share (c)	281.86	348.70
Cash flow per share (c)	351.38	434.65
Dividend (c)	158	189
Percentage franked	100	100
Net tangible assets per share ($)	4.48	4.18
Interest cover (times)	53.6	48.7
Return on equity (%)	26.9	30.6
Debt-to-equity ratio (%)	9.5	4.9
Current ratio	1.7	1.5

Reece Limited

ASX code: REH

group.reece.com

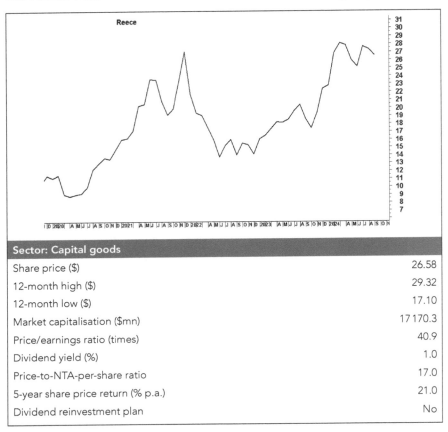

Sector: Capital goods	
Share price ($)	26.58
12-month high ($)	29.32
12-month low ($)	17.10
Market capitalisation ($mn)	17 170.3
Price/earnings ratio (times)	40.9
Dividend yield (%)	1.0
Price-to-NTA-per-share ratio	17.0
5-year share price return (% p.a.)	21.0
Dividend reinvestment plan	No

Melbourne-based plumbing supplies company Reece traces its origins back to 1919, when Harold Reece started selling his products from the back of a truck. It is today one of the country's leading suppliers of plumbing products, with operations also in the US and New Zealand, and it has expanded into related fields. These include a network of businesses in the heating, ventilation, air conditioning and refrigeration sectors and specialist stores for the landscape and agricultural industries. At June 2024 it operated 661 branches in Australia and New Zealand, up from 655 a year earlier, and 243 in the US, up from 231.

Latest business results (June 2024, full year)

In a subdued housing environment, Reece achieved modest gains in sales and profits. Most of the growth came from the US, where the company continues to build its business. There were also benefits from favourable currency exchange rates. Australia and New Zealand revenues and profits were generally in line with the previous year. Stringent cost control measures helped mitigate the impact of inflation, particularly related to wages, and profit margins actually edged up. However, despite the positive result from the US, profit margins there remained substantially below those prevailing in Australia.

Outlook

Reece's operations are quite heavily geared to housing and renovation markets in Australia, New Zealand and the US and the company expects demand to remain subdued in the near term, though with positive structural fundamentals in all regions that will support its longer-term business. It continues to strengthen its networks. In Australia it is investing heavily in digital innovation, to make business as smooth as possible for customers, and it also expects to continue opening new branches, as well as refurbishing and upgrading existing stores. It also hopes to add further non-plumbing businesses to its domestic network. In April 2024 it opened its new central distribution centre in Auckland, tripling its storage capacity and supporting the further growth of its operations in New Zealand. However, it is in the US that Reece sees its best growth prospects, and its restructuring efforts there are steadily raising margins. It operates in 16 states and is carrying out trials of new branch formats and service concepts in order to expand business and lower costs. It expects to rebrand all US stores to the Reece brand by the end of 2024. It has opened a new distribution centre in Texas to support its expansion. It is also seeking further US acquisitions.

Year to 30 June	2023	2024
Revenues ($mn)	8839.6	9104.8
US (%)	56	58
Australia/New Zealand (%)	44	42
EBIT ($mn)	660.1	693.9
EBIT margin (%)	7.5	7.6
Gross margin (%)	28.4	28.6
Profit before tax ($mn)	567.8	589.6
Profit after tax ($mn)	387.6	419.2
Earnings per share (c)	60.03	64.92
Cash flow per share (c)	104.92	115.31
Dividend (c)	25	25.75
Percentage franked	100	100
Net tangible assets per share ($)	1.25	1.56
Interest cover (times)	7.7	7.6
Return on equity (%)	11.2	11.2
Debt-to-equity ratio (%)	20.0	13.3
Current ratio	2.3	2.2

Reliance Worldwide Corporation Limited

ASX code: RWC

www.rwc.com

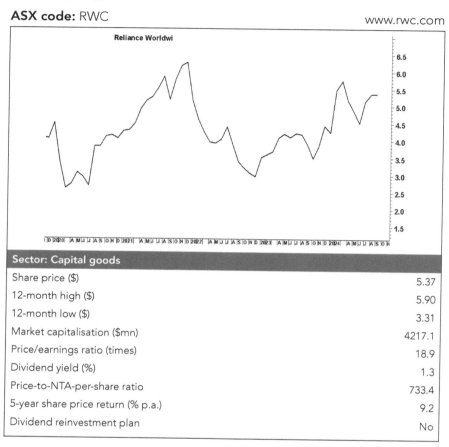

Sector: Capital goods	
Share price ($)	5.37
12-month high ($)	5.90
12-month low ($)	3.31
Market capitalisation ($mn)	4217.1
Price/earnings ratio (times)	18.9
Dividend yield (%)	1.3
Price-to-NTA-per-share ratio	733.4
5-year share price return (% p.a.)	9.2
Dividend reinvestment plan	No

Melbourne-based engineering firm Reliance dates back to 1949 and the establishment of a small tool shop in Brisbane. It is today a major global manufacturer and distributor of a range of products, particularly for the plumbing and heating industries. Its businesses and brands include SharkBite, Speedfit, HoldRite, MultiSafe, Reliance Valves and John Guest. In March 2024 it acquired Holman Industries.

Latest business results (June 2024, full year)

For the second straight year revenues rose but profits fell. However, a four-month contribution from the Holman acquisition lay behind the rise in sales. Excluding Holman, revenues fell 2 per cent, reflecting weaker residential construction and renovation activity in all regions. American sales fell by only 1 per cent and profits there rose. Asia-Pacific sales fell 3 per cent with the Europe/Middle East/Africa segment down 10 per cent, and both regions recorded profit declines. Restructuring initiatives delivered significant cost savings in overseas operations, and helped limit the decline in profits. A range of new products in the Americas generated a solid sales performance in that region and also helped mitigate the impact of inflation. Note that Reliance reports its results in US dollars. The Australian dollar figures in this book — converted at prevailing exchange rates — are for guidance only.

Outlook

Reliance has a significant exposure to housing markets in many countries, including both new house construction and renovation activity. Consequently, it is wary about the outlook for its businesses, with economic conditions expected to remain challenging across most of its markets. In particular, rising inflation and higher interest rates have hit consumer confidence, and the company forecasts little sales growth for at least the first half of the June 2025 year. In response, it is working to lower its cost base further. It also expects some significant new product ranges to continue generating strong sales. One of these is SharkBite Max, a new generation of brass push-to-connect plumbing fittings. This product range comes after several years of development work and is the first major update of Reliance's SharkBite product line in 20 years. Another new product range is an innovative new pipe and fitting system known as PEX-A, which was introduced to the US market during the June 2024 year. Reliance sees great potential in the $160 million acquisition of Australian plumbing supplies specialist Holman Industries, which will help double sales for its Asia-Pacific segment. The acquisition is also expected to generate annual cost savings of some $5 million.

Year to 30 June	2023	2024
Revenues ($mn)	1856.4	1887.6
Americas (%)	71	70
Europe/Middle East/Africa (%)	19	18
Asia Pacific (%)	10	12
EBIT ($mn)	331.9	326.0
EBIT margin (%)	17.9	17.3
Gross margin (%)	38.4	39.2
Profit before tax ($mn)	283.1	278.2
Profit after tax ($mn)	232.4	222.6
Earnings per share (c)	29.61	28.37
Cash flow per share (c)	39.63	39.96
Dividend (c)	14.24	7.24
Percentage franked	5	0
Net tangible assets per share ($)	0.05	0.01
Interest cover (times)	6.9	7.0
Return on equity (%)	13.0	11.8
Debt-to-equity ratio (%)	35.2	33.1
Current ratio	3.0	2.8

Ricegrowers Limited

ASX code: SGL   investors.sunrice.com.au

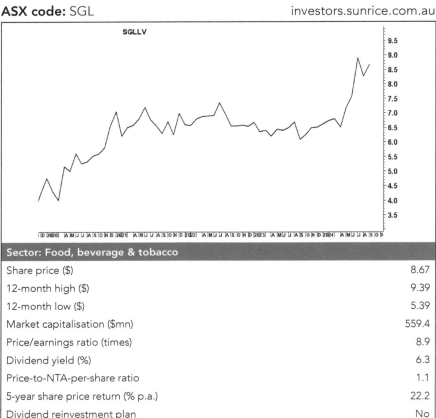

Sector: Food, beverage & tobacco	
Share price ($)	8.67
12-month high ($)	9.39
12-month low ($)	5.39
Market capitalisation ($mn)	559.4
Price/earnings ratio (times)	8.9
Dividend yield (%)	6.3
Price-to-NTA-per-share ratio	1.1
5-year share price return (% p.a.)	22.2
Dividend reinvestment plan	No

Ricegrowers Limited, based in Leeton in the Riverina region of NSW, is the official ASX name for the rice company SunRice. Founded in 1950, it is today one of Australia's largest foodstuffs companies, with operations in many countries. It divides its many businesses into five core divisions. International Rice manages the global processing, manufacturing, marketing and distribution of bulk or branded rice products. Rice Pool involves the receipt, storage, milling, marketing and distribution of Riverina rice. The CopRice division manufactures and distributes bulk stockfeed. Riviana Foods markets specialty gourmet food products. The Rice Food business handles rice-based products, such as rice flour and rice cakes. Note that Ricegrowers has a dual-class share structure, with A Class shares held by the company's ricegrower partners and B class shares held by outside investors.

Latest business results (April 2024, full year)

Ricegrowers overcame inflationary pressures, increasing competition and supply chain disruptions to post a pleasing increase in sales and profits. All main businesses were strong, with a particularly good performance from the International Rice division, with sales up 22 per cent and the pre-tax profit soaring by 53 per cent, thanks to volume growth in key global markets, effective sales pricing strategies and cost efficiencies. The high-margin Rice Food division benefited from product innovation and manufacturing efficiencies. The underperforming CopRice business achieved a significant turnaround, with the pre-tax profit nearly doubling. The low-margin Riviana Foods division saw modest growth, though it was affected by unfavourable exchange rates and a shift in consumer spending toward cheaper products. Altogether, 43 per cent of sales were to Australia and New Zealand, with 22 per cent to the Pacific Islands, 14 per cent to the Middle East and 13 per cent to the US.

Outlook

Ricegrowers dominates the Australian rice industry, with a solid presence in around 50 overseas markets, and stands to benefit as global food demand grows. It has a particular focus on the development of a strong and popular portfolio of brands, and branded products now represent some 70 per cent of total sales. In addition, it has initiated a review of its growth strategies with the aim of identifying new markets and product segments. It is also seeking strategic acquisitions that will deliver growth. Nevertheless, sales and profits for Ricegrowers can be buffeted by a multiplicity of influences, including weather patterns, droughts and floods, global rice prices, competition from low-cost foreign growers, exchange rates, inflationary pressures, supply chain issues and shipping disruptions.

Year to 30 April	2023	2024
Revenues ($mn)	1634.5	1874.2
International Rice (%)	45	47
Rice Pool (%)	21	21
CopRice (%)	14	14
Riviana (%)	13	12
Rice Food (%)	7	6
EBIT ($mn)	83.7	105.7
EBIT margin (%)	5.1	5.6
Profit before tax ($mn)	69.7	86.7
Profit after tax ($mn)	52.6	63.1
Earnings per share (c)	83.77	97.50
Cash flow per share (c)	128.95	142.01
Dividend (c)	50	55
Percentage franked	100	100
Net tangible assets per share ($)	7.13	7.68
Interest cover (times)	6.1	5.8
Return on equity (%)	10.3	11.4
Debt-to-equity ratio (%)	48.8	34.0
Current ratio	1.4	1.5

Ridley Corporation Limited

ASX code: RIC

www.ridley.com.au

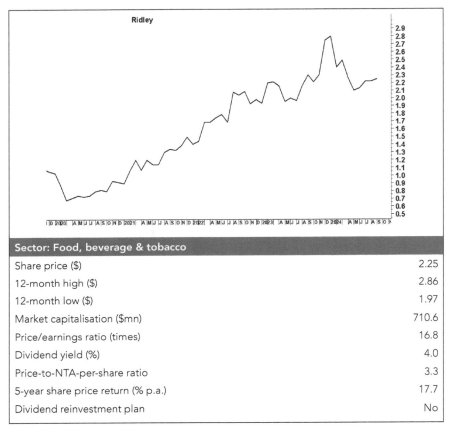

Sector: Food, beverage & tobacco	
Share price ($)	2.25
12-month high ($)	2.86
12-month low ($)	1.97
Market capitalisation ($mn)	710.6
Price/earnings ratio (times)	16.8
Dividend yield (%)	4.0
Price-to-NTA-per-share ratio	3.3
5-year share price return (% p.a.)	17.7
Dividend reinvestment plan	No

Melbourne-based Ridley, founded in 1987, is a leading producer of animal feed. It operates from some 20 sites in Victoria, New South Wales, Queensland and South Australia, producing around two million tonnes annually of finished feeds and feed ingredients, based on locally grown cereal grains. It also owns an aquafeed manufacturing facility in Thailand. It classifies its production into two broad segments. Bulk stockfeeds comprises the company's animal nutrition feed that is delivered in bulk. Packaged feeds and ingredients represents animal nutrition feed and ingredients that are delivered in packaged form, ranging from three-kilogram bags to one-tonne containers. In March 2024 it acquired New Zealand pet food manufacturer Oceania Meat Processors (OMP).

Latest business results (June 2024, full year)

Revenues and profits edged up in a mixed year for the company. The bulk stockfeeds segment enjoyed a double-digit rise in profits, with particularly solid growth in demand for cattle feed. Feedstuffs for some other sectors experienced a small decline in sales, despite a recovery late in the year for poultry feed, although efficiency initiatives helped maintain profit margins. The packaged feeds and ingredients segment saw profits down, with lower prices for tallows and protein meals only partially offset by stronger demand. Earnings for this segment would have fallen further but for a contribution from the OMP acquisition. Nevertheless, profit margins for the feeds and ingredients segment remained substantially higher than for bulk stockfeeds.

Outlook

Ridley occupies a prominent place in the Australian agricultural sector as one of the leading producers of stockfeeds, nutritional blocks, mineral concentrates, supplements and other products for a wide range of animal species that include cattle, poultry, pigs, horses, sheep, working dogs, pets and fish. It has an extensive research and development program and strong partnerships with industry bodies, universities and key research organisations. It benefits as the Australian agricultural sector expands and has adopted an ambitious three-year growth plan. The streamlining of its bulk stockfeeds facilities is expected to lead to increased production and the company is hoping to move into new markets. It also wishes to boost exports for the packaged feeds and ingredients segment. It sees particular potential in the premium pet food market, and its NZ$57 million OMP acquisition is designed to boost this business. OMP has factories in Timaru, New Zealand, and in Melbourne, and is a leading supplier of premium meat to the global pet industry. Ridley believes it is on track for further earnings growth in the June 2025 year.

Year to 30 June	2023	2024
Revenues ($mn)	1260.1	1262.9
Bulk stockfeeds (%)	69	70
Packaged feeds & ingredients (%)	31	30
EBIT ($mn)	64.1	67.5
EBIT margin (%)	5.1	5.3
Gross margin (%)	8.8	9.2
Profit before tax ($mn)	58.6	58.9
Profit after tax ($mn)	41.8	42.3
Earnings per share (c)	13.24	13.39
Cash flow per share (c)	21.09	21.67
Dividend (c)	8.25	9.05
Percentage franked	100	100
Net tangible assets per share ($)	0.76	0.68
Interest cover (times)	12.6	8.6
Return on equity (%)	13.2	13.2
Debt-to-equity ratio (%)	9.3	19.8
Current ratio	1.2	1.1

Rio Tinto Limited

ASX code: RIO   www.riotinto.com

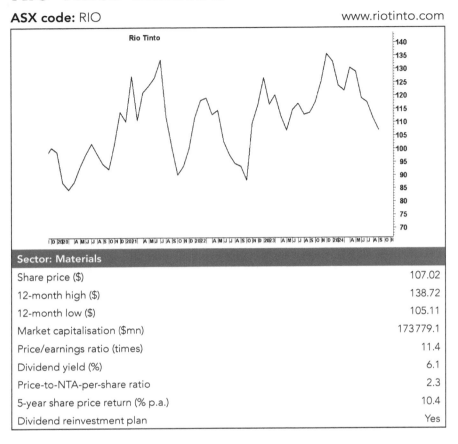

Sector: Materials	
Share price ($)	107.02
12-month high ($)	138.72
12-month low ($)	105.11
Market capitalisation ($mn)	173779.1
Price/earnings ratio (times)	11.4
Dividend yield (%)	6.1
Price-to-NTA-per-share ratio	2.3
5-year share price return (% p.a.)	10.4
Dividend reinvestment plan	Yes

British-based Rio Tinto, one of the world's largest mining companies, was founded by European investors in 1873 in order to reopen some ancient copper mines at the Tinto River in Spain. It maintains an ASX presence in a dual-listing structure and continues to pay franked dividends to Australian shareholders. Its products include iron ore, copper, gold, industrial minerals, diamonds and aluminium. Subsidiaries include the 86 per cent-owned uranium miner Energy Resources of Australia.

Latest business results (June 2024, half year)

Profits rose, although this in part reflected reduced impairment charges and some benefits from currency movements. Otherwise, some lower commodities prices outpaced modest increases in sales volumes, and the company's operations were also hit by inflationary pressures. Iron ore represented 57 per cent of total company revenues, and lower prices sent profits down. Nevertheless, this division again accounted for around 80 per cent of total underlying earnings during the period. The Aluminium division, representing 24 per cent of revenues, rebounded from the previous year, with increased production helping boost profits. Copper division profits benefited from rising prices and higher output at all three of the company's key operations, Oyu Tolgoi in Mongolia, Escondida in Chile and Kennecott in the US. The Minerals division, incorporating iron ore pellets and concentrates, titanium dioxide, borates and diamonds, posted an earnings decline. Altogether, 58 per cent of total company sales were to China and a further 13.5 per cent to the rest of Asia. Note that Rio Tinto reports its results in US dollars. The figures in this book are based on prevailing exchange rates.

Outlook

Rio Tinto maintains a substantial portfolio of well-run assets across many countries, and with generally low operating costs. It forecasts capital expenditure of up to US$10 billion in each of 2025 and 2026. It continues to boost production at the major Oyu Tolgoi project, and copper is set to become a growing contributor to Rio Tinto's business operations. It is also working to bring the giant Simandou iron ore project in Guinea into production during 2025. In Argentina it has acquired the Rincon lithium project and sees this as a further engine of growth. The company has expressed its interest in acquiring further copper and lithium assets. It also maintains a strong portfolio of greenfield exploration projects incorporating eight commodities in 18 countries. Nevertheless, in the short term Rio Tinto remains highly exposed to Chinese iron ore demand.

Year to 31 December	2022	2023
Revenues ($mn)	80513.0	81880.3
EBIT ($mn)	27531.9	22351.5
EBIT margin (%)	34.2	27.3
Profit before tax ($mn)	27046.4	20886.4
Profit after tax ($mn)	18000.0	15239.4
Earnings per share (c)	1111.25	939.89
Cash flow per share (c)	1559.51	1438.34
Dividend (c)	710.19	653.67
Percentage franked	100	100
Interest cover (times)	121.8	34.2
Return on equity (%)	25.0	19.7
Half year to 30 June	2023	2024
Revenues ($mn)	39216.2	40609.1
Profit before tax ($mn)	10191.2	12295.5
Profit after tax ($mn)	7525.0	8800.0
Earnings per share (c)	464.26	542.27
Dividend (c)	260.89	261.7
Percentage franked	100	100
Net tangible assets per share ($)	43.91	46.60
Debt-to-equity ratio (%)	6.9	6.3
Current ratio	2.0	1.7

Santos Limited

ASX code: STO

www.santos.com

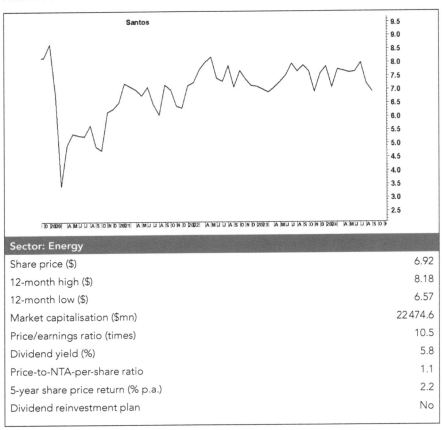

Sector: Energy	
Share price ($)	6.92
12-month high ($)	8.18
12-month low ($)	6.57
Market capitalisation ($mn)	22 474.6
Price/earnings ratio (times)	10.5
Dividend yield (%)	5.8
Price-to-NTA-per-share ratio	1.1
5-year share price return (% p.a.)	2.2
Dividend reinvestment plan	No

Adelaide-based Santos, established in 1954, is one of Australia's leading producers of oil and gas. It arranges its operations into three regional business units: the Eastern Australia and Papua New Guinea (PNG) unit produces natural gas, gas liquids and crude oil at the Cooper Basin and liquefied natural gas (LNG) in Queensland and PNG; the Western Australia, Northern Australia and Timor-Leste unit produces natural gas at the Bayu-Undan field in Timor-Leste and LNG at Darwin, along with natural gas, gas liquids and crude oil in Western Australia; the Alaskan unit incorporates three oil and gas development projects. In addition to the three regional business units, Santos also manages Santos Energy Solutions, which provides mid-stream processing of gas and liquids along with decarbonisation and carbon management services and long-term portfolio strategy services.

Latest business results (June 2024, half year)

Lower production and falling prices sent revenues and profits down. Production of 44 million barrels of oil equivalent (boe) was 2 per cent lower than in the June 2023 half, due primarily to lower volumes from Bayu-Undan as the field approaches the end of its life. The average realised oil price rose 4 per cent, but this was more than offset by a 9 per cent decline in the average realised LNG price. Note that Santos reports its results in US dollars. The Australian dollar figures in this book — converted at prevailing exchange rates — are for guidance only.

Outlook

Santos is involved in some large development projects aimed at securing long-term supplies of oil and gas, and with the potential to double the company's output by 2028. One of the biggest is the $5.8 billion Barossa gas project in the Timor Sea, which is aimed at supplying gas for the Darwin LNG plant to replace supplies from the Bayu-Undan field. This is 80 per cent complete and the company expects the first gas deliveries from the third quarter of 2025. The initial phase of the Pikka project in Alaska is 60 per cent complete, and the company expects the first oil from early 2026. It will decide during 2025 whether to proceed with three major projects — a new LNG development in PNG, the Dorado oil and gas project in Western Australia and the Narrabri domestic gas project in New South Wales. Santos has abandoned talks with Woodside on a possible corporate merger. The company expects to produce between 84 million boe and 90 million boe during 2024.

Year to 31 December	2022	2023
Revenues ($mn)	11 289.9	8922.7
EBIT ($mn)	4718.8	3260.6
EBIT margin (%)	41.8	36.5
Gross margin (%)	49.9	37.7
Profit before tax ($mn)	4272.5	2756.1
Profit after tax ($mn)	3060.9	2156.1
Earnings per share (c)	91.35	66.10
Cash flow per share (c)	166.92	152.42
Dividend (c)	33.29	40.23
Percentage franked	0	0
Interest cover (times)	12.8	9.5
Return on equity (%)	15.1	10.0
Half year to 30 June	**2023**	**2024**
Revenues ($mn)	4363.2	4107.6
Profit before tax ($mn)	1435.3	1331.8
Profit after tax ($mn)	1161.8	963.6
Earnings per share (c)	35.44	29.70
Dividend (c)	13.4	19.11
Percentage franked	0	0
Net tangible assets per share ($)	6.35	6.49
Debt-to-equity ratio (%)	20.9	24.9
Current ratio	1.6	1.1

Schaffer Corporation Limited

ASX code: SFC

schaffer.com.au

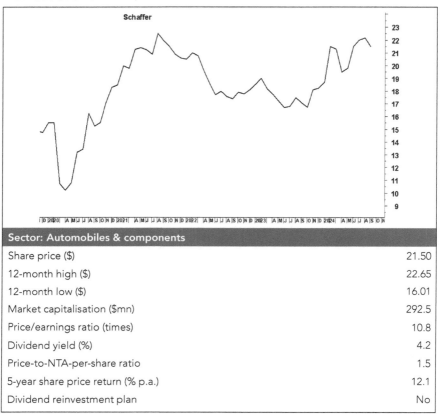

Sector: Automobiles & components	
Share price ($)	21.50
12-month high ($)	22.65
12-month low ($)	16.01
Market capitalisation ($mn)	292.5
Price/earnings ratio (times)	10.8
Dividend yield (%)	4.2
Price-to-NTA-per-share ratio	1.5
5-year share price return (% p.a.)	12.1
Dividend reinvestment plan	No

Perth company Schaffer was founded in 1955 to manufacture sand-lime bricks for the construction industry. Today its Delta Corporation subsidiary produces precast and prestressed concrete floors, beams and wall products, aimed mainly at the Western Australian construction market. However, its primary business now is the manufacture of leather goods, with a particular emphasis on products for the automotive industry, through its 83 per cent–owned subsidiary Automotive Leather. This business operates from facilities in Australia, China and Slovakia and supplies leading auto makers around the world. A third business for Schaffer is investments and property development, and it owns a portfolio of rental and development sites, mainly in Western Australia.

Latest business results (June 2024, full year)

Revenues and profits rose strongly, with all businesses reporting good results. The core Automotive Leather division saw sales up 27 per cent to $181.9 million, with the after-tax profit up 39 per cent to $15.3 million, thanks especially to good business from the launch of a new program for Mercedes and increased demand from Land

Rover. Sales in the previous year had been hurt by purchasing delays from a major European customer, high energy costs and adverse currency movements. The Building Materials division achieved sales growth of 8 per cent to $31.1 million, and an after-tax profit more than doubling to $4.5 million, thanks especially to improved operational efficiencies. Profits in the previous year had been affected by design and engineering problems on a large project. The company's Investments division benefited from an $8.1 million unrealised revaluation gain on its major South Connect property holding at Jandakot.

Outlook

Schaffer's core automotive leather goods business is highly dependent on trends in the global car-making sector, with a large part of demand coming from luxury automobile manufacturers. Thanks to increasing demand from Audi and Porsche the company believes that profits should continue to rise for at least the first half of the June 2025 year, bolstered by a series of operational efficiencies. It also expects a further strong performance from its construction-related activities, thanks especially to continuing government investment in large-scale civil engineering projects. However, it is concerned about skilled labour shortages, supply disruptions and inflationary cost pressures. It also expects further growth in its investment portfolio, valued at $210.9 million — or $15.53 per share — at June 2024. It continues development work on its 34-hectare Jandakot Road land holding, 15 minutes from the Perth CBD, and has received approval for the first phase of logistics warehouses on the site.

Year to 30 June	2023	2024
Revenues ($mn)	174.0	216.2
EBIT ($mn)	26.0	46.5
EBIT margin (%)	14.9	21.5
Gross margin (%)	20.2	21.3
Profit before tax ($mn)	22.9	42.8
Profit after tax ($mn)	13.6	27.1
Earnings per share (c)	99.84	198.84
Cash flow per share (c)	158.48	260.84
Dividend (c)	90	90
Percentage franked	100	100
Net tangible assets per share ($)	11.85	14.15
Interest cover (times)	13.4	19.9
Return on equity (%)	6.7	12.4
Debt-to-equity ratio (%)	20.5	11.9
Current ratio	2.1	2.1

Servcorp Limited

ASX code: SRV www.servcorp.com.au

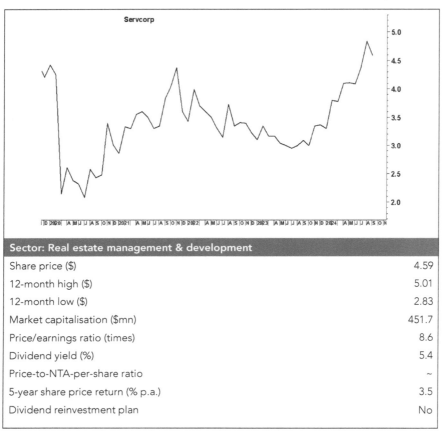

Sector: Real estate management & development	
Share price ($)	4.59
12-month high ($)	5.01
12-month low ($)	2.83
Market capitalisation ($mn)	451.7
Price/earnings ratio (times)	8.6
Dividend yield (%)	5.4
Price-to-NTA-per-share ratio	~
5-year share price return (% p.a.)	3.5
Dividend reinvestment plan	No

Sydney-based Servcorp was founded in 1978 to provide serviced office space to small businesses. It has expanded to provide advanced corporate infrastructure, including IT and telecommunications services, and office support services. It also offers what it terms virtual offices, providing a prestigious address and a range of services for people or businesses not needing a physical office. More than a third of the company's business is in Europe and the Middle East, with more than a quarter in North Asia. In June 2024 it was operating 132 floors of offices in 40 cities across 20 countries.

Latest business results (June 2024, full year)

Profits posted a double-digit rise, with strength in most regions, in another good result. For a third consecutive year the Europe/Middle East segment showed strong growth, with double-digit rises in sales and profits, as two new operations were added to the portfolio. The Australia/New Zealand/South East Asia region was also strong, with double-digit increases in revenues and profits as the company achieved success in boosting occupancy rates. By contrast, North Asia was weak, with revenues and profits down, following challenges in China, together with an unfavourable impact from the falling Japanese yen. The small US segment suffered a widening loss. During the year the company increased net capacity by 176 offices.

Outlook

Servcorp is a world leader in its business, with good market shares and a reputation for quality. After a period of disruption during the COVID pandemic, when many workers abandoned their offices to work from home, the company has been investing heavily to build its business. It has spent more than $60 million on a steady expansion of its operations, with further new locations still to come, along with a major new digital platform, which was completed in December 2023. It expects to add 205 new offices during the June 2025 year. Much of the growth is from the Europe/Middle East segment and Servcorp has become the first company in the shared workspace sector to receive a licence to operate in Saudi Arabia. It has created a new company for its Middle East and European operations and is working towards a stock market listing of this entity during 2025, with Servcorp retaining a 55 per cent holding in this new company. At June 2024 Servcorp had no debt and more than $103 million in cash holdings. Its early forecast is for underlying profits to rise by at least 8 per cent in the June 2025 year.

Year to 30 June	2023	2024
Revenues ($mn)	293.8	314.1
Europe/Middle East (%)	33	39
North Asia (%)	35	28
Australia/NZ/South East Asia (%)	24	25
USA (%)	7	6
EBIT ($mn)	59.0	70.6
EBIT margin (%)	20.1	22.5
Profit before tax ($mn)	47.8	56.6
Profit after tax ($mn)	42.6	52.1
Earnings per share (c)	44.00	53.24
Cash flow per share (c)	169.90	170.30
Dividend (c)	22	25
Percentage franked	11	20
Net tangible assets per share ($)	~	~
Interest cover (times)	7.0	6.2
Return on equity (%)	22.1	27.2
Debt-to-equity ratio (%)	~	~
Current ratio	0.8	0.8

Smartgroup Corporation Limited

ASX code: SIQ   www.smartgroup.com.au

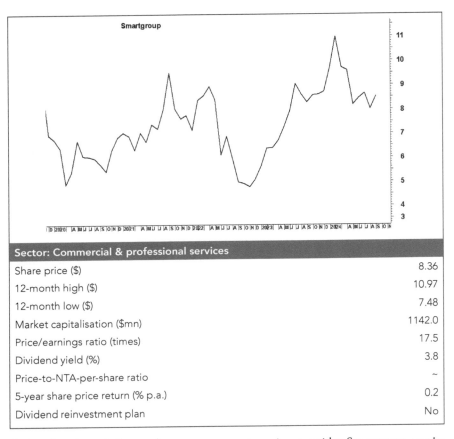

Sector: Commercial & professional services	
Share price ($)	8.36
12-month high ($)	10.97
12-month low ($)	7.48
Market capitalisation ($mn)	1142.0
Price/earnings ratio (times)	17.5
Dividend yield (%)	3.8
Price-to-NTA-per-share ratio	~
5-year share price return (% p.a.)	0.2
Dividend reinvestment plan	No

Sydney-based specialist employee management services provider Smartgroup got its start in 1999 as Smartsalary, a salary packaging specialist. It later branched into other businesses and has grown significantly, both organically and through acquisition. It is now engaged in salary packaging services, vehicle novated leasing and fleet management.

Latest business results (June 2024, half year)

Revenues rose again and profits bounced back from the previous year's decline as improvements to vehicle supply and a stabilisation of interest rates led to stronger business. The novated lease business was particularly buoyant. The company noted that vehicle supply disruptions were steadily easing, and the number of leases under management, which had fallen in the June 2023 half, rose 11 per cent to 64 600, with increasingly strong demand for electric vehicles. Salary packaging customer numbers of 402 000 were up from 385 000 a year earlier, thanks to new clients and organic growth from existing clients. The high-margin managed fleet vehicle business saw numbers rise 17 per cent to 30 600.

Outlook

Smartgroup is one of Australia's largest companies involved in the salary packaging and novated leasing businesses. Essentially this latter business involves taking advantage of complex legislation to provide tax deductions for employees, mainly those working in the non-profit or public sectors. Following the establishment of a new operating model and the divestment of two non-core businesses, the company is now focused on its core operations of salary packaging, novated leasing and fleet management. As it grows it achieves economies of scale, and profit margins increase. It has been achieving success in renewing or extending the contracts of its leading clients. From July 2024 it initiated an important new contract with the South Australian government, opening its services to some 110 000 employees. Following severe constraints on new car supply during and after the COVID pandemic, deliveries are steadily returning to a normal pattern, and this has stimulated a solid rise in demand. In addition, the abolition of the fringe benefits tax on many electric vehicles has led to a sharp increase in demand for these, with electric vehicles representing 42 per cent of all new car novated lease orders in the June 2024 half. The company believes that as new, cheaper electric vehicle models are released this demand will continue to grow. It is enjoying success with its new online car leasing portal, which allows customers to obtain quotes and to process applications, and the company is rolling it out progressively to the bulk of its clients.

Year to 31 December	2022	2023
Revenues ($mn)	224.7	251.6
EBIT ($mn)	86.0	91.1
EBIT margin (%)	38.3	36.2
Profit before tax ($mn)	83.6	88.1
Profit after tax ($mn)	58.8	61.9
Earnings per share (c)	45.33	47.74
Cash flow per share (c)	51.47	53.85
Dividend (c)	32	31.5
Percentage franked	100	100
Interest cover (times)	41.3	40.3
Return on equity (%)	23.2	25.6
Half year to 30 June	**2023**	**2024**
Revenues ($mn)	116.6	148.5
Profit before tax ($mn)	41.6	49.6
Profit after tax ($mn)	28.9	34.3
Earnings per share (c)	22.30	26.40
Dividend (c)	15.5	17.5
Percentage franked	100	100
Net tangible assets per share ($)	~	~
Debt-to-equity ratio (%)	17.2	23.0
Current ratio	0.9	1.0

Southern Cross Electrical Engineering Limited

ASX code: SXE

www.scee.com.au

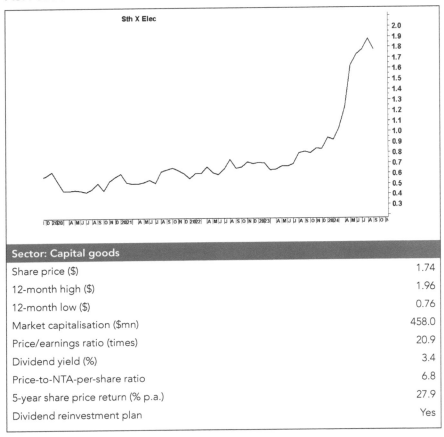

Sector: Capital goods	
Share price ($)	1.74
12-month high ($)	1.96
12-month low ($)	0.76
Market capitalisation ($mn)	458.0
Price/earnings ratio (times)	20.9
Dividend yield (%)	3.4
Price-to-NTA-per-share ratio	6.8
5-year share price return (% p.a.)	27.9
Dividend reinvestment plan	Yes

Perth-based Southern Cross Electrical Engineering (SCEE) was founded in 1978. A series of acquisitions have generated some strong expansion and the company is now a leading national provider of specialised electrical, instrumentation, maintenance and communication services, operating through seven dedicated businesses. In May 2024 it acquired electrical and communications specialist MDE Group.

Latest business results (June 2024, full year)

Its fast-expanding strength in infrastructure work helped deliver SCEE gains in revenues and profits. Infrastructure division revenue of $233.7 million was up by 65 per cent from the previous year, thanks especially to continuing work on the Western Sydney International Airport project. The supply of Westgate Tunnel switchboards in Victoria was completed during the year. The Commercial division reported revenues of $171.1 million, up 10 per cent. The third division, Resources, saw revenues fall 13 per cent, having completed large-scale construction work in the previous year for the Kemerton lithium plant and the Gudai-Darri iron ore mine. The year-end order book of $720 million was up 18 per cent from the previous year.

Outlook

As a diversified national electrical contractor SCEE believes it is well positioned to benefit from three structural trends. The first is growing demand for data centres, due to developments in cloud computing and artificial intelligence and the consequent growth in data storage requirements. Electrical work is the largest component of data centre construction costs. The company expects revenues from data centres alone of at least $100 million annually from the June 2025 year, and it expects to tender for some $500 million of data centre work over the coming two years. The second trend is the electrification and decarbonisation of the economy, requiring a huge investment in renewable energy. In May 2024 SCEE received the largest initial contract in its history, the $160 million Collie Battery project in Western Australia. The third trend is the growth of infrastructure projects in Australia. SCEE expects to tender for further work for the Western Sydney International Airport. It is also involved in Australia's largest public transport project, Sydney Metro. The $10.55 million acquisition of Sydney-based MDE Group enlarges Southern Cross's core activities. This company has strong synergies with Southern Cross business Heyday Group, and will enable Heyday to expand its offerings to clients. SCEE is seeking further acquisition opportunities. Its early forecast is for June 2025 EBITDA of at least $53 million, compared to $40.1 million in June 2024, and with expectations of further growth in ensuing years.

Year to 30 June	2023	2024
Revenues ($mn)	464.7	551.9
Infrastructure (%)	31	42
Commercial (%)	33	31
Resources (%)	36	27
EBIT ($mn)	30.8	35.1
EBIT margin (%)	6.6	6.4
Gross margin (%)	16.4	15.0
Profit before tax ($mn)	29.0	31.7
Profit after tax ($mn)	20.1	21.9
Earnings per share (c)	7.69	8.34
Cash flow per share (c)	11.01	11.17
Dividend (c)	5	6
Percentage franked	100	100
Net tangible assets per share ($)	0.23	0.26
Interest cover (times)	59.7	34.8
Return on equity (%)	11.3	11.7
Debt-to-equity ratio (%)	~	~
Current ratio	1.5	1.4

Steadfast Group Limited

ASX code: SDF　　　　　　　　investor.steadfast.com.au

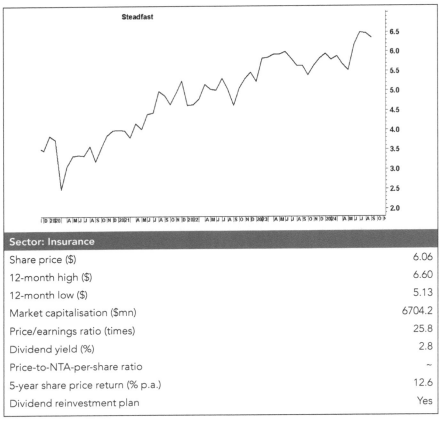

Sector: Insurance	
Share price ($)	6.06
12-month high ($)	6.60
12-month low ($)	5.13
Market capitalisation ($mn)	6704.2
Price/earnings ratio (times)	25.8
Dividend yield (%)	2.8
Price-to-NTA-per-share ratio	~
5-year share price return (% p.a.)	12.6
Dividend reinvestment plan	Yes

Melbourne-based insurance broking firm Steadfast launched in 1996 with the aim of boosting the buying power of small independent general insurance brokers in their dealings with insurers. It has since grown to become the largest insurance broker network and underwriting group in Australasia, with further operations abroad. It also manages a range of complementary businesses that include back office services, risk services guidance, work health consultancy, reinsurance and legal advice. It has a 60 per cent stake in Hamburg-based UnisonSteadfast, one of the world's largest networks of general insurance brokers. In October 2023 it acquired ISU Group, a network of independent agencies in the US.

Latest business results (June 2024, full year)

Steadfast reported another excellent result, with further double-digit rises in revenues and profits. It was the company's 11th consecutive profit increase. Its core Steadfast Australasian Network broking business recorded gross written premium of $13 billion, up 12.1 per cent from the previous year, thanks to increased sales volumes and premium rate increases. Underlying EBITDA was up 19.6 per cent. At June 2024

Steadfast incorporated a network of 318 brokerages in Australia, 69 in New Zealand and 31 in Singapore. It had equity holdings in 68 of the brokerages. The 60 per cent–owned UnisonSteadfast incorporated a further 294 brokerages across 110 countries. The Steadfast Underwriting Agencies business, comprising 29 specialist agencies offering over 100 niche products, generated gross written premium of $2.3 billion, up 13.4 per cent, with EBITDA up 18.9 per cent.

Outlook

Steadfast continues its strong growth trajectory. After spending $457.8 million in the June 2024 year for 48 acquisitions, it expects to spend a further $300 million in the June 2025 year. It sees particular potential in its US$55 million ISU Group acquisition. This is a network of 228 agencies across 40 US states, and Steadfast believes it can provide products and services that will substantially enhance ISU's current offerings and offer a platform for long-term growth. Steadfast operates nine complementary businesses supporting its network. It claims that through its Steadfast Technologies business it is a global leader in broker insurance technology that supports interactions with broker partners and clients and underpins its strong market position. Its fast-growing Steadfast Client Trading Platform provides brokers with automated access to its network and the ability to make comparisons of policies and prices on a single screen. Steadfast is forecasting a June 2025 after-tax profit of $290 million to $300 million, with EPS growth of 12 per cent to 16 per cent.

Year to 30 June	2023	2024
Revenues ($mn)	1409.5	1676.2
EBIT ($mn)	379.1	478.7
EBIT margin (%)	26.9	28.6
Profit before tax ($mn)	348.1	425.0
Profit after tax ($mn)	207.0	252.2
Earnings per share (c)	20.19	23.45
Cash flow per share (c)	28.81	32.52
Dividend (c)	15	17.1
Percentage franked	100	100
Net tangible assets per share ($)	~	~
Interest cover (times)	49.9	111.3
Return on equity (%)	11.1	11.5
Debt-to-equity ratio (%)	31.7	33.6
Current ratio	1.4	1.5

Super Retail Group Limited

ASX code: SUL   www.superretailgroup.com.au

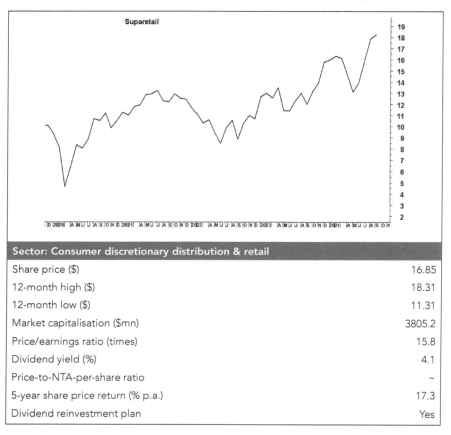

Sector: Consumer discretionary distribution & retail	
Share price ($)	16.85
12-month high ($)	18.31
12-month low ($)	11.31
Market capitalisation ($mn)	3805.2
Price/earnings ratio (times)	15.8
Dividend yield (%)	4.1
Price-to-NTA-per-share ratio	~
5-year share price return (% p.a.)	17.3
Dividend reinvestment plan	Yes

Specialist retail chain Super Retail Group was established as a mail-order business in 1972 and has its headquarters in Strathpine, Queensland. It now comprises four retail brands, with around 760 stores throughout Australia and New Zealand. Supercheap Auto is a retailer of automotive spare parts and related products. Rebel is a prominent sporting goods chain. BCF is a retailer of boating, camping and fishing products. Macpac is an outdoor adventure and activity specialist retailer.

Latest business results (June 2024, full year)

The opening of 28 new stores and further growth in online business boosted revenues, but inflationary pressures and weakened consumer sentiment hit profits, which were down. On a like-for-like basis sales were little changed from the previous year. The best result came from BCF, with sales up by nearly 5 per cent and pre-tax profit up 6.5 per cent, although this partly reflected new store openings. The company reported particularly strong demand for fishing-related products, supported by the roll-out of a series of in-store tackle specialty outlets. The biggest division, Supercheap Auto, recorded a small increase in sales, but with the pre-tax profit edging down. The Rebel sporting goods business was hit by a decline in consumer discretionary spending, with sales down by 1 per cent and the pre-tax profit plunging by 30 per cent. Macpac achieved positive sales growth, with particular strength in New Zealand. However, higher operating expenses sent the pre-tax profit down by 34.5 per cent. Total online sales of $485 million were up 9 per cent.

Outlook

Super Retail controls four prominent brands with strong positions in their respective markets. Nevertheless, it operates in a competitive retail environment at a time when rising interest rates and inflationary pressures have been dampening consumer spending. With much of its product range imported, it is also vulnerable to currency fluctuations and supply chain disruptions. It plans a roll-out of 25 new stores during the June 2025 year. Its Supercheap Auto division generates the strongest profit margins of the four businesses, and the company expects solid sales as car numbers continue to grow in Australia and New Zealand. A particular focus is meeting growing demand for electric vehicle aftermarket products. It sees scope for leveraging its loyalty programs, with some 11.5 million active club members, one of the largest such schemes in Australia. Already more than three-quarters of group sales come from club members. At June 2024 Super Retail had no debt and cash holdings of $217 million.

Year to 29 June*	2023	2024
Revenues ($mn)	3802.6	3882.6
Supercheap Auto (%)	38	38
Rebel (%)	34	33
BCF (%)	22	23
Macpac (%)	5	6
EBIT ($mn)	426.8	397.6
EBIT margin (%)	11.2	10.2
Gross margin (%)	46.2	46.3
Profit before tax ($mn)	379.4	339.8
Profit after tax ($mn)	263.0	240.1
Earnings per share (c)	116.46	106.32
Cash flow per share (c)	262.41	256.08
Dividend (c)	78	69
Percentage franked	100	100
Net tangible assets per share ($)	~	~
Interest cover (times)	9.9	8.0
Return on equity (%)	19.8	17.5
Debt-to-equity ratio (%)	~	~
Current ratio	1.3	1.2

*1 July 2023

Supply Network Limited

ASX code: SNL   www.supplynetwork.com.au

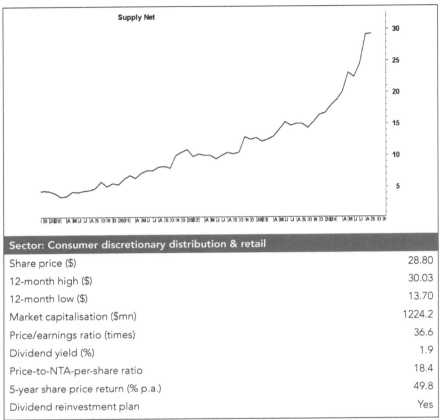

Sector: Consumer discretionary distribution & retail	
Share price ($)	28.80
12-month high ($)	30.03
12-month low ($)	13.70
Market capitalisation ($mn)	1224.2
Price/earnings ratio (times)	36.6
Dividend yield (%)	1.9
Price-to-NTA-per-share ratio	18.4
5-year share price return (% p.a.)	49.8
Dividend reinvestment plan	Yes

Sydney-based Supply Network is a supplier of truck and bus parts in the commercial vehicle aftermarket, operating under the brand name Multispares, which was established in 1976. It manages offices, distribution centres and workshops at 20 locations throughout Australia and five in New Zealand.

Latest business results (June 2024, full year)

Strong demand for its products and services generated another excellent result for Supply Network. Profit margins remained stable, despite inflationary pressures, especially for wages, and continuing investments in growth initiatives. Disruptions during the year in Red Sea shipping did not have a material impact on the result. Sales in Australia were up 21 per cent, with EBIT rising 16 per cent. New Zealand, representing 15 per cent of total income, saw revenues up 16 per cent and EBIT up 12 per cent.

Outlook

Supply Network is one of the leaders in the Australian market for the supply of truck and bus parts. It is a fragmented market, and the majority of truck operators are small businesses with only a single vehicle. With a great diversity of vehicle makes and models, and with a considerable difference in requirements between various regions of the country, the company has established a decentralised management structure with a strong regional focus. Its core activity has become the supply of truck components, and this now represents more than 80 per cent of total income. Company fleets are the largest customer group, and these are sophisticated buyers of parts with a focus on costs, making this business highly competitive. Independent repair workshops are the next-largest customer group. The company is a beneficiary of the increasing complexity of trucks, which require an ever-growing range of expensive components. It also benefits from a slow rise in the average age of trucks in Australia. It has a range of projects designed to lay the foundations for future growth, with a view to reaching annual revenues of $350 million. In particular, it plans a major upgrade of its technology systems, targeting transaction efficiency and the speed and accuracy of customer service, as well as standardising its internal catalogue and rolling out new scanning technologies. It expects the expansion of its Truganina Distribution Centre in Melbourne to be completed by the end of the June 2025 year. It is also building a new centre in Wangara, Perth. Anticipating an increase in road freight volumes and market share gains the company forecasts revenue growth of around 14 per cent for the June 2025 year.

Year to 30 June	2023	2024
Revenues ($mn)	252.3	302.6
EBIT ($mn)	40.9	49.5
EBIT margin (%)	16.2	16.4
Profit before tax ($mn)	39.0	47.1
Profit after tax ($mn)	27.4	33.0
Earnings per share (c)	66.51	78.61
Cash flow per share (c)	84.71	100.24
Dividend (c)	48	56
Percentage franked	100	100
Net tangible assets per share ($)	0.96	1.56
Interest cover (times)	23.4	22.2
Return on equity (%)	40.0	36.5
Debt-to-equity ratio (%)	2.8	3.6
Current ratio	2.5	2.7

Technology One Limited

ASX code: TNE   www.technologyonecorp.com

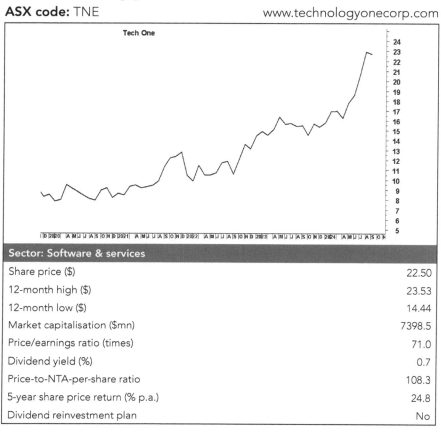

Sector: Software & services	
Share price ($)	22.50
12-month high ($)	23.53
12-month low ($)	14.44
Market capitalisation ($mn)	7398.5
Price/earnings ratio (times)	71.0
Dividend yield (%)	0.7
Price-to-NTA-per-share ratio	108.3
5-year share price return (% p.a.)	24.8
Dividend reinvestment plan	No

Brisbane-based Technology One, founded in 1987, designs, develops, implements and supports a wide range of financial management, accounting and business software. It enjoys particular strength in local government. Its software is also used by educational institutions, including many Australian universities. Other key markets are financial services, central government, and health and community services. It derives revenues not only from the supply of its products but also from annual licence fees. It operates from offices in Australia, New Zealand, Malaysia and the UK.

Latest business results (March 2024, half year)

Technology One posted another solid result, with profits up for the 15th straight March half year and strength across all its businesses. Once again it enjoyed success in moving its customers onto its Software as a Service (SaaS) cloud platforms, and this now represents 90 per cent of company income. Total annual recurring revenue was a 21 per cent jump from a year before. Consulting services — essentially the business of implementing the company's software, and representing about 13 per cent of company turnover — saw sales rise but profits fall. British operations continued to expand, although the pre-tax profit there fell from $3 million to $1 million. The company maintained its high level of research and development spending, up 15 per cent to $56.9 million.

Outlook

Technology One has become a star among Australian high-tech companies, with growing profits and regular dividend increases. In large part this reflects a strong product line, a solid flow of recurring income and a heavy investment in new products and services, which it believes will enable it to double in size every five years. It has achieved great success with its SaaS offerings, which put software in the cloud, rather than on the customers' own computers, meaning that the customers always have the latest software versions, and giving them greater flexibility than previously. It currently receives annual recurring revenues of $424 million from its SaaS business, and believes it is on track to boost this to more than $500 million by 2025, with growing profit margins. As the move to SaaS continues the company expects its low-margin consulting business to shrink. It believes it can enhance its competitive position in the UK through its new Scientia business, which provides academic timetabling and resource scheduling software to educational institutions. It is also considering expansion to other markets. At March 2024 Technology One had no debt and cash holdings of $103 million.

Year to 30 September	2022	2023
Revenues ($mn)	368.2	429.4
EBIT ($mn)	114.2	132.0
EBIT margin (%)	31.0	30.7
Profit before tax ($mn)	112.3	129.9
Profit after tax ($mn)	88.8	102.9
Earnings per share (c)	27.51	31.71
Cash flow per share (c)	39.31	48.20
Dividend (c)	15.02	16.52
Percentage franked	60	60
Interest cover (times)	80.3	~
Return on equity (%)	41.4	37.7
Half year to 31 March	2023	2024
Revenues ($mn)	201.0	240.8
Profit before tax ($mn)	52.7	61.5
Profit after tax ($mn)	41.3	48.0
Earnings per share (c)	12.73	14.75
Dividend (c)	4.62	5.08
Percentage franked	60	65
Net tangible assets per share ($)	0.12	0.21
Debt-to-equity ratio (%)	~	~
Current ratio	1.1	1.2

Wesfarmers Limited

ASX code: WES www.wesfarmers.com.au

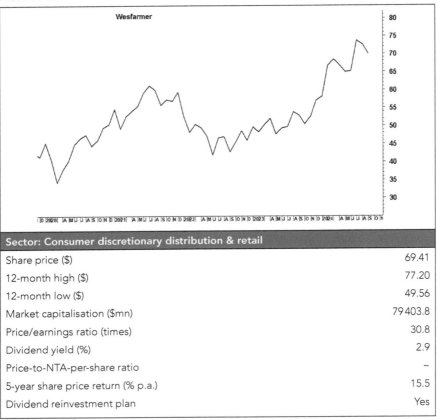

Sector: Consumer discretionary distribution & retail

Share price ($)	69.41
12-month high ($)	77.20
12-month low ($)	49.56
Market capitalisation ($mn)	79 403.8
Price/earnings ratio (times)	30.8
Dividend yield (%)	2.9
Price-to-NTA-per-share ratio	~
5-year share price return (% p.a.)	15.5
Dividend reinvestment plan	Yes

Perth-based Wesfarmers, founded in 1914 as a farmers' cooperative, is now a conglomerate with many areas of operation. Its primary business is the Bunnings network of hardware stores. Other retail businesses include the Officeworks, Kmart, Priceline, Soul Pattinson Chemist and Target chains and the Catch online marketplace. In addition, it produces fertilisers, chemicals and industrial safety products. It holds 50 per cent of the Flybuys loyalty card business, owns a 25 per cent interest in the ASX-listed BWP property trust — which owns many Bunnings warehouses — and holds half the equity in the financial services business Gresham Partners, the timber business Wespine Industries and the lithium producer Covalent Lithium. At June 2024 Wesfarmers operated 1926 stores across Australia and New Zealand.

Latest business results (June 2024, full year)

Sales and profits rose moderately, with strength across most areas of business. The Kmart division, which includes Target stores, achieved another excellent result, with sales up 4 per cent and profits jumping 25 per cent, having surged by more than 50 per cent in the previous year. The Bunnings business saw sales and profits edge up in an environment of weakening building activity. Officeworks also saw sales and profits rise modestly, boosted by above-market growth in technology. Strong sales growth at Priceline helped deliver a rise in revenues and profits for the Health division. By contrast, the WesCEF division, which manages a portfolio of businesses in the chemicals, energy, fertilisers and lithium sectors, was weak, with profits dropping 34 per cent on a 17 per cent decline in sales, driven largely by lower global commodity prices. Despite the decline, profit margins for this division remained higher than for other Wesfarmers businesses.

Outlook

Wesfarmers depends on its retail businesses for more than 80 per cent of its income, and is highly exposed to trends in consumer sentiment as well as to the state of the economy. Its Kmart stores have achieved particular success with the Anko range of low-cost products, which have helped drive the recovery in this division. Target stores now also sell the Anko range, and the company is trialling export sales. A transformation program, including an expansion of the Priceline pharmacy network, continues to drive profitable growth for the Health division. The company's Covalent Lithium joint venture is constructing a $1.9 billion mine and refinery in Western Australia with the goal of producing 50 000 tonnes annually of lithium hydroxide for use in lithium batteries, with initial output expected in mid 2025.

Year to 30 June	2023	2024
Revenues ($mn)	43 550.0	44 189.0
Bunnings Group (%)	43	43
Kmart Group (%)	24	25
Health (%)	12	13
Officeworks (%)	8	8
WesCEF (%)	8	6
EBIT ($mn)	3644.0	3753.0
EBIT margin (%)	8.4	8.5
Profit before tax ($mn)	3509.0	3587.0
Profit after tax ($mn)	2465.0	2557.0
Earnings per share (c)	217.76	225.68
Cash flow per share (c)	368.02	384.55
Dividend (c)	191	198
Percentage franked	100	100
Net tangible assets per share ($)	~	~
Interest cover (times)	30.6	27.2
Return on equity (%)	30.3	30.3
Debt-to-equity ratio (%)	45.4	45.7
Current ratio	1.2	1.1

Westpac Banking Corporation

ASX code: WBC   www.westpac.com.au

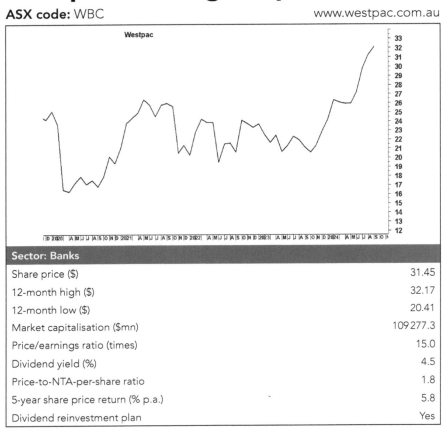

Sector: Banks	
Share price ($)	31.45
12-month high ($)	32.17
12-month low ($)	20.41
Market capitalisation ($mn)	109 277.3
Price/earnings ratio (times)	15.0
Dividend yield (%)	4.5
Price-to-NTA-per-share ratio	1.8
5-year share price return (% p.a.)	5.8
Dividend reinvestment plan	Yes

Sydney-based Westpac, which began trading in 1817 as the Bank of New South Wales, is one of Australia's big four banks, with interests in most areas of financial services. It is also one of New Zealand's leading banks and has some smaller businesses in the Pacific region. It owns St George Bank, BankSA and Bank of Melbourne. Its wealth management arm is BT and it also operates the Asgard investment advisory service and the RAMS home loans business.

Latest business results (March 2024, half year)

Revenues and profits fell as intense home loans competition drove down the bank's net interest margin by seven basis points to 1.89 per cent. The result was also affected by an 8 per cent rise in operating costs, due to higher software amortisation charges and inflationary pressures on wages and third-party vendor costs. Loans increased by 5 per cent to $785 billion, with deposits up 4 per cent to $651 billion. Of the four key divisions, the Consumer division performed the worst, with profits down 32 per cent. The Institutional Bank division also suffered a modest profit decline. However, New Zealand business experienced an 11 per cent increase in profits, although this largely reflected a fall in impairment charges, with rising costs more than offsetting growth in operating income. The Business and Wealth division saw a small rise in profits, as operating income grew at a faster pace than costs.

Outlook

Westpac has said it expects a soft landing for the Australian economy, although it believes inflation and interest rates could remain high for some time. However, it has reported signs of an easing in the intense competition among home loan providers. Thanks to investments made over recent years, the bank has succeeded in reducing mortgage and business lending approval times and has upgraded merchant payment services for business customers. It has announced a $2 billion program, named Unite and running until 2028, to streamline its operating structure and reduce the number of its technology platforms and systems. Under this program it has started work on 14 initiatives aimed at improving service for customers. It is also introducing new technology aimed at protecting its customers from scams. It has expanded its presence in the healthcare sector with the acquisition of the electronic healthcare claiming service HealthPoint. It is considering strategic options for the future of its RAMS mortgage broking operation after failing to find a buyer for this business early in 2024.

Year to 30 September	2022	2023
Operating income ($mn)	19905.0	21542.0
Net interest income ($mn)	16606.0	18414.0
Operating expenses ($mn)	10181.0	10232.0
Profit before tax ($mn)	9389.0	10662.0
Profit after tax ($mn)	6568.0	7368.0
Earnings per share (c)	184.29	210.09
Dividend (c)	125	142
Percentage franked	100	100
Non-interest income to total income (%)	16.6	14.5
Cost-to-income ratio (%)	51.9	47.3
Return on equity (%)	9.2	10.3
Return on assets (%)	0.7	0.7
Half year to 31 March	2023	2024
Operating income ($mn)	10871.0	10816.0
Profit before tax ($mn)	5493.0	5059.0
Profit after tax ($mn)	3823.0	3506.0
Earnings per share (c)	109.10	100.30
Dividend (c)	70	75
Percentage franked	100	100
Net tangible assets per share ($)	17.64	17.79

WiseTech Global Limited

ASX code: WTC www.wisetechglobal.com

Sector: Software & services	
Share price ($)	122.94
12-month high ($)	124.40
12-month low ($)	57.79
Market capitalisation ($mn)	40 994.0
Price/earnings ratio (times)	143.5
Dividend yield (%)	0.1
Price-to-NTA-per-share ratio	~
5-year share price return (% p.a.)	26.5
Dividend reinvestment plan	Yes

Sydney-based logistics software specialist WiseTech was founded in 1994 to supply code for local freight forwarders. Today it is a global leader in international logistics software, with customers that include most of the world's largest global third-party logistics providers and global freight forwarders. It has more than 50 offices worldwide and 40 product development centres. Its flagship product, CargoWise, is sold in 183 countries, with more than 17 000 customers. It has become the largest technology stock on the ASX.

Latest business results (June 2024, full year)

Revenues and profits rose strongly, with new customers, increased usage by existing customers and favourable foreign exchange movements all adding to the good result. Acquisitions over two years contributed revenues of $83.8 million. Price increases designed to offset the impact of inflation also helped boost revenues and profits. Recurring revenues edged up from 96 per cent to 97 per cent of total income. The customer attrition rate remained below 1 per cent. The research and development expense jumped 41 per cent to $368.2 million, with the product design and development budget up 37 per cent to $255.3 million.

Outlook

WiseTech's strategy is to target the 25 leading global freight forwarders and the 200 leading global logistics providers, and it benefits as these companies consolidate and increasingly dominate their industries. It says its focus is on growth through six key development priorities — landside container haulage logistics, warehousing, Neo (the company's global integrated platform for consumers of logistics services), digital documents, customs and compliance, and international eCommerce. The company continues to seek out new markets, and the CargoWise product is gaining traction among Asian freight companies, with China's Sinotrans and Japan's Yamato Transport secured as customers during the June 2024 year. Early in the June 2025 year Japan's largest global freight forwarder Nippon Express also became a customer. The company sees great potential in three important new products to be introduced during the June 2025 year. The first of these, CargoWise Next, is a next-generation platform for its customers with a significant portfolio of new product features. Container Transport Optimisation is a product that is intended dramatically to lower costs and boost revenues for transportation companies. The third product, ComplianceWise, helps to automate customer audits, inspections and other compliance procedures. A company-wide cost efficiency program continues to lower expenses. WiseTech's early forecast is for June 2025 revenues of $1.3 billion to $1.35 billion, with EBITDA of $660 million to $700 million, compared to $495.6 million in June 2024.

Year to 30 June	2023	2024
Revenues ($mn)	816.8	1041.7
EBIT ($mn)	349.5	411.4
EBIT margin (%)	42.8	39.5
Profit before tax ($mn)	342.4	394.5
Profit after tax ($mn)	247.6	283.5
Earnings per share (c)	75.60	85.65
Cash flow per share (c)	101.74	120.36
Dividend (c)	15	16.9
Percentage franked	100	100
Net tangible assets per share ($)	~	~
Interest cover (times)	~	28.8
Return on equity (%)	15.4	13.8
Debt-to-equity ratio (%)	4.3	~
Current ratio	0.6	1.0

Woolworths Group Limited

ASX code: WOW   www.woolworthsgroup.com.au

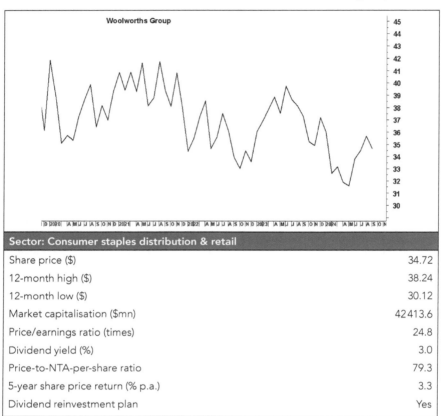

Sector: Consumer staples distribution & retail	
Share price ($)	34.72
12-month high ($)	38.24
12-month low ($)	30.12
Market capitalisation ($mn)	42413.6
Price/earnings ratio (times)	24.8
Dividend yield (%)	3.0
Price-to-NTA-per-share ratio	79.3
5-year share price return (% p.a.)	3.3
Dividend reinvestment plan	Yes

Woolworths, founded in Sydney in 1924, is one of Australia's retail giants. Its 1734 outlets across Australia and New Zealand are centred on Woolworths and Countdown supermarkets, Big W mixed goods stores and Petstock pet supplies stores. Its Australian B2B division manages wholesale food and drinks operations. Among its brands are PFD Food Services, Australian Grocery Wholesalers, Everyday Rewards, Everyday Insurance, Healthylife Pharmacy, Primary Connect, Cartology, Quantium and Wpay.

Latest business results (June 2024, full year)

In an environment of reduced consumer spending, Woolworths again reported increased sales and profits, although a higher tax bill sent the after-tax profit down. The core Australian Food division achieved a 5.6 per cent increase in sales, or 3.7 per cent on a normalised basis, as the June 2024 year comprised 53 weeks, compared to 52 weeks for June 2023. EBIT rose by a normalised 6 per cent, with the WooliesX digital operation responsible for about three-quarters of this. The Australian Food division represents three-quarters of company sales but contributed more than 90 per cent of earnings. The Australian B2B division reported an 87.1 per cent leap in EBIT on a small rise in revenues, though actual profit margins remain very low. New Zealand sales edged up but profits again dropped sharply, down 57.2 per cent in a weak economic environment. Big W fell back again, having staged a recovery in the previous year, with sales down 3.9 per cent and EBIT crashing 90.3 per cent.

Outlook

Woolworths enjoys roughly a 37 per cent share of the Australian food and grocery market, compared to around 28 per cent for its big rival Coles. It relies to a large degree on non-discretionary spending, and can expect to continue growing. The company is finding that many customers are trading down to own-brand items, and it is boosting the range of these products. However, rising costs, particularly wage increases and inflation in energy and transport, are a concern. It is working on a makeover program for its NZ operations, which have been hit by sharply rising costs. This includes a store rebranding from Countdown to Woolworths. It is revitalising Big W stores with the introduction of specialised instore health and beauty shops, a large range of new toy products and transformed clothing lines. Woolworths believes the pet industry has great potential and has taken a 55 per cent holding in the Petstock chain of stores. It is working to enter the pharmacy sector through its Healthylife Pharmacy online business.

Year to 30 June*	2023	2024
Revenues ($mn)	64 294.0	67 922.0
Australian food (%)	75	75
New Zealand food (%)	11	11
Big W (%)	7	7
Australian B2B (%)	7	7
EBIT ($mn)	3165.0	3295.0
EBIT margin (%)	4.9	4.9
Gross margin (%)	26.7	27.3
Profit before tax ($mn)	2439.0	2483.0
Profit after tax ($mn)	1721.0	1711.0
Earnings per share (c)	141.73	140.27
Cash flow per share (c)	354.03	368.01
Dividend (c)	104	104
Percentage franked	100	100
Net tangible assets per share ($)	0.60	0.44
Interest cover (times)	4.5	4.2
Return on equity (%)	27.7	28.9
Debt-to-equity ratio (%)	39.9	58.9
Current ratio	0.5	0.5

*25 June 2023

PART II
THE TABLES

Table A

Market capitalisation

A company's market capitalisation is determined by multiplying the share price by the number of shares. To be included in this book, a company must be in the All Ordinaries Index, which comprises the 500 largest companies by market capitalisation.

	$mn
Commonwealth Bank	239 891.9
BHP Group	194 952.0
Rio Tinto	173 779.1
CSL	146 918.4
National Australia Bank	120 826.7
Westpac Banking Corp.	109 277.3
ANZ Group	95 431.6
Macquarie Group	86 231.7
Wesfarmers	79 403.8
Fortescue	49 584.6
Woolworths Group	42 413.6
WiseTech Global	40 994.0
Aristocrat Leisure	34 774.3
REA Group	27 039.1
Brambles Industries	25 945.4
Coles Group	24 907.9
Santos	22 474.6
Cochlear	18 911.4
Insurance Australia Group	18 414.9
Reece	17 170.3
Computershare	16 623.4
Origin Energy	16 507.7
Pro Medicus	16 202.6
CAR Group	13 894.7
ASX	12 234.3
Medibank Private	10 547.8
JB Hi-Fi	8 965.4
Evolution Mining	7 923.7
AGL Energy	7 756.8
Technology One	7 398.5
Steadfast Group	6 704.2
Premier Investments	5 614.6
Netwealth Group	5 307.7
Breville Group	4 860.9
IDP Education	4 422.8
Reliance Worldwide Corp.	4 217.1
Metcash	3 918.7
Super Retail Group	3 805.2
Lovisa Holdings	3 557.9
ARB Corp.	3 280.9
Pinnacle Investment	3 254.7
NIB Holdings	2 915.3

Codan	2 734.2
Ramelius Resources	2 503.1
Iluka Resources	2 413.5
Perpetual	2 191.2
Nine Entertainment	2 034.3
Gold Road Resources	1 679.2
Magellan Financial Group	1 626.7
IPH	1 533.5
NRW Holdings	1 524.6
Elders	1 422.6
Amotiv	1 419.5
Accent Group	1 295.0
Nick Scali	1 284.4
Objective Corp.	1 282.8
Supply Network	1 224.2
Data#3	1 183.5
Monadelphous Group	1 158.8
Smartgroup Corp.	1 142.0
Mader Group	1 056.0
Johns Lyng Group	1 021.0
Credit Corp Group	1 019.0
PWR Holdings	927.5
Collins Foods	905.4
Jumbo Interactive	849.4
Clinuvel Pharmaceuticals	737.1
Ridley Corp.	710.6
Macmahon Holdings	675.7
GWA Group	617.9
Beacon Lighting Group	592.0
Ricegrowers	559.4
Platinum Asset Management	521.2
Lycopodium	458.9
Southern Cross Electrical	458.0
Servcorp	451.7
Monash IVF Group	444.2
Australian Ethical Investment	435.3
Adairs	338.9
Acrow	295.4
Schaffer Corp.	292.5
Grange Resources	289.3
Lindsay Australia	278.1
Fiducian Group	253.4

Table B

Revenues

This list ranks the companies in the book according to their most recent full-year revenues figures (operating income for the banks). The figures include revenues from sales and services, but other revenues — such as interest receipts and investment income — are not generally included.

	$mn
BHP Group	84 330.3
Rio Tinto	81 880.3
Woolworths Group	67 922.0
Wesfarmers	44 189.0
Coles Group	43 571.0
Fortescue	27 606.1
Commonwealth Bank	26 921.0
CSL	22 424.2
Westpac Banking Corp.	21 542.0
ANZ Group	20 893.0
National Australia Bank	20 654.0
Macquarie Group	16 887.0
Origin Energy	16 138.0
Metcash	15 912.4
Insurance Australia Group	15 425.0
AGL Energy	13 583.0
Brambles Industries	9 917.3
JB Hi-Fi	9 592.4
Reece	9 104.8
Santos	8 922.7
Medibank Private	7 623.1
Aristocrat Leisure	6 295.7
Computershare	4 421.0
Super Retail Group	3 882.6
NIB Holdings	3 337.7
Elders	3 321.4
Evolution Mining	3 215.8
NRW Holdings	2 913.0
Nine Entertainment	2 629.8
Cochlear	2 235.6
Macmahon Holdings	2 031.3
Monadelphous Group	2 015.9
Reliance Worldwide Corp.	1 887.6
Ricegrowers	1 874.2
Steadfast Group	1 676.2
Premier Investments	1 643.5
Breville Group	1 530.0
Collins Foods	1 488.9
Accent Group	1 448.1
REA Group	1 430.0
Perpetual	1 357.5
Iluka Resources	1 291.0

Ridley Corp.	1 262.9
Johns Lyng Group	1 158.9
CAR Group	1 098.7
WiseTech Global	1 041.7
IDP Education	1 037.2
ASX	1 034.3
Amotiv	987.2
Ramelius Resources	882.6
Data#3	805.7
Lindsay Australia	804.4
Mader Group	774.5
Lovisa Holdings	698.7
ARB Corp.	693.2
Grange Resources	614.7
IPH	605.6
Adairs	594.4
Southern Cross Electrical	551.9
Codan	550.5
Credit Corp Group	519.6
Gold Road Resources	472.1
Nick Scali	468.2
Technology One	429.4
GWA Group	413.5
Lycopodium	344.5
Beacon Lighting Group	323.1
Servcorp	314.1
Supply Network	302.6
Magellan Financial Group	278.3
Monash IVF Group	255.0
Smartgroup Corp.	251.6
Netwealth Group	249.5
Schaffer Corp.	216.2
Acrow	215.3
Platinum Asset Management	174.3
Pro Medicus	161.5
Jumbo Interactive	159.3
Pinnacle Investment	139.8
PWR Holdings	139.4
Objective Corp.	117.5
Australian Ethical Investment	100.5
Clinuvel Pharmaceuticals	88.2
Fiducian Group	79.3

Table C

Year-on-year revenues growth

Companies generally strive for growth, though profit growth is usually of more significance than a boost in revenues. In fact, it is possible for a company to increase its revenues by all kinds of means — including cutting profit margins or acquiring other companies — and year-on-year revenues growth is of little relevance if other ratios are not also improving. The figures used for this calculation are the latest full-year figures.

	%
Evolution Mining	44.4
CAR Group	40.6
Ramelius Resources	39.8
Jumbo Interactive	34.2
Perpetual	31.3
Pro Medicus	29.3
Acrow	27.8
WiseTech Global	27.5
Mader Group	27.2
Schaffer Corp.	24.2
Australian Ethical Investment	23.9
Pinnacle Investment	23.9
IPH	23.6
Gold Road Resources	23.3
REA Group	20.9
Codan	20.6
Supply Network	20.0
Monash IVF Group	19.4
Lindsay Australia	18.9
Steadfast Group	18.9
Southern Cross Electrical	18.8
Netwealth Group	18.0
PWR Holdings	17.8
Monadelphous Group	17.1
Lovisa Holdings	17.1
Technology One	16.6
Cochlear	15.5
Ricegrowers	14.7
National Australia Bank	13.0
Aristocrat Leisure	13.0
CSL	12.9
ANZ Group	12.6
Clinuvel Pharmaceuticals	12.6
Smartgroup Corp.	12.0
Insurance Australia Group	11.5
Collins Foods	10.4
Credit Corp Group	9.8
Premier Investments	9.7
Fortescue	9.6
Fiducian Group	9.6
Brambles Industries	9.3
NIB Holdings	9.3

	%
NRW Holdings	9.2
Westpac Banking Corp.	8.2
Amotiv	7.7
Coles Group	7.6
Medibank Private	7.6
Servcorp	6.9
Computershare	6.6
Macmahon Holdings	6.6
Objective Corp.	6.5
Lycopodium	6.4
Woolworths Group	5.6
IDP Education	5.6
BHP Group	5.0
Beacon Lighting Group	3.6
Breville Group	3.5
Grange Resources	3.4
ARB Corp.	3.3
Reece	3.0
Accent Group	2.8
ASX	2.4
Super Retail Group	2.1
Rio Tinto	1.7
Reliance Worldwide Corp.	1.7
Wesfarmers	1.5
Metcash	0.7
GWA Group	0.4
Ridley Corp.	0.2
JB Hi-Fi	−0.4
Data#3	−0.4
Commonwealth Bank	−1.8
Origin Energy	−2.1
Nine Entertainment	−2.8
Elders	−3.6
AGL Energy	−4.1
Adairs	−4.3
Nick Scali	−7.8
Johns Lyng Group	−9.6
Macquarie Group	−11.7
Platinum Asset Management	−14.0
Magellan Financial Group	−18.8
Iluka Resources	−19.9
Santos	−21.0

Table D

EBIT margin

A company's earnings before interest and taxation (EBIT) is sometimes regarded as a better measure of its profitability than the straight pre-tax or post-tax profit figure. EBIT is derived by adding interest payments to the pre-tax profit. Different companies choose different methods of financing their operations; by adding back interest payments to their profits we can help minimise these differences and make comparisons between companies more valid.

The EBIT margin is the EBIT figure as a percentage of annual sales. Clearly a high figure is to be desired, though of course this can be achieved artificially by inflating borrowings (and hence interest payments). And it is noteworthy that efficient companies with strong cashflow like some of the retailers can operate most satisfactorily on low margins.

The EBIT margin figure has little relevance for banks, and they have been excluded.

	%		
ASX	110.7	ARB Corp.	20.6
Magellan Financial Group	86.2	IDP Education	20.6
Pro Medicus	72.1	Lycopodium	20.5
Pinnacle Investment	69.9	Australian Ethical Investment	19.5
Clinuvel Pharmaceuticals	57.5	Brambles Industries	19.4
REA Group	48.7	Lovisa Holdings	18.4
Netwealth Group	48.5	GWA Group	17.9
CAR Group	47.7	Reliance Worldwide Corp.	17.3
Fortescue	47.7	Amotiv	17.1
BHP Group	44.6	Monash IVF Group	17.0
Platinum Asset Management	42.0	Supply Network	16.4
Jumbo Interactive	40.3	Beacon Lighting Group	16.0
WiseTech Global	39.5	Nine Entertainment	14.1
Gold Road Resources	37.2	Origin Energy	12.3
Iluka Resources	37.1	Breville Group	12.3
Santos	36.5	Adairs	11.3
Smartgroup Corp.	36.2	AGL Energy	10.9
Grange Resources	35.7	Super Retail Group	10.2
Objective Corp.	33.2	Mader Group	9.6
Ramelius Resources	31.4	Medibank Private	9.4
Technology One	30.7	Wesfarmers	8.5
IPH	30.4	NIB Holdings	8.5
Aristocrat Leisure	29.0	Johns Lyng Group	8.4
Steadfast Group	28.6	Collins Foods	8.2
Computershare	28.4	Data#3	7.8
Nick Scali	28.4	Accent Group	7.8
Credit Corp Group	27.4	Reece	7.6
Rio Tinto	27.3	Macmahon Holdings	7.0
Fiducian Group	27.0	JB Hi-Fi	6.9
Evolution Mining	26.5	Lindsay Australia	6.7
Perpetual	26.1	Southern Cross Electrical	6.4
CSL	26.0	Ricegrowers	5.6
PWR Holdings	25.4	NRW Holdings	5.6
Acrow	24.9	Ridley Corp.	5.3
Premier Investments	24.3	Elders	4.9
Servcorp	22.5	Woolworths Group	4.9
Cochlear	22.1	Monadelphous Group	4.7
Schaffer Corp.	21.5	Coles Group	4.7
Codan	20.7	Metcash	2.8

Table E
Year-on-year EBIT margin growth

The EBIT (earnings before interest and taxation) margin is one of the measures of a company's efficiency. So a rising margin is much to be desired, as it suggests that a company is achieving success in cutting its costs. This table does not include banks.

	%		
AGL Energy	140.2	Computershare	2.0
Ramelius Resources	71.3	Wesfarmers	1.5
Objective Corp.	63.1	Mader Group	1.0
Evolution Mining	53.9	Supply Network	0.9
Medibank Private	51.3	Australian Ethical Investment	−0.2
Schaffer Corp.	44.1	Collins Foods	−0.2
Gold Road Resources	43.9	Jumbo Interactive	−0.7
NIB Holdings	43.6	Technology One	−0.9
Origin Energy	37.4	Amotiv	−0.9
Data#3	16.4	Clinuvel Pharmaceuticals	−1.2
Magellan Financial Group	16.3	Woolworths Group	−1.5
Macmahon Holdings	13.0	Adairs	−1.8
Fortescue	12.3	PWR Holdings	−2.3
ARB Corp.	12.0	Reliance Worldwide Corp.	−3.4
Servcorp	11.9	Southern Cross Electrical	−4.0
Acrow	11.4	Metcash	−4.0
Johns Lyng Group	11.2	IPH	−4.1
Fiducian Group	10.7	Pinnacle Investment	−4.4
Ricegrowers	10.2	Monash IVF Group	−4.6
Brambles Industries	9.8	Smartgroup Corp.	−5.3
ASX	7.8	CSL	−6.3
Codan	7.4	WiseTech Global	−7.7
Monadelphous Group	6.2	Nick Scali	−8.1
Steadfast Group	6.2	Super Retail Group	−8.8
Breville Group	5.3	Beacon Lighting Group	−8.8
Netwealth Group	5.2	IDP Education	−9.5
GWA Group	5.0	Premier Investments	−9.5
Ridley Corp.	5.0	CAR Group	−10.4
NRW Holdings	4.9	Credit Corp Group	−10.9
Pro Medicus	4.6	Santos	−12.6
REA Group	4.5	Nine Entertainment	−14.0
Cochlear	3.7	JB Hi-Fi	−14.6
Lovisa Holdings	3.5	Grange Resources	−16.0
Lycopodium	3.4	Iluka Resources	−18.7
Coles Group	2.8	Rio Tinto	−20.2
BHP Group	2.4	Accent Group	−22.1
Perpetual	2.1	Lindsay Australia	−24.0
Reece	2.1	Platinum Asset Management	−27.2
Aristocrat Leisure	2.0	Elders	−31.8

Table F
After-tax profit
This table ranks all the companies according to their most recent full-year after-tax profit.

	$mn
BHP Group	20 697.0
Rio Tinto	15 239.4
Commonwealth Bank	9 836.0
Fortescue	8 610.6
National Australia Bank	7 731.0
ANZ Group	7 405.0
Westpac Banking Corp.	7 368.0
CSL	4 112.1
Macquarie Group	3 522.0
Wesfarmers	2 557.0
Santos	2 156.1
Woolworths Group	1 711.0
Aristocrat Leisure	1 454.1
Origin Energy	1 183.0
Brambles Industries	1 181.7
Coles Group	1 128.0
Insurance Australia Group	898.0
AGL Energy	812.0
Computershare	747.2
Medibank Private	492.5
Evolution Mining	481.8
ASX	474.2
REA Group	460.5
JB Hi-Fi	438.8
Reece	419.2
Cochlear	356.8
CAR Group	344.0
Iluka Resources	342.6
WiseTech Global	283.5
Metcash	282.3
Premier Investments	271.1
Steadfast Group	252.2
Super Retail Group	240.1
Reliance Worldwide Corp.	222.6
Perpetual	206.1
Ramelius Resources	200.3
Nine Entertainment	189.4
NIB Holdings	182.6
Magellan Financial Group	177.9
Grange Resources	150.1
IDP Education	132.7
Breville Group	118.5

Gold Road Resources	115.7
IPH	112.4
NRW Holdings	105.1
Technology One	102.9
ARB Corp.	102.7
Elders	100.8
Amotiv	99.8
Macmahon Holdings	91.9
Pinnacle Investment	90.4
Netwealth Group	83.4
Pro Medicus	82.8
Lovisa Holdings	82.4
Nick Scali	82.0
Codan	81.4
Credit Corp Group	81.2
Ricegrowers	63.1
Monadelphous Group	62.2
Smartgroup Corp.	61.9
Accent Group	59.5
Collins Foods	55.6
Servcorp	52.1
Lycopodium	50.7
Mader Group	50.4
Johns Lyng Group	48.0
GWA Group	45.6
Platinum Asset Management	45.0
Jumbo Interactive	43.3
Data#3	43.3
Ridley Corp.	42.3
Clinuvel Pharmaceuticals	35.6
Adairs	35.5
Supply Network	33.0
Acrow	33.0
Objective Corp.	31.3
Beacon Lighting Group	30.1
Monash IVF Group	29.9
Lindsay Australia	27.3
Schaffer Corp.	27.1
PWR Holdings	24.8
Southern Cross Electrical	21.9
Australian Ethical Investment	18.4
Fiducian Group	15.0

Table G

Year-on-year earnings per share growth

The earnings per share (EPS) figure is a crucial one. It tells you — the shareholder — what your part is of the company's profits, for each of your shares. So investors invariably look for EPS growth in a stock. The year–on–year EPS growth figure is often one of the first ratios that investors look to when evaluating a stock. The figures used for this calculation are the latest full–year figures.

	%
AGL Energy	189.0
Evolution Mining	124.8
Ramelius Resources	112.5
Schaffer Corp.	99.2
Gold Road Resources	66.3
NIB Holdings	64.4
Medibank Private	59.6
Origin Energy	58.2
Australian Ethical Investment	56.3
Objective Corp.	48.3
Aristocrat Leisure	47.6
Pro Medicus	36.5
Macmahon Holdings	35.5
Mader Group	30.9
Jumbo Interactive	30.9
Netwealth Group	24.1
REA Group	23.7
Fiducian Group	22.1
NRW Holdings	21.8
Servcorp	21.0
Fortescue	20.2
Brambles Industries	20.2
Codan	20.0
Lovisa Holdings	19.2
Supply Network	18.2
Cochlear	17.3
Monash IVF Group	17.3
Data#3	16.9
CAR Group	16.8
Pinnacle Investment	16.4
Ricegrowers	16.4
Steadfast Group	16.1
ARB Corp.	15.7
Clinuvel Pharmaceuticals	15.5
Technology One	15.3
Monadelphous Group	14.7
Westpac Banking Corp.	14.0
PWR Holdings	13.9
WiseTech Global	13.3
National Australia Bank	11.7
Insurance Australia Group	10.0
Lycopodium	8.4

	%
Southern Cross Electrical	8.4
Reece	8.1
ANZ Group	7.9
Breville Group	7.1
Collins Foods	6.9
Amotiv	6.5
IPH	5.6
CSL	5.4
Smartgroup Corp.	5.3
Computershare	4.5
Wesfarmers	3.6
GWA Group	3.4
BHP Group	3.2
Magellan Financial Group	2.9
Coles Group	2.7
Ridley Corp.	1.1
Acrow	–0.9
Woolworths Group	–1.0
Commonwealth Bank	–1.4
Johns Lyng Group	–3.4
ASX	–3.5
Reliance Worldwide Corp.	–4.2
Premier Investments	–5.1
Super Retail Group	–8.7
Perpetual	–9.3
IDP Education	–10.6
Metcash	–11.1
Credit Corp Group	–11.1
Beacon Lighting Group	–11.3
Adairs	–12.3
Grange Resources	–12.6
Rio Tinto	–15.4
JB Hi–Fi	–16.4
Nick Scali	–19.5
Lindsay Australia	–23.2
Nine Entertainment	–25.2
Santos	–27.6
Macquarie Group	–31.8
Iluka Resources	–34.3
Accent Group	–34.3
Elders	–38.1
Platinum Asset Management	–43.6

Table H

Return on equity

Shareholders' equity is the company's assets minus its liabilities. It is, in theory, the amount owned by the shareholders of the company. Return on equity is the after-tax profit expressed as a percentage of that equity. Thus, it is the amount of profit that the company managers made for you — the shareholder — from your assets. For many investors it is one of the most important gauges of how well a company is doing. It is one of the requirements for inclusion in this book that all companies have a return on equity of at least 10 per cent in their latest financial year.

	%
Lovisa Holdings	102.8
Australian Ethical Investment	64.8
Netwealth Group	62.3
Data#3	60.5
Pro Medicus	50.7
Lycopodium	41.8
Jumbo Interactive	40.3
Objective Corp.	37.8
Technology One	37.7
Nick Scali	37.5
Supply Network	36.5
Mader Group	36.0
Coles Group	32.4
REA Group	30.6
BHP Group	30.6
Wesfarmers	30.3
Fortescue	30.3
JB Hi-Fi	29.5
Woolworths Group	28.9
Fiducian Group	28.5
Servcorp	27.2
Acrow	27.1
PWR Holdings	26.3
Brambles Industries	25.6
Smartgroup Corp.	25.6
IDP Education	25.5
Computershare	24.1
Aristocrat Leisure	22.8
Metcash	21.8
Medibank Private	21.7
Pinnacle Investment	20.6
Cochlear	19.9
Lindsay Australia	19.7
Rio Tinto	19.7
Clinuvel Pharmaceuticals	19.4
Beacon Lighting Group	19.1
Codan	19.1
IPH	18.6
NIB Holdings	18.2
Magellan Financial Group	18.0
Ramelius Resources	17.7
Super Retail Group	17.5

	%
Iluka Resources	16.9
Adairs	16.7
NRW Holdings	16.6
CSL	16.4
ARB Corp.	16.2
Premier Investments	15.9
Grange Resources	15.5
AGL Energy	15.4
GWA Group	14.9
Macmahon Holdings	14.8
Breville Group	14.6
Platinum Asset Management	14.0
Accent Group	13.8
WiseTech Global	13.8
Monadelphous Group	13.8
Collins Foods	13.7
Commonwealth Bank	13.6
Insurance Australia Group	13.5
Ridley Corp.	13.2
Gold Road Resources	13.0
Evolution Mining	13.0
ASX	12.9
Origin Energy	12.9
National Australia Bank	12.9
Schaffer Corp.	12.4
Johns Lyng Group	11.9
Reliance Worldwide Corp.	11.8
Elders	11.7
Southern Cross Electrical	11.7
Monash IVF Group	11.6
Nine Entertainment	11.6
CAR Group	11.6
Steadfast Group	11.5
Ricegrowers	11.4
Reece	11.2
Amotiv	10.9
ANZ Group	10.9
Macquarie Group	10.6
Westpac Banking Corp.	10.3
Perpetual	10.2
Credit Corp Group	10.0
Santos	10.0

Table I
Year-on-year return on equity growth

Company managers have a variety of strategies they can use to boost profits. It is much harder to lift the return on equity (ROE). Find a company with a high ROE figure, one that is growing year by year, and it is possible you have found a real growth stock. This figure is simply the percentage change in the ROE figure from the previous year to the latest year.

	%
AGL Energy	218.7
Evolution Mining	106.9
Ramelius Resources	94.7
Schaffer Corp.	84.5
Origin Energy	62.7
Medibank Private	59.7
NIB Holdings	49.6
Australian Ethical Investment	41.4
Gold Road Resources	30.4
Macmahon Holdings	27.8
Servcorp	23.5
Monash IVF Group	23.2
Objective Corp.	21.4
Jumbo Interactive	17.5
NRW Holdings	16.8
REA Group	14.0
Fiducian Group	13.4
Aristocrat Leisure	12.8
Cochlear	11.9
Westpac Banking Corp.	11.8
Pinnacle Investment	10.9
Fortescue	10.7
National Australia Bank	10.3
Smartgroup Corp.	10.2
Ricegrowers	10.1
Monadelphous Group	9.3
Codan	9.0
Lovisa Holdings	8.9
ANZ Group	8.7
Computershare	6.6
ARB Corp.	6.5
Data#3	6.2
Netwealth Group	5.5
Woolworths Group	4.2
Southern Cross Electrical	4.1
Insurance Australia Group	3.9
Steadfast Group	3.8
GWA Group	3.3
Brambles Industries	3.1
Collins Foods	2.8
Magellan Financial Group	2.4
Amotiv	1.5

BHP Group	1.2
Perpetual	0.9
Pro Medicus	0.6
Reece	0.0
Wesfarmers	0.0
Ridley Corp.	0.0
PWR Holdings	−0.4
Commonwealth Bank	−2.3
ASX	−2.4
Lycopodium	−3.9
Mader Group	−4.3
Coles Group	−4.5
CSL	−5.4
IPH	−5.6
Breville Group	−8.0
Clinuvel Pharmaceuticals	−8.1
Supply Network	−8.7
Technology One	−8.8
Reliance Worldwide Corp.	−9.4
WiseTech Global	−10.5
Premier Investments	−10.7
Super Retail Group	−11.5
Johns Lyng Group	−14.1
Credit Corp Group	−14.6
CAR Group	−15.3
IDP Education	−16.4
Adairs	−16.9
Acrow	−17.3
Beacon Lighting Group	−19.5
Grange Resources	−19.8
Rio Tinto	−21.1
Nine Entertainment	−21.3
Metcash	−23.7
JB Hi-Fi	−24.2
Accent Group	−31.2
Santos	−33.9
Lindsay Australia	−34.3
Macquarie Group	−37.1
Nick Scali	−40.5
Elders	−41.2
Iluka Resources	−43.0
Platinum Asset Management	−43.5

Table J
Debt-to-equity ratio

A company's borrowings as a percentage of its shareholders' equity is one of the most common measures of corporate debt. Many investors will be wary of a company with a ratio that is too high. However, a company with a steady business and a regular income flow — such as an electric power company or a large supermarket chain — is generally considered relatively safe with a high level of debt, whereas a small company in a new business field might be thought at risk with even moderate debt levels. Much depends on surrounding circumstances, including the prevailing interest rates. Of course, it is often from borrowing that a company grows, and some investors are not happy buying shares in a company with little or no debt.

There are various ways to calculate the ratio, but for this book the net debt position is used. That is, a company's cash has been deducted from its borrowings. For inclusion in this book no company was allowed a debt-to-equity ratio of more than 70 per cent. Some of the companies had no net debt — their cash position was greater than the amount of their borrowings, or they had no borrowings at all — and so have been assigned a zero figure in this table. The ratio has no relevance for banks, and they have been excluded.

	%
ARB Corp.	0.0
Aristocrat Leisure	0.0
ASX	0.0
Australian Ethical Investment	0.0
Beacon Lighting Group	0.0
Breville Group	0.0
Clinuvel Pharmaceuticals	0.0
Cochlear	0.0
Data#3	0.0
Fiducian Group	0.0
Gold Road Resources	0.0
Grange Resources	0.0
Iluka Resources	0.0
JB Hi-Fi	0.0
Johns Lyng Group	0.0
Jumbo Interactive	0.0
Lindsay Australia	0.0
Lycopodium	0.0
Magellan Financial Group	0.0
Medibank Private	0.0
Monadelphous Group	0.0
Netwealth Group	0.0
NIB Holdings	0.0
Nick Scali	0.0
Objective Corp.	0.0

Platinum Asset Management	0.0
Premier Investments	0.0
Pro Medicus	0.0
PWR Holdings	0.0
Ramelius Resources	0.0
Servcorp	0.0
Southern Cross Electrical	0.0
Super Retail Group	0.0
Technology One	0.0
WiseTech Global	0.0
Fortescue	2.5
Supply Network	3.6
REA Group	4.9
NRW Holdings	5.1
Rio Tinto	6.3
Schaffer Corp.	11.9
Reece	13.3
Pinnacle Investment	14.8
Metcash	16.5
BHP Group	16.7
Codan	16.9
Mader Group	19.4
Monash IVF Group	19.6
Ridley Corp.	19.8
Smartgroup Corp.	23.0
Macmahon Holdings	23.1
Computershare	23.7

Santos	24.9
Insurance Australia Group	26.2
Coles Group	27.0
Adairs	28.7
Origin Energy	29.0
Accent Group	29.2
Lovisa Holdings	29.2
GWA Group	31.4
IDP Education	32.5
AGL Energy	33.1
Reliance Worldwide Corp.	33.1
Steadfast Group	33.6
CAR Group	33.7
Ricegrowers	34.0
Amotiv	35.2
Perpetual	35.4
Nine Entertainment	35.8
Evolution Mining	36.7
Collins Foods	38.7
Credit Corp Group	42.4
Elders	42.8
Wesfarmers	45.7
Acrow	48.7
Brambles Industries	51.4
CSL	54.3
IPH	56.5
Woolworths Group	58.9

Table K
Current ratio

The current ratio is simply the company's current assets divided by its current liabilities. Current assets are cash or assets that can, in theory, be converted quickly into cash. Current liabilities are normally those payable within a year. The current ratio helps measure the ability of a company to repay in a hurry its short-term debt, should the need arise. Banks are not included.

Platinum Asset Management	16.4	GWA Group	1.6
Pinnacle Investment	11.5	IDP Education	1.6
Clinuvel Pharmaceuticals	8.8	Objective Corp.	1.6
Grange Resources	7.8	REA Group	1.5
Magellan Financial Group	7.2	Ricegrowers	1.5
Credit Corp Group	6.1	Steadfast Group	1.5
Pro Medicus	6.0	Southern Cross Electrical	1.4
Netwealth Group	5.1	NRW Holdings	1.3
Iluka Resources	4.9	Johns Lyng Group	1.3
ARB Corp.	4.1	Macmahon Holdings	1.3
Ramelius Resources	3.4	Technology One	1.2
Aristocrat Leisure	3.1	Acrow	1.2
PWR Holdings	3.0	JB Hi-Fi	1.2
Computershare	2.9	Super Retail Group	1.2
Reliance Worldwide Corp.	2.8	Nick Scali	1.1
IPH	2.8	Wesfarmers	1.1
Supply Network	2.7	Metcash	1.1
Fiducian Group	2.7	ASX	1.1
Fortescue	2.7	Ridley Corp.	1.1
Lycopodium	2.3	Elders	1.1
Australian Ethical Investment	2.3	Santos	1.1
Cochlear	2.3	Evolution Mining	1.1
Gold Road Resources	2.3	Origin Energy	1.1
Breville Group	2.3	Data#3	1.1
CSL	2.2	AGL Energy	1.1
Reece	2.2	Accent Group	1.0
Premier Investments	2.1	Nine Entertainment	1.0
NIB Holdings	2.1	WiseTech Global	1.0
Schaffer Corp.	2.1	Lindsay Australia	1.0
Amotiv	2.0	Smartgroup Corp.	1.0
CAR Group	2.0	Lovisa Holdings	0.9
Jumbo Interactive	1.9	Servcorp	0.8
Medibank Private	1.9	Adairs	0.8
BHP Group	1.7	Brambles Industries	0.6
Rio Tinto	1.7	Coles Group	0.6
Mader Group	1.7	Collins Foods	0.5
Beacon Lighting Group	1.7	Woolworths Group	0.5
Codan	1.7	Perpetual	0.5
Monadelphous Group	1.6	Monash IVF Group	0.5

Table L

Price/earnings ratio

The price/earnings ratio (PER) — the current share price divided by the earnings per share figure — is one of the best known of all sharemarket ratios. Essentially it expresses the amount of money investors are ready to pay for each cent or dollar of a company's profits, and it allows you to compare the share prices of different companies of varying sizes and with widely different profits. A high PER suggests the market has a high regard for the company and its growth prospects; a low one may mean that investors are disdainful of the stock. The figures in this table are based on share prices as of 6 September 2024.

Company	PER	Company	PER
Grange Resources	1.9	Beacon Lighting Group	19.5
Fortescue	5.8	Jumbo Interactive	19.6
Iluka Resources	7.0	JB Hi-Fi	20.4
Macmahon Holdings	7.3	Clinuvel Pharmaceuticals	20.6
Acrow	8.5	Premier Investments	20.7
Servcorp	8.6	Insurance Australia Group	20.8
Ricegrowers	8.9	Southern Cross Electrical	20.9
Magellan Financial Group	9.2	Mader Group	20.9
Lycopodium	9.2	Johns Lyng Group	21.2
BHP Group	9.4	Medibank Private	21.4
Adairs	9.5	Accent Group	21.7
AGL Energy	9.6	Brambles Industries	21.9
Lindsay Australia	10.2	Coles Group	22.1
Perpetual	10.5	Computershare	22.6
Santos	10.5	Australian Ethical Investment	23.4
Schaffer Corp.	10.8		
Nine Entertainment	10.9	Macquarie Group	23.6
Rio Tinto	11.4	Commonwealth Bank	24.4
Platinum Asset Management	11.7	Aristocrat Leisure	24.7
Ramelius Resources	12.1	Woolworths Group	24.8
Credit Corp Group	12.5	ASX	25.8
Metcash	12.7	Steadfast Group	25.8
ANZ Group	12.9	Data#3	27.3
IPH	13.4	Wesfarmers	30.8
GWA Group	13.6	ARB Corp.	31.9
Origin Energy	14.0	IDP Education	33.3
Elders	14.0	Codan	33.5
Amotiv	14.2	CSL	35.7
Gold Road Resources	14.4	Pinnacle Investment	35.8
NRW Holdings	14.5	Supply Network	36.6
Monash IVF Group	14.9	PWR Holdings	37.4
Westpac Banking Corp.	15.0	CAR Group	40.4
Nick Scali	15.0	Reece	40.9
National Australia Bank	15.8	Breville Group	41.0
Super Retail Group	15.8	Objective Corp.	41.0
Evolution Mining	15.9	Lovisa Holdings	43.0
NIB Holdings	15.9	Cochlear	53.0
Collins Foods	16.3	REA Group	58.7
Ridley Corp.	16.8	Netwealth Group	63.7
Fiducian Group	16.8	Technology One	71.0
Smartgroup Corp.	17.5	WiseTech Global	143.5
Monadelphous Group	18.6	Pro Medicus	195.7
Reliance Worldwide Corp.	18.9		

Table M

Price-to-NTA-per-share ratio

The NTA-per-share figure expresses the worth of a company's net tangible assets — that is, its assets minus its liabilities and intangible assets — for each share of the company. Intangible assets, such as goodwill or the value of newspaper mastheads, are excluded because it is deemed difficult to place a value on them (though this proposition is debatable), and also because they might not have much worth if separated from the company. The price-to-NTA-per-share ratio relates this figure to the share price.

A ratio of one means that the company is valued exactly according to the value of its assets. A ratio below one suggests that the shares are a bargain, though usually there is a good reason for this. Profits are more important than assets.

In some respects, this is an 'old economy' ratio. For many high-tech companies in the 'new economy' the most important assets are human ones whose worth does not appear on the balance sheet.

Companies with a negative NTA-per-share figure, as a result of having intangible assets valued at more than their net assets, have been omitted from this table.

Company	Ratio	Company	Ratio
Grange Resources	0.3	NIB Holdings	6.2
Iluka Resources	1.1	Southern Cross Electrical	6.8
Santos	1.1	Mader Group	6.9
Macmahon Holdings	1.1	Insurance Australia Group	7.1
Ricegrowers	1.1	Pinnacle Investment	7.3
Credit Corp Group	1.3	Brambles Industries	7.7
ANZ Group	1.4	Premier Investments	9.1
Schaffer Corp.	1.5	Fiducian Group	9.5
Fortescue	1.7	PWR Holdings	11.0
Platinum Asset Management	1.7	ASX	11.0
Westpac Banking Corp.	1.8	Elders	11.1
Magellan Financial Group	1.8	Breville Group	13.0
Ramelius Resources	1.9	Aristocrat Leisure	14.2
Evolution Mining	2.0	Johns Lyng Group	15.0
Gold Road Resources	2.0	Beacon Lighting Group	15.7
National Australia Bank	2.1	Australian Ethical Investment	16.0
Rio Tinto	2.3	Cochlear	16.1
Origin Energy	2.4	Reece	17.0
Monadelphous Group	2.6	Supply Network	18.4
BHP Group	3.0	Jumbo Interactive	19.0
Macquarie Group	3.0	Codan	25.2
Ridley Corp.	3.3	Data#3	26.7
AGL Energy	3.3	Netwealth Group	43.8
Clinuvel Pharmaceuticals	3.6	Objective Corp.	46.1
Commonwealth Bank	3.7	REA Group	49.0
NRW Holdings	3.8	Woolworths Group	79.3
Acrow	3.9	Pro Medicus	97.7
Lycopodium	4.1	Technology One	108.3
ARB Corp.	5.7	Reliance Worldwide Corp.	733.4
Medibank Private	5.7		

Table N

Dividend yield

Many investors buy shares for income, rather than for capital growth. They look for companies that offer a high dividend yield (the dividend expressed as a percentage of the share price). This table ranks the companies in this book according to their historic dividend yields. Note that the franking credits available from most companies in this book can make the dividend yield substantially higher. The dividend yield changes with the share price. The figures in this table are based on share prices as of 6 September 2024.

	%
Fortescue	12.2
Platinum Asset Management	10.8
Grange Resources	8.0
Magellan Financial Group	7.2
Nine Entertainment	6.6
Lycopodium	6.6
GWA Group	6.4
Ricegrowers	6.3
Adairs	6.2
Perpetual	6.1
Rio Tinto	6.1
Acrow	6.0
Santos	5.8
BHP Group	5.7
Origin Energy	5.7
IPH	5.7
Accent Group	5.7
Lindsay Australia	5.5
ANZ Group	5.5
Servcorp	5.4
Metcash	5.4
AGL Energy	5.3
Elders	5.1
Fiducian Group	4.9
Monadelphous Group	4.9
NIB Holdings	4.8
NRW Holdings	4.6
Westpac Banking Corp.	4.5
Nick Scali	4.5
Monash IVF Group	4.4
Medibank Private	4.3
National Australia Bank	4.3
Schaffer Corp.	4.2
Super Retail Group	4.1
Jumbo Interactive	4.0
Ridley Corp.	4.0
Amotiv	4.0
Smartgroup Corp.	3.8
Coles Group	3.6
Collins Foods	3.6
Insurance Australia Group	3.5
Southern Cross Electrical	3.4

	%
Data#3	3.3
ASX	3.3
Macmahon Holdings	3.3
Commonwealth Bank	3.2
Premier Investments	3.2
JB Hi-Fi	3.2
Beacon Lighting Group	3.0
Woolworths Group	3.0
Computershare	2.9
Wesfarmers	2.9
Macquarie Group	2.8
Steadfast Group	2.8
Brambles Industries	2.8
Lovisa Holdings	2.7
Johns Lyng Group	2.6
Pinnacle Investment	2.6
Credit Corp Group	2.5
Australian Ethical Investment	2.3
Ramelius Resources	2.3
IDP Education	2.1
CAR Group	2.0
Supply Network	1.9
Evolution Mining	1.8
ARB Corp.	1.7
PWR Holdings	1.5
Codan	1.5
Mader Group	1.5
Cochlear	1.4
Gold Road Resources	1.4
Reliance Worldwide Corp.	1.3
CSL	1.3
Netwealth Group	1.3
Objective Corp.	1.3
Iluka Resources	1.2
Aristocrat Leisure	1.2
Breville Group	1.0
Reece	1.0
REA Group	0.9
Technology One	0.7
Clinuvel Pharmaceuticals	0.3
Pro Medicus	0.3
WiseTech Global	0.1

Table O

Year-on-year dividend growth

Most investors hope for a rising dividend, and this table tells how much each company raised or lowered its dividend in its latest financial year.

	%
Ramelius Resources	150.0
AGL Energy	96.8
Insurance Australia Group	80.0
Evolution Mining	75.0
Origin Energy	50.7
Adairs	50.0
Gold Road Resources	46.7
Macmahon Holdings	40.0
Mader Group	34.5
Pro Medicus	33.3
Acrow	33.0
Brambles Industries	31.6
Fiducian Group	29.7
Australian Ethical Investment	28.6
Jumbo Interactive	26.7
Lovisa Holdings	26.1
Objective Corp.	25.9
Cochlear	24.2
Aristocrat Leisure	23.1
Codan	21.6
Santos	20.8
Southern Cross Electrical	20.0
ANZ Group	19.9
CAR Group	19.7
REA Group	19.6
Monadelphous Group	18.4
Computershare	17.1
Netwealth Group	16.7
Pinnacle Investment	16.7
Supply Network	16.7
Data#3	16.4
GWA Group	15.4
Steadfast Group	14.0
Premier Investments	14.0
Medibank Private	13.7
Servcorp	13.6
Monash IVF Group	13.6
Westpac Banking Corp.	13.6
WiseTech Global	12.7
Fortescue	12.6
PWR Holdings	12.0

ARB Corp.	11.3
National Australia Bank	10.6
Ricegrowers	10.0
Technology One	10.0
Ridley Corp.	9.7
CSL	9.5
Breville Group	8.2
IPH	6.1
Johns Lyng Group	4.4
Amotiv	3.8
Collins Foods	3.7
Wesfarmers	3.7
NIB Holdings	3.6
Commonwealth Bank	3.3
Coles Group	3.0
Reece	3.0
Clinuvel Pharmaceuticals	0.0
Lindsay Australia	0.0
Schaffer Corp.	0.0
Woolworths Group	0.0
Smartgroup Corp.	–1.6
Perpetual	–1.7
Beacon Lighting Group	–4.8
Lycopodium	–4.9
NRW Holdings	–6.1
Rio Tinto	–8.0
ASX	–8.9
Nick Scali	–9.3
Super Retail Group	–11.5
Metcash	–13.3
Macquarie Group	–14.7
BHP Group	–16.0
JB Hi-Fi	–16.3
IDP Education	–17.1
Elders	–17.9
Nine Entertainment	–22.7
Magellan Financial Group	–24.9
Accent Group	–25.7
Platinum Asset Management	–28.6
Credit Corp Group	–45.7
Reliance Worldwide Corp.	–49.2
Grange Resources	–50.0
Iluka Resources	–84.4

Table P

Five-year share price return

This table ranks the approximate annual average return to investors from a five-year investment in each of the companies in the book, as of September 2024. It is an accumulated return, based on share price appreciation or depreciation plus dividend payments.

	% p.a.
Supply Network	49.8
Pro Medicus	36.2
Mader Group	34.3
Acrow	32.9
Pinnacle Investment	32.0
Southern Cross Electrical	27.9
Objective Corp.	27.8
Codan	27.5
Fortescue	26.5
WiseTech Global	26.5
Data#3	25.2
Technology One	24.8
Lindsay Australia	24.2
JB Hi-Fi	23.8
Lovisa Holdings	22.6
Netwealth Group	22.6
Ricegrowers	22.2
Beacon Lighting Group	21.4
Nick Scali	21.3
Premier Investments	21.2
CAR Group	21.0
Reece	21.0
Lycopodium	19.9
Grange Resources	18.8
ARB Corp.	18.1
Ridley Corp.	17.7
Johns Lyng Group	17.5
Super Retail Group	17.3
PWR Holdings	16.8
Breville Group	16.2
Wesfarmers	15.5
Commonwealth Bank	15.4
REA Group	15.1
Australian Ethical Investment	15.0
Macquarie Group	14.9
Computershare	14.8
Aristocrat Leisure	13.9
Fiducian Group	13.2
Brambles Industries	12.6
Steadfast Group	12.6
Ramelius Resources	12.5
Schaffer Corp.	12.1

Accent Group	11.5
Macmahon Holdings	10.6
National Australia Bank	10.5
Rio Tinto	10.4
Elders	9.8
BHP Group	9.6
NRW Holdings	9.6
Reliance Worldwide Corp.	9.2
Iluka Resources	9.1
Metcash	9.1
Adairs	8.7
Coles Group	8.3
Origin Energy	8.1
ANZ Group	7.5
Monash IVF Group	7.0
Cochlear	6.9
Amotiv	6.2
Medibank Private	5.8
Westpac Banking Corp.	5.8
CSL	5.7
Gold Road Resources	3.6
Servcorp	3.5
Woolworths Group	3.3
Santos	2.2
Insurance Australia Group	1.0
Collins Foods	0.9
NIB Holdings	0.4
IDP Education	0.2
Smartgroup Corp.	0.2
Nine Entertainment	−0.5
Evolution Mining	−1.8
Monadelphous Group	−1.9
GWA Group	−2.1
ASX	−2.8
IPH	−3.2
Perpetual	−4.8
AGL Energy	−5.2
Jumbo Interactive	−7.8
Credit Corp Group	−8.7
Clinuvel Pharmaceuticals	−9.3
Platinum Asset Management	−14.2
Magellan Financial Group	−19.6

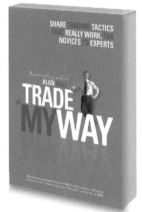

Best-selling author Alan Hull presents the complete sharemarket solution for novices to experts. Whether you're managing your portfolio, trading tactically on the sharemarket or investing in blue chip shares, Alan Hull explains the ins and outs of investing and trading in easy-to-understand and engaging language.

Available in print and e-book formats